C000295703

STROUDLEY
and his
'TERRIERS'

The story of a classic locomotive and its designer

TOM MIDDLEMASS

PENDRAGON

Determined to oppose new electric tramway opposition, and reduce its own short distance passenger train costs, the LB&SCR instituted motor-trains between Brighton and Worthing, and provided five conveniently sited halts en route. No.82 *Boxhill* was one of two 'Terriers' which commenced motor-train work in September 1905, and is seen here in duly modified 2-4-0 form. The leading wheels were a 3ft pair of Class D3 No.393's bogie. Condensing pipes have gone, but sandboxes and pipes have been re-positioned to deposit sand in front of the driving wheels. The 'Terrier', meanwhile, has retained its Stroudley green livery. It's typical new trailer-type coach cost £750 to build and accommodated 52 passengers in smoking and non-smoking compartments.

STROUDLEY
and his
'TERRIERS'

Tom Middlemass

PENDRAGON

INTRODUCTION

As modern life becomes more and more frenetic, and innumerable mediocrities, particularly in 'show biz', are accorded strident, and quite disproportionate, publicity, I find myself, as a railway historian, turning with relief to ever more sympathetic consideration of the men who laboured throughout the nineteenth century to develop the British locomotive. Such men, of course, wielded enormous authority in their day, and, hardly surprisingly, they varied in character. Workshop disciplines were of paramount importance in the cause of making enormous strides and one is obliged, however reluctantly, to record that one or two celebrated locomotive engineers were, in fact, downright bullies. A few others maintained rather too lax a regime; and I find it doubly intriguing that William Stroudley, brim full of ideas, contrived at all times to invoke respect and affection from railway management and workforce alike. Make no mistake, he was a strict disciplinarian — and Brighton Works blossomed accordingly — but so self-evident were his convictions, and the technical knowledge which backed them, that this dapper little figure rarely had occasion to raise his voice. In his own quiet way he was a truly remarkable man — a rare mixture of sheer artistry and acute mechanical perception. His stubborn disdain for leading bogies, compounding, and injectors, coupled with a marked enthusiasm for the Westinghouse brake and Gresham & Craven sanding gear, and a peculiarly parochial preference for place names, made him an odd 'mix' indeed.

The irony is that had Stroudley practised his trade longer — he died at the age of 56 — his very conservatism would have placed him at ever-increasing odds with the mainstream of locomotive development over the last decades of the nineteenth century. The standardisation he so earnestly advocated could have coped; but the front-coupled principle he clung to, particularly as regards express locomotives, was soon superseded, both on the LB&SCR and other major Companies. Yet, despite that, ten of his immortal 'Terrier' 0-6-0 tanks (an incredible 20% of those built) are lovingly preserved to this day. One has even found a home in Canada.

I need hardly add that these gallant centenarians were very much in the forefront of my mind when I decided to assume the privilege of writing a detailed history of the species.

T.M. — Theydon Bois, Essex.

© Tom Middlemass and The Pendragon Partnership 1995

Published by The Pendragon Partnership, PO Box No.3, Easingwold, York, YO6 3YS. All rights reserved

Layout and Design by Barry C. Lane, Sutton-in-Craven

Set in 9pt Galliard by Ian D. Luckett (Typesetting), St. Austell, Cornwall

Reproduction and printing by The Amadeus Press Ltd., Huddersfield, West Yorkshire

All rights reserved. No part of this publication may be reproduced, stored in a retrieval system, transmitted in any form by any means electronic or manual or photocopied or recorded by any other information storage and retrieval system without prior permission in writing from the publisher

British Cataloguing-in-Publication Data: a catalogue reference for this book is held by the British Library

ISBN No. 1 899816 00 3

Note: *Unless annotated otherwise, all illustrations appearing in this book are from the author's private collection and the publisher regrets that copies cannot be made available to readers.*

CONTENTS

Seen here at Inverness, after reboiling in October 1894, the second *Aldourie* now carries a Jones chimney, but the distinctive cab and number plate remain as Stroudley hallmarks. Mainly employed on Thurso branch work, No.2 spent its last years shunting at Inverness, before being withdrawn in 1903. *(Author's Collection)*

Chapter 1
THE MAN — WILLIAM STROUDLEY
(1833–1889

WHEN A COMPARATIVELY UNKNOWN locomotive superintendent joins a modest southern English railway company in 1870, and emerges fêted by the national engineering Press five years later, he has, to be sure, thoroughly earned the title 'eminent Victorian railway engineer'. Yet, one wonders if, in Stroudley's case, that rather facile expression does not tend to camouflage the man's true significance. For, gaze as one might at two of the National Railway Museum's loveliest locomotive exhibits, *Gladstone* and *Boxhill*, it still takes an act of imagination to appreciate that William Stroudley was, in fact, born a pre-Victorian.

Consider 1833, the year in which he arrived on the scene, on 6th March, at Sandford, near Oxford. William IV was on the throne with seven more years to reign, the legendary *Rocket* was only four years old, and the Stephensons, father and son, bestrode the contemporary railway scene like the giants they were. 1833, too, was the year during which the London & Birmingham Railway earned Royal Assent; though Stroudley was five ere London sampled its first main line. Five years later, this gifted boy, armed only with minimal formal education, could be found assisting his machinist father in a Birmingham paint shop. An engineer he met there, John Inshaw (and his wife), played crucial roles in advancing Stroudley's technical education to match his patently restless ambition.

Came 1848, and Stroudley, still only fifteen, was off. Vulcan Foundry saw him for a year; then back he went to Inshaw, there to glean further invaluable experience, mostly in maritime engineering. In 1853, however, his ambitions crystallised, and, opting to specialise in locomotive engineering, he joined the Great Western Railway, under Daniel Gooch, in May that year. Looking back now, there can be little doubt that Gooch's masterful way of obtaining both discipline and respect from the men who served under him found deep and sympathetic echoes in Stroudley's mind. One would have thought, too, that in the year 1853 Swindon offered a secure niche for a young man determined to make his mark in the locomotive world. Yet, within twelve months, Stroudley could not resist the offer of a job which was made to him by his old friend, John Inshaw. Rather remarkably, the job entailed supervision of the erection of a pair of mill engines in *Australia*. The financial inducement, nevertheless, of £15 a month was more than double the amount he was then earning at Swindon. So, he terminated his connection with the GWR — only to find that his parents were desperately unhappy at the prospect of losing their son to Australia. As became a dutiful son, Stroudley then abandoned Australian horizons and, boats burned as far as Swindon was concerned, back he went on the labour market.

Assisted by his father, Stroudley soon found employment as a fitter at the Great Northern Railway's Peterborough running shed. There, both S. W. Johnson, the Works manager, and Charles Sacré, GNR's assistant locomotive superintendent, perceived Stroudley's talent and inventiveness, and promotion followed. Latterly he was appointed shed foreman, under W. S. Brown, at a salary of £104 per annum. An engaging diversion came his way in 1857, when he was seconded for a year to supervise the working of the Edenham & Little Bytham Railway, a four mile long private railway which had been opened on 1st November 1856 by Lord Willoughby de Eresby. Single throughout, the line terminated in the goods yard of the GNR's Little Bytham station. However, once passenger service was authorised by the Board of Trade in December 1857, Stroudley was able to resume normal GNR employment at Peterborough. The next development came less than four years later, in October 1861, when W. S. Brown succeeded William Paton as Locomotive Superintendent to the Edinburgh & Glasgow Railway. Shrewdly, Brown invited the 28 year old Stroudley to join him as Works manager at Cowlairs, Glasgow. The invitation was accepted.

At Cowlairs Stroudley soon justified his free house, free coal, and £200 a year. Apart from effecting major improvements to the Works themselves, he eagerly grasped the opportunity presented by Brown's failing health to introduce locomotive innovations of his own. Two new (though partly second-hand) double-framed 2-4-0s duly emerged from Cowlairs Works in 1862. Although the locomotives were ostensibly designed by Brown, we know now that their strong boiler manholes and copper-capped chimneys were but early manifestations of palmy days to come at Brighton. The 2-4-0s, numbered E&GR 101 and 102, entered North British Railway stock in 1865, and lasted for another 50 years. Meanwhile, it was at Cowlairs that Stroudley met and formed a close rapport with Dugald Drummond, a fiery Scots colleague seven years his junior. Tempera-

mentally, the two men were poles apart; yet this strange highly productive relationship was to persist over the next thirteen years.

The next important change in Stroudley's life came in 1864, when S. W. Johnson, his former superior at Peterborough, arrived on the Edinburgh & Glasgow Railway scene as W. S. Brown's successor. Familiar with Johnson's ambitions and work at Peterborough, and content to concede that there was room for only one artiste on the Cowlairs trapeze, Stroudley chose to move on. Thus, in July 1865, after matching himself against 29 other applicants, he was awarded the post of Locomotive & Carriage Superintendent to the Highland Railway. His salary of £500 per annum was quite a substantial sum in those days.

Again, the money was well earned. The Highland Railway, a newly-formed amalgam of two impecunious Scottish companies, the Inverness & Aberdeen Junction and the Inverness & Perth Junction Railways, may well have owned 242 miles of track; but its motive power consisted of only 55 locomotives, and almost half of those were Crewe-type 'singles', quite unsuited for tackling mountainous terrain. The problem was further aggravated by the stark fact that capital funds were in short supply. Nevertheless, Stroudley confronted his new job head on. Lochgorm Works, at Inverness, were reconstructed at his behest, and two HR 'singles', No.1 *Raigmore* and No.2 *Aldourie* (Hawthorns Works Nos.129 and 130/1855) emerged therefrom in 1869, rebuilt as 6ft 3in 2-4-0s. Both were very elaborately liveried in dark green. Presumably, however, the rebuilds were no great success: *Raigmore* was laid aside in 1873, while *Aldourie* was replaced by a virtually new engine, bearing the same name, but Lochgorm-built, in February 1871.

February 1869, however, also saw the emergence of Lochgorm Works' first completely *new* engine: Stroudley's maiden design, and a distinct forerunner of his immortal 'Terriers'; it was a small 0-6-0 tank named *Balnain*. Two more, *Lochgorm*

HR No.57 *Lochgorm,* shopped from Lochgorm Works, Inverness in November 1872, was the first of two additional 0-6-0Ts which were added by David Jones, Stroudley's successor. Its boiler came from ex-Inverness & Aberdeen Junction 2-2-2 No.4 *Ardross. (Pendragon Collection)*

and *St Martins* (later *Fort George*), were added by David Jones, Stroudley's successor, in 1872 and 1874. *Balnain*, incidentally, was also the first Highland engine to be fitted with Stephenson link motion.

All in all, by dint of a remarkable demonstration of personal example, tact, and engineering skill, Stroudley completely transformed Highland Railway fortunes within four years. He even pioneered the use of snow ploughs, and succeeded in keeping the HR main line clear all through the severe winter of 1866-67; a feat which proved to be beyond the capability of many a larger English company.

Highland Railway management duly appreciated Stroudley's efforts; but, alas, it did not have the foresight to reward him in practical terms. As a result, it lost a loyal servant when, once more in the teeth of fierce competition, Stroudley won the coveted appointment of Locomotive, Carriage & Wagon Superintendent to the London, Brighton & South Coast Railway. He took over from J. C. Craven on 1st February 1870 at a salary of £800 per annum.

Stroudley must have rubbed his eyes when he arrived at Brighton, for conditions there were little less chaotic than those he had already conquered at Cowlairs and Lochgorm. Craven's 22 years of service, however well meaning, had bequeathed a veritable hotchpot of locomotives and rolling stock; and repair facilities at Brighton, with the honourable exception of the boiler shop, were grossly inadequate.

Reaction was typical of the man. Content to spend a few months quietly assessing the situation, Stroudley peered into every corner of Brighton Works, examined every old engine which lay idle, occupying valuable space, and, perhaps most importantly of all, noted that such workshop disciplines as existed at Brighton sprang from fear of Craven rather than respect. Then, on 31st May 1870, he confronted a slightly startled Board with a frank recital of his conclusions. Restoration of LB&SCR fortunes, he argued, could only commence with provision of efficient locomotive construction and repair facilities. It followed, he went on, that even with the incorporation of intelligent economies a minimum capital investment of £20,000 would be required. The Board, swallowing hard, but deeply impressed by their new man's logical presentation, approved.

The scene is Dingwall, the year 1926, and lurking beneath LMS livery as No.16118 is No.56 *Balnain*, the 0-6-0T Stroudley designed for the Highland Railway in 1869, primarily for shunting duties at Inverness. Peter Drummond installed a coal bunker in the early 1900s in place of Stroudley's familiar toolbox. In 1917 the side tanks were extended back to the cab, and a Drummond chimney of sorts was added three years later. Despite that, and the engine's spokeless cast-iron 3ft 7in wheels, enough remains to indicate that here, in fact, was the future Brighton 'Terrier'. Renamed *Dornoch* in 1902 to mark the opening of the Dornoch Light Railway, the little tank remained in the Dornoch vicinity for nearly two decades, before moving on to Inverness and, latterly, Strathpeffer. When the locomotive was withdrawn in January 1928 its boiler was transferred to *Lochgorm*. *(Author's Collection)*

Reboilered in August 1897, and Duplicate Listed as No.57A in 1920, *Lochgorm* lost its name in 1898, and acquired LMS No.16119 in 1925. Many of its original Stroudley characteristics are still in evidence, notably the cab, copper-capped chimney, sloping smokebox front, and dome over the firebox. Ross pop safety valves, however, have since replaced the earlier Salter pattern. The locomotive still carries its short tank, with rounded edges, and the cab sheets still extend to meet the rear of the tank. No bunker was provided originally and fuel was kept between the right-hand cab sheet and the firebox casing. Early in the engine's life, the front and rear wheels were partly spoked, and in course of a 1927 overhaul it was fitted at Lochgorm with *Dornoch*'s boiler and *Fort George*'s flare-reduced Stroudley chimney. Not required to perform any passenger work, however, *Lochgorm* was never fitted with vacuum brake. Names were removed from the class as and when LMS black livery was applied and, last to go, No.16119 worked on until 26th December 1932. *(Locomotive & General)*

Left

The impact of William Stroudley on Highland Railway affairs was equal to the worst the weather could summon. Here, possibly in the midst of a minor snow flurry, the proud inventor reflects on one of the massive snow ploughs he introduced. The locomotive, No.21 (Works No.1427), was one of ten 5ft 1½in 'Small Goods' 2-4-0s which were supplied to the Inverness & Aberdeen Junction Railway by Sharp Stewart in 1863. Poor No.21, which carried the name *Forres* for a brief period, was the unlucky member of the class. Apart from suffering a boiler explosion on 4th January 1872, it was also involved in the HR's only passenger fatality, when a head-on collision occurred, mercifully at low speed, at Newtonmore on 2nd August 1894. Despite that, No.21, renumbered 39 in 1902, soldiered on until September 1909, when it was sold to a party whose identity still remains unknown. *(Author's Collection)*

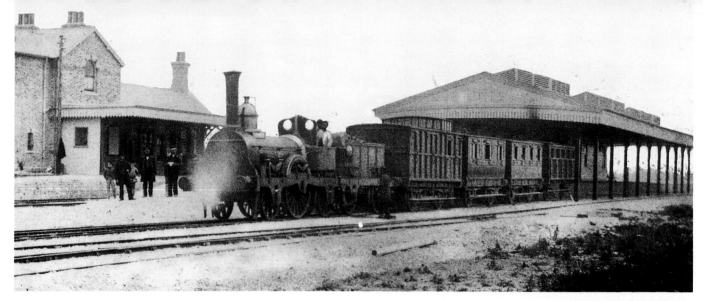

Thus, Stroudley's meteoric transformation of Brighton affairs got under way. Meanwhile, Dugald Drummond, having already followed Stroudley to Inverness, quit northern parts to reappear at Brighton as principal works foreman. The new Brighton Works were substantially completed by early 1873; though Stroudley, ever the perfectionist, continued to inspire further capital investments well into 1880. To its everlasting credit the LB&SCR Board stumped up without complaint. Running sheds were also the subject of major rehabilitation.

One consequence of Stroudley's shrewd initial policy was that for the first few years, precious little money was available for new locomotive construction. Accepting the inevitable, he contented himself with smartening up the design of two 0-4-2 tanks which had already been placed on order under Craven's aegis. Then came two powerful 0-6-0 tender engines of his own design. Liveried in dark green, they entered traffic in December 1871. A year later they were joined by four 'Belgravia' class 2-4-0s. The latter had, perforce, to be built on frames ordered by Craven in 1869; but their design clearly reflected that of the two Edinburgh & Glasgow 2-4-0s which had been shopped from Cowlairs in 1862. Then in 1872 came the first six 'Terriers'. Tailor-made by Stroudley to meet urgent London suburban traffic demands, the immediate impact of these little tanks and the subsequent history of the class were so remarkable as to command the remaining chapters of this book.

Thus, within two years Stroudley succeeded in firmly stamping his imprimatur on Brighton affairs. In that brief period he even acquired his Board's complete trust as unofficial 'Marine Superintendent'. Shades of John Inshaw! In short, his confident demeanour, backed by demonstrable knowledge of all aspects of his craft and allied to an infallible sense of tact when dealing with other human beings, earned him automatic and universal respect. He was a disciplinarian, to boot; yet his weekly descents upon New Cross shed, after attending Board Meetings at London Bridge, were not feared by Brighton men as Dugald Drummond's lightning forays on Nine Elms were by London & South Western men 25 years later. Stroudley, who openly regarded every engine he built — and he built over 370 — as almost private property, never hesitated to indicate displeasure when occasion demanded. But when this dapper figure visited the shop floor, and the ferrule of his umbrella beat an irritated tattoo thereon, a hugely significant silent look was sufficient to chasten the offender. Every man present knew that he could, and probably would, offer a valid explanation of his vexation. Colour blind and short-sighted Stroudley may have been, but very little escaped his attention.

This early view of a down passenger train leaving Barnham Junction conveys something of the conditions which obtained on the LB&SCR as Stroudley assumed office in 1870. The locomotive is one of nine 5ft 6in single wheelers which were supplied by Sharp Bros. in 1847. Craven began 'renewing' the class in 1855 and four ultimately emerged as tanks. All but one lived to add to the hopeless miscellany which greeted Stroudley on his arrival at Brighton. One can see, too, from this photograph, why Stroudley later considered provision of new coaching stock on the South London line to be a matter of urgency. *(Author's Collection)*

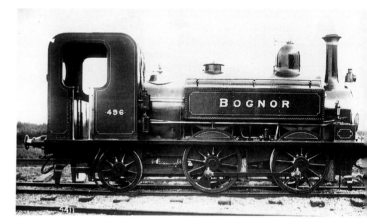

An interesting example of Stroudley modernisation, coupled with respect shown for locomotives introduced by his predecessor. Purchased from Kitson & Co. for £1,140 in December 1868, this LB&SCR saddle tank, numbered 76, worked awhile in London, before moving to Littlehampton. In January 1872 Stroudley fitted stylish cabsides, replaced the locomotive's stovepipe with a copper-capped chimney, and added a dome cover which was later crowned by two balance safety valves. Renumbered 358 (1877) and 496 (1886), and named *Bognor*, the engine found full employment around Bognor, Littlehampton, and Eastbourne. Between 1890 and 1894 it also worked on the Hayling Island branch, until 'Terriers' arrived to take the branch over completely. *(Author's Collection)*

Today, Stroudley's concern for men working under him would be styled 'industrial psychology'. In the late 1870s, however, his ardent advocacy of free-steaming locomotives, comfortable cabs, and flamboyant locomotive livery simply brought a new pride to all who served the LB&SCR. Each locomotive was allocated its own crew, and Stroudley's shrewd tactic of inscribing the driver's name and cumulative mileage in gold letters

Bramley and Wonersh, two small Surrey villages, shared a common railway station on the LB&SCR's Guildford–Christ's Hospital branch. Each village name was taken up just the same when Stroudley produced his later batches of 'Terriers'. *(Steamchest)*

inside each cab had a wonderfully stimulative effect of offering each man a *share* in his locomotive's welfare. The practice was only abandoned in later years, when vastly improved working conditions for the men required locomotives to be worked in two, or more, shifts.

Stroudley's passion for naming his passenger engines displayed another facet of his undoubtedly artistic temperament. Yet, curiously, not until his later express tender locomotives arrived did his imagination rise beyond the provision of place names. As a result, no village in Sussex was too tiny to be denied recognition! His ex-pupil, Dugald Drummond, on the NBR,

shared this peculiar limitation. Nevertheless, Stroudley's partiality for locomotive names, no matter how mundane the end product might be, was warmly shared by train crews and travelling public alike. In any case, the names were so beautifully and boldly inscribed that even dear old ladies could not possibly mistake them for destination boards! So one would like to think . . .

Thus, 90% of the 377 locomotives which Stroudley designed bore names. Of the 34 which did not, 32 were Class C and C1 goods engines, while the remaining pair were class '18' 0-4-2Ts, ordered from Brighton Works by Craven but redesigned by Stroudley. It seems that names were to be bestowed on these tanks too, but for some reason intention was never translated into practice. In fairness, it should be added that Stroudley, in modifying many other Craven-inspired engines, lavished names on them quite impartially, despite his understandable lack of affection for the locomotives concerned.

Like all great locomotive engineers, Stroudley had both convictions, and failings; and, of course, they clearly emerged as his work with LB&SCR got under way. All through the 1870s, for instance, and on into the 1880s, a current fashion for express passenger 'single wheelers', exercised by many major British railway companies, carried with it the corollary that large driving wheels and cylinders should be matched with moderate boilers and small fireboxes. Stroudley, though, would have none of it. Thus, when his first 'true' 2-2-2, No.151 *Grosvenor*, emerged from Brighton Works on 24th December 1874, at a cost, for locomotive alone, of £3,075, its design patently ran against the tide of popular engineering opinion. The boiler, to start with, was extra generous. So, too, was the firebox; yet *Grosvenor's* 17in × 24in cylinders and 6ft 9in driving wheels were no larger than those of contemporary coupled engines. Whatever else, Stroudley correctly deduced, there would be no shortage of steam as and when the 'single' was called upon to perform arduous express duties. Inevitably, feedwater heating, another passion of Stroudley's, was employed; but the locomotive's initial powerful steam brake was replaced by the Westinghouse vacuum

LB&SCR No.203 started life as one of twelve 'singles' which were delivered by Robert Stephenson & Co. in 1864. As they incorporated a certain amount of material from a cancelled Egyptian order, the locomotives were bought at a reduced price of £2,500 each. This did not prevent the LB&SCR, however, from selling four of them back to the Egyptian Government Railways a year later, as 'low mileage passenger engines', for £3,000 each! From their inception, alas, the 'singles' were heavy on coal, and during 1866–67 five of the eight which remained in LB&SCR ownership were modified under Craven's aegis. Stroudley dealt with another in 1871, by rebuilding No.203 at a rather exorbitant cost of £1,870. Still in 2-2-2 form, the locomotive was given the name *Sussex*. Five years later, the Adams safety valves on the domeless boiler were eliminated in favour of a pair of balanced safety valves attached to a typical Stroudley dome; and the latter, plus Westinghouse brake, Stroudley cab and livery, are clearly in evidence in our photograph. Laid aside, under cover, early in 1895, and renumbered 503 in January 1897 to make way for a new Billinton Class B2 4-4-0, *Sussex* was eventually sold for scrap to Moss Isaacs in February 1897. *(Author's Collection)*

brake ere *Grosvenor* took part in the inter-company brake trials at Newark in 1875. Results there, in fact, convinced Stroudley that the Westinghouse air brake was superior still; and on 19th December 1877 this remarkable man persuaded the LB&SCR directorate to spend £20,000 on so equipping 50 engines and 500 carriages. In due course, *Grosvenor* was appropriately converted. Meanwhile, in rather quaint contrast, Stroudley, ever mindful of *sensible* economies, introduced a new type of tender, with inside bearings to all three axles. The argument here was that worn locomotive trailing wheels could be used under the tenders before ultimate re-tyring was required! Consequent difficulty in getting at tender springs and boxes was, it seems, considered the lesser of two evils.

Initially classified 'B', *Grosvenor* was joined in January 1877 by No.325 *Abergavenny*, a Class 'F' 2-2-2 of scaled down proportions which was built at Brighton at a reduced cost, including tender, of £2,970. Experience in this instance, however, with 16in × 22in cylinders and 6ft 6in driving wheels suggested that power was being sacrificed in the interests of economy; and 24 subsequent Class 'G' 2-2-2s, shopped from Brighton in 1880–82, though still only costing £2,675, restored the balance by employing 17in diameter cylinders and lighter steel frames. Finally, in December 1884, all 26 'singles' were grouped under Class 'G' and, subjected to various modifications in their time, they served LB&SCR well into the early 1900s. *Grosvenor*, withdrawn in May 1907 with a top mileage of 1,048,090, was one of several which were shipped to Italy in August 1907, destined to end their days as 'high quality' scrap metal. The reconditioned boiler of No.329 *Stephenson*, the last survivor of the class, left Brighton in October 1915, duly fitted with a tall hinged stovepipe chimney, for subsequent stationary use at No.7 Base Hospital, Rennes.

Two more of Stroudley's heartfelt antipathies thrust him into even deeper conflict with currently accepted locomotive development. Apart from declining to employ injectors, he also turned his face against compounding. That was one thing; but his stubborn refusal to introduce leading bogies on his engines really placed him in a minority. By now most leading British locomotive engineers embraced the theory that leading bogies on express engines helped to 'iron out the track ahead', thus easing the passage of large driving wheels. Stroudley, for his part, never tired of advocating the merits of employing front-coupled driving wheels. 'Large leading wheels', he insisted, 'pass over points, crossings etc very easily, causing less disturbance than small ones'. In addition to arguing that maximum adhesion should also be exerted well forward in such engines, he threw in a further conviction that merit could be gained by adopting a higher centre of gravity than was customary at the time. The slight rolling motion this induced, he avowed, eased a locomotive's passage, and eliminated the violent lateral lurches which often afflicted those with a lower centre of gravity.

Beautifully liveried as usual, Stroudley's large 'single', No.151 *Grosvenor*, is seen here at Battersea shortly before being renumbered 326 in December 1880, to coincide with 25 successors. Shopped in 1874, carrying a spare Craven tender and wooden brake shoes, the locomotive's appearance has altered somewhat, with the addition of Westinghouse air brake and new Stroudley tender. Interestingly, the small cylindrical casing of another Stroudley innovation, his speed indicator — an odd amalgam of footplate water gauges, motivated by a four-bladed paddle wheel which was linked to the crank axle — can be seen below the firebox. (*Author's Collection*)

The true test of Stroudley's dictums came in the mid-1870s, when the undoubted success with which his recently introduced Class 'D' 0-4-2 tanks were handling semi-fast traffic around London convinced him that, given increased water capacity, the same wheel formula was capable of wider traffic implications. Thus, in September 1876, Stroudley's first 0-4-2 tender engine, 'D' class (later D2) No.300 *Lyons*, left Brighton Works. Apart from possessing a larger boiler and firebox, the new engine mirrored the already proven 'D-Tanks' in most other details — and, as such, the success of this 5ft 6in class was never in doubt. The first eight, shopped in 1876–78, ran with rebuilt Craven tenders; but six more, added in 1883, were given the additional sophistication of Westinghouse brake and new inside-framed 2,238 gallon tenders. Named after a wide range of European resorts which were served by the LB&SCR's Newhaven-Dieppe connections, the D2s worked on for some 30 years before bowing the knee; and, so substantial was their construction, wheels and motion from five of them were re-used when Marsh I1 4-4-2Ts Nos.5 and 7–10 were built in 1906–07.

Useful though the D2s proved to be, they were, however, essentially mixed-traffic machines and could hardly be expected to handle heavy fast expresses. This sober fact was not lost on Stroudley, and as he watched LB&SCR express traffic burgeon during the winter of 1877–78 he resolved to enlarge the 'D-Tank' formula further still. Cautious as ever, however, he confined himself to the production of one large-wheeled 0-4-2 tender engine. It duly emerged from Brighton Works on 11th September 1878 in the form of No.208 *Richmond*. Cylinders of 17¼ in × 26in were not unexpected — but *Richmond's* 6ft 6in driving wheels raised a few eyebrows at Brighton! Nevertheless, the new 0-4-2 soon proved its worth on crack express service and justified the completion of five more in 1879–80. Ten years later, all six were transferred to St Leonards. Fireboxes had already been renewed and, with new cylinders also fitted between 1892 and 1899, the 'Richmonds' served the Hastings area extremely well. Renumbered 508–13 in 1897, then 608–13 at the turn of the century, all accumulated healthy mileages before a final withdrawal in November 1904 saw the end of the class.

No.199 *Samuel Laing* was one of seventeen B1s which were allocated to Brighton by April 1891. Battersea and New Cross accounted for sixteen more, the remaining trio went to Eastbourne and this distribution remained pretty static until April 1910, when the first of ten pre-World War One withdrawals was effected. Two months later, No.199 was placed on the LB&SCR's Duplicate List. This, however, did not prevent the locomotive from entering Southern Railway stock in 1923, with a cumulative mileage of 1,141,526. Most of the B1s taken into SR stock acquired Maunsell's dark green livery from 1924 onwards and lost their names in the process. *Samuel Laing* enjoyed the unique privilege of going to the breakers in July 1925 with name and pre-Grouping umber livery still intact. *(W. G. Tilling — Author's Collection)*

Historically, the real significance of the 'Richmond' class locomotives lay in the fact that they paved the way for Stroudley's masterpiece, his much more prolific 'Gladstone' 0-4-2s. Once again, although an order was placed in March 1882 for six engines and tenders, at a combined cost of £16,000, Stroudley was careful to assess the initial performance of the December 1882 prototype, No.214 *Gladstone*, before authorising Brighton Works to proceed with the remainder. Thus, twelve more months elapsed before a second 'Gladstone', No.215 *Salisbury*, was shopped. Indeed, the last pair did not enter traffic until November 1885. Initially, the new engines were classified 'B', but this was later altered to 'B1'.

The prototype B1, No.214 *Gladstone*, renumbered 618 in July 1920 to permit rationalisation of the 'D-Tanks' growing ranks, also survived to enter SR stock; though it was condemned in April 1927, with a total mileage of 1,346,918. Fortunately, the Stephenson Locomotive Society intervened to urge its preservation and an agreed contribution by the Society of £140 saw *Gladstone* taken into Brighton Works, where it was painstakingly restored to original LB&SCR condition. Renovations at the Science Museum, South Kensington, however, thwarted an intention to see the locomotive installed there as a permanent exhibit; instead, *Gladstone* was granted 'temporary' accommodation at the LNER's York Railway Museum, with effect from 31st May 1927. Our photograph, taken in August 1935, testifies that residence there lasted rather longer than was anticipated! In the event, ownership passed on to the British Transport Commission, and *Gladstone* later found a safe home in the National Railway Museum at York. *(Steamchest)*

Stroudley was too consummate an artist to be a vain man. Thus, it was the LB&SCR Board which recommended that a 'Terrier' should be displayed at the Paris Exhibition of 1878 and promptly set aside the sum of £90 for special preparation of the engine. It was, incidentally, the only 'Terrier' to be fitted with Stroudley's patent speed indicator. After *Brighton's* triumphal return to England an appropriate legend was painted in gilt letters on her tank sides, while the Gold Medal she won was, at the insistence of the Board, presented to Stroudley at a brief ceremony held on 2nd July 1879. *(Author's Collection)*

However one might view Stroudley's innate conservatism in sticking to his 0-4-2 wheel arrangement, it cannot be denied that the 'Gladstones' were superlative engines, both in appearance and performance. Seen at their best in full LB&SCR livery, they were a source of great pride to the men who handled them. Their 18¼in × 26in cylinders, akin to those previously fitted to Stroudley's Class C1 0-6-0 goods engines, had been unashamedly adopted to give greater power — and the formula worked. It should be added, though, that only foresight on Stroudley's part in providing highly flexible coil springs for their 6ft 6in driving wheels, and less resilient leaf springs for the leading coupled wheels and 4ft 6in trailing wheels, forestalled potentially embarrassing disproof of his contention that heavily weighted front-coupled engines could negotiate curves and crossovers at speed in perfect safety and comfort. 'Gladstones', it was soon discovered, behaved rather alarmingly in such circumstances and, once bitten, their drivers unearthed a new respect for speed restrictions. But firing was uncomplicated, fuel consumption was moderate, and all agreed that the cabs on the B1s were tailor-made for maximum comfort and convenience. Thus, there were few complaints from Traffic Department when 24 more 'Gladstones' were introduced during Stroudley's remaining period of office. Even his successor, R. J. Billinton, who held no great brief for the class, agreed, as an interim measure, to the construction of six more; shopped between November 1890 and April 1891, these brought the final 'Gladstone' tally to 36.

How, then, does one sum up this mercurial figure, William Stroudley? His versatility as an engineer, particularly when coupled with his undoubted ability for obtaining genuine respect from those who served under him, came as a breath of fresh air at a critical time in LB&SCR affairs. He designed locomotives which gave his Company a new dignity and status in the railway world; yet he had energy left to employ his skills on Brighton's Newhaven–Dieppe steamships. No sooner, too, had Edison invented the incandescent lamp, than Stroudley transformed one of the LB&SCR's American-built Pullman cars into the world's first electrically-lit carriage. Special first-class bogie coaches, designed to convey business men to and from Brighton and London Bridge, embodied much the same opulence. These, however, offered a disturbing contrast to the skeletal four-wheelers which ferried the London suburbs so industriously. How strange it was that such a gifted man should be capable of such contradiction!

History provides us with an answer to that paradox: strong-minded men find compromise a difficult, if not impossible, exercise. Stroudley's unshakeable faith in standardisation, for instance, rescued the LB&SCR initially from the locomotive quagmire it inherited from J. C. Craven. But once it joined forces with his equally impregnable distrust of leading bogies, it placed him at a distinct disadvantage *vis-à-vis* those British locomotive engineers who chose to blaze the 4-4-0 trail. Truth to tell, Stroudley reached the end of a self-made *cul de sac* with his 'Gladstones' — for the design was incapable of further enlargement. Yet, conversely, another of his standardised products, his beautifully machined 'Terriers', played as vital a role in resolving the LB&SCR's inner London problems as did Stanier's 'Black Fives' and Gresley's V2s during the 'blitz' of 1940–41. These, then — plus, of course, his untimely demise — were the kinds of contradiction which inhibited the progress one might have expected from such a brilliant practitioner. Nevertheless, Stroudley's fame spread abroad.

Eleven years after the 'Terrier's' 1878 Paris success, this time at the 1889 Paris Exhibition, a beautifully prepared 'Gladstone', No.189 *Edward Blount*, graced the British Stand, together with SER 4-4-0 No.240 *Onward* and MR 4-2-2 No.1853. All were awarded Gold Medals and the three British exhibits so intrigued the Paris, Lyons & Mediterranean Railway management that the

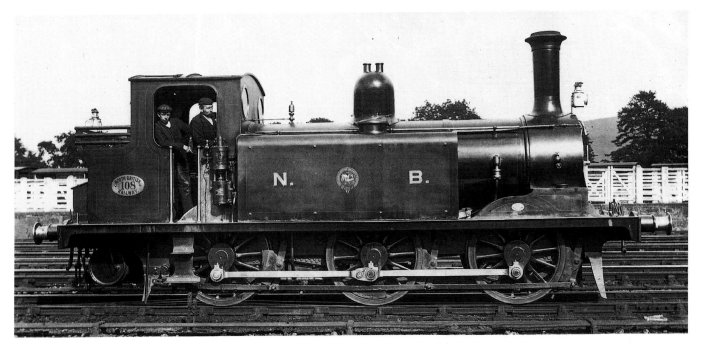

respective companies were invited to conduct a series of joint trials on French metals. The Midland Railway declined; but *Onward* and *Edward Blount* duly locked horns on the Paris–Laroche route. Results were not totally conclusive — the 'Gladstone' kept better time and burned less fuel, while *Onward* proved to be slightly faster. French railway authorities, though, were favourably impressed by the way the two British engines tackled strange conditions. Then — tragedy struck, quite suddenly. A chill Stroudley had contracted during the trials worsened. It developed into acute bronchitis, and he died at the Grand Hotel St Lazare, Paris, aged 56, on 20th December 1889.

His funeral at Brighton on Christmas Eve was an astonishing affair and drew a procession half a mile long. First, led by four Brighton cross-channel captains, came 70 officers and seamen. Behind them, marching four abreast, no fewer than 1600 men from Brighton Works doggedly paid their respects; while, immediately preceding the cortège, five carriages conveyed departmental heads and foremen. Innumerable private carriages brought up the rear.

Too often, funerals on this scale can be viewed a little cynically as stage-managed events. But there is a poignancy — is there not? — in the memory of that solid phalanx of marching Brighton men which somehow hallmarks the true nature of the man they were laying to rest.

Stroudley's influence revealed itself in Dugald Drummond's maiden design when the latter became Locomotive Superintendent to the North British Railway in 1875. The NBR, employing ageing Wheatley saddletanks on branch passenger work, badly needed reinforcements. Drummond's response was to design a new six-coupled side tank. Twenty-four were built in 1875–78, and this view of No.108 illustrates Drummond's close adherence to his late master's practices. The locomotives were really a larger version of the 'Terrier'. Another Stroudley touch lay in the provision of local place names. No.108 first bore the name *Hamilton*, then *St Andrews*. By 1926, however, when all had gone, more than two dozen 'Terriers' were still working hard down South. *(Author's Collection)*

Again in the year 1875, an even more striking compliment came from New South Wales, Australia, when eight locally-built 0-6-0Ts entered suburban traffic at Sydney. The coal bunker was slightly larger, the cab, understandably, offered greater ventilation to enginemen; but in all other respects the Australian N67s were facsimiles of Stroudley's 'Terrier'. The rugged life they led was not dissimilar, either — and the last was not scrapped until 1938. Comparative dimensions of both this and the previously illustrated NBR 'spin off' are shown in Table 3. *(Author's Collection)*

N-67 Class
N.S.W.R.

DRAWING · KEN UPTON

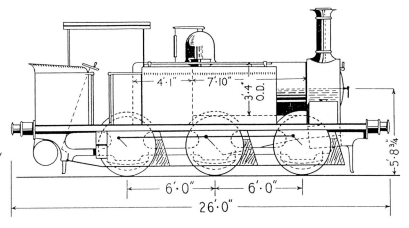

Valediction

Had Stroudley not been the perfectionist he was, the paeans of praise which were lavished on him, particularly where his 'Terriers' were concerned, might easily have turned his head. As it was, being human, he enjoyed success; but, being Stroudley, he was never content to rest upon his laurels. To his dying day, therefore, he probed, perfected — and encouraged others to do likewise.

Others, far beyond his immediate environment, certainly did. Dugald Drummond, deeply influenced by his early associations with William Stroudley, carried many of his convictions back North with him.

One final tribute came 60 years later, in the mid-1930s, when the Southern Railway, under the aegis of R. E. L. Maunsell, summoned all seven of L. B. Billinton's magnificent 'Baltic' tanks to Eastleigh. Within a matter of months Weir pumps and Westinghouse equipment were removed and the locomotives, destined now for Western Section duties, re-emerged rebuilt as Class N15X 4-6-0s. All were fitted with tenders which were previously carried by Urie S15 class 4-6-0 goods engines. For obvious reasons N15X No.2333 retained the name *Remembrance*, as did No.2329 the name *Stephenson*. The remaining five, however,

As they re-entered traffic after rebuild the N15X 4-6-0s were allocated to Nine Elms. Performance, however, proved disappointing, and they were soon relegated to main line semi-fast duties. Equipped with Maunsell superheater and displaying the appropriate smokebox-top snifting valves, No.2332 *Stroudley* was duly photographed at Nine Elms. The tender she carries came from S15 class No.510. *(Author's Collection)*

Nos.2327/28/30–32, now commemorated the names of Locomotive Engineers of the pre-Grouping companies. *Trevithick, Hackworth, Cudworth* and *Beattie* could all be found in this miniature hall of fame — and, fittingly, No.2332, rebuilt in November 1935, was named *Stroudley*.

Alas, for a variety of reasons, mainly connected with rapidly expanding electrification, life was comparatively short for the species. The first N15X withdrawal, that of No.32328 *Hackworth*, came in January 1955 and exactly one year later, No.32332 *Stroudley* paid its final visit to Eastleigh Works. During its lifetime as a 'Baltic' tank and N15X 4-6-0 the locomotive completed a total of 1,066,737 miles.

In mid-1947 the N15X rebuilds were transferred en bloc to Basingstoke. Freshly liveried in BR malachite Green and now carrying No.32332, *Stroudley* is seen here passing Vauxhall on a Southampton express in July 1948. Four and a half years later the locomotive was given BR lined-black livery, and a second coat came its way in April 1954. *(Steamchest)*

Chapter 2
THE 'TERRIERS' — 1872–1880

IN THE EVENT, the LB&SCR was thrice blessed in acquiring Stroudley's services when it did; for the preceding decade had been one of unremitting expansion, particularly in the Metropolitan area. First of all, the Company's ambition to pierce the heart of London's West End had been realised at last in the form of a half share in a new terminus at Victoria. The remainder was leased jointly to LCDR and GWR; but symptomatic of Brighton's zeal, the LB&SCR platforms opened first, on 1st October 1860. Next, on 30th June 1862, came the South London Act authorising construction of a rail link between London Bridge and Victoria. LB&SCR suburban traffic prospects brightened accordingly as this important 8½ mile artery opened for public use on 1st May 1867. Alas, they soon dulled again as operational problems reared their ugly head.

Meanwhile, incorporation of a new Company, the East London Railway, in 1865 added substance to the prospect of a direct link between the Great Eastern Railway on the north bank of the Thames and LB&SCR and South Eastern Railway in the south. Surely enough, Brunel's abortive pedestrian tunnel at Wapping was duly converted to railway use, and on 7th December 1869 a brand new double track between Wapping and New Cross (Gate) received its public baptism. Extension to Shoreditch followed on 10th April 1876 and the LB&SCR, closely implicated from the start, eventually instituted a service between Liverpool Street and Croydon. In light of these developments, the LB&SCR Board, bleakly surveying the hopeless multiplicity of Craven types which constituted its total stock of 155 locomotives, decided it was high time its Locomotive Superintendent abandoned his well-known antipathy towards standardisation. Pressure was duly applied. Craven, an ingenious and loyal servant in most respects, stubbornly refused to comply on this issue, and his resignation was accepted by the Board with effect from 31st January 1870. Happily, history depones that his departure was accompanied by a refreshing absence of mutual recrimination.

Thus, the situation in 1870 was such that it hardly required a Stroudley to perceive that the LB&SCR was coping ill with its increased share of London suburban traffic. But someone of Stroudley's calibre was badly needed to supply an *answer* to the problem; that he did, most spectacularly, with his 'Terriers'.

The East London line, with its formidable gradients of 1:40 on either side of the Thames Tunnel, posed problems enough. But it was the South London line which presented the greater challenge. To begin with, its light iron rails, shoddy sleepers, and shallow ballast called for locomotives of much lighter axle loading and shorter wheelbase than anything the LB&SCR could presently summon. Again, the close proximity of many of the ten stations which had been crammed in between London Bridge and Victoria demanded a locomotive versatility hitherto unknown in Brighton calculations; eight of the stations were less than a mile apart. Most were perched on gradients ranging from 1:200 to 1:96 and at the Victoria end, a standing start invoked an almost immediate scramble at 1:64 up Grosvenor Road bank. Add to this the discomfiting factor that South London traffic was 'peak hour' by nature and it is clear that the need for economic, as well as efficient, locomotive practice loomed large, perforce, in Stroudley's mind.

The LB&SCR's urgent requirement to see so many virtues embodied in one locomotive design led Stroudley unerringly to the conclusion that only a very special type of light six-coupled side tank would suffice. Not unnaturally, his thoughts reverted to *Balnain*, the 0-6-0T he built for the Highland Railway in 1869. The dimensions, he knew, were not far out; though many refinements would have to be made. Curiously enough, his first thoughts, as revealed in drawings dated June 1870, postulated a considerably smaller tank engine, with domeless boiler and Adams safety valves. Then, concluding correctly that such a diminutive machine would not be rugged enough to cope with London suburban traffic requirements, he prepared fresh drawings the following year. This time the design was larger, albeit the domeless boiler, wooden front buffer beam, and over-modest side tanks were retained. But it was still not right, and it took a third, and final, set of drawings that year to bring to light all the 'Terrier' features we know so well. Well, *nearly* all — for the boiler remained stubbornly domeless. Only after March 1872, by which time work had commenced on construction of the first six 'Terriers', did Stroudley relent, by substituting a larger boiler surmounted by steam dome and spring balance safety valves.

The 'Terrier' as first built — no Westinghouse brake, so link couplings were employed. The pipe joining the tanks in front of the cab tended to conduct water as well as steam, and was soon abandoned. So, too, was the small lever on the smokebox just below the condensing pipe. (*Author's Collection*)

Twelve years after Stroudley's death, *Stepney*'s immaculate livery still fires the imagination as the 'Terrier' prepares to leave Brighton Central on a Kemp Town train. The little locomotive has just been Duplicate Listed, and its new running number, 655, now appears in neat gold transfer numerals on the bunker side. Brake blocks are still wooden, and the locomotive has not yet been adapted for motor-train work. *(Author's Collection)*

The result, at a reasonable building cost of £1,800, was a finely proportioned little engine which was to prove more than a match for the tasks it was set. To keep axle loading to a minimum the frames were slotted, and so low were the bufferbeams — iron, not *wooden* as originally intended — the castings of the buffers projected above platform level. The boiler, too, was pitched so low that only a single-arm regulator could be accommodated in the cab. Despite its modest proportions, however, the boiler contrived to produce plenty of steam and it was beautifully complemented by a copper-capped chimney, 3ft 6in high. The cab, with its distinctive white-painted roof, dished to eliminate drumming, was both neat and functional. Inside, stone-coloured paint offset the white under-roof, and both boiler backplate and spectacle glasses were encased in brass. Trouble was the glasses were rigid and this could at times hinder both vision and ventilation. Adding further to the lightness factor, marine-type big ends were employed, while connecting rods, 5ft long and round in section, were machined in Stroudley tradition to precise proportions. A 'Terrier' in average trim weighed only 24 tons 12 cwts, but Stroudley, ever the perfectionist, saw to it that the centre of gravity came directly over the driving axle. This offered ideal weight distribution to a locomotive which simply had to be capable of working with equal efficiency in either direction. Firing, except at speed, presented no problems, for coal consumption was masterfully low. As E. L. Ahrons observed in later years: "A 'Terrier' would run on coal which a Webb compound would throw out of the chimney".

The first six 'Terriers' bore many other Stroudley hallmarks. The side tanks were really a form of saddle tank, for they were solely supported by a frame which passed over the boiler top and were not in any way bracketed to the footplate. Cylinders, inclined at 1:11, were originally 13in × 20in, but considerable variation was later introduced, for a variety of reasons, by both Stroudley and his successor, R. J. Billinton.

Perhaps Stroudley's most controversial innovation was the feedwater pump he devised specially for the 'Terriers'. Having conducted tests which persuaded him that the practice of feeding hot water rather than cold to a locomotive boiler lent itself to significant decrease in fuel consumption, he deduced further that feed pumps were superior to injectors. In any case the latter did not tolerate hot water kindly. Thus, where 'Terriers' were concerned, exhaust steam, when influenced by a valve operated from the footplate, entered a pipe on the left-hand tank. After circulating there and heating the water, it passed on to the right-hand tank. In due course any surplus steam was taken off by the right-hand condensing pipe and was released to the atmosphere through the locomotive chimney. Unfortunately, two problems emerged to confound this tidy arrangement. First, when, as sometimes happened, the footplate-operated valve stuck, the only way to bring the feed pump into operation was for the driver to edge his way along the running plate and open the pet-cock by hand. Alas, all against Company regulations, the practice was only too frequently observed whilst locomotives were still in motion; bruises and abrasions were commonplace and it took a more serious accident in February 1901 (see under No.41 *Piccadilly*) to bring matters finally to a head. The second objection centred on periodic floodbacks which occurred within the smokebox when tanks were full. Apart from causing cylinder damage, on the premise that oil and water do not mix, such calamities caused equally grievous offence to members of the public, who took exception to being showered with dirty hot water.

Another subject close to Stroudley's heart was that of locomotive brakes. At the time he acceded to office at Brighton, hand brakes were being employed almost universally on British railways and power-operated brake systems were very much in their infancy. The urgency, however, with which the 'Terriers' were required left little room for experiment and, bowing to the inevitable, Stroudley fitted the first six with wooden brake blocks. These were capable of being applied by either hand or steam power. In the event the latter proved so temperamental in practice that London suburban train crews soon resorted to exclusive use of the less powerful hand brake in course of their exacting daily routines. An improved layout, however, was introduced in 1873 and subsequent developments led to complete adoption of the Westinghouse air brake.

Where locomotive livery was concerned, green had long been the LB&SCR's chosen colour. Brunswick was the shade favoured when Craven took over in 1847; but a darker glossy green had gained precedence by the time Stroudley arrived on the scene. Harry Wainwright was to employ such a colour when he revolutionised SE&CR locomotive livery half a century later. Fresh from Highland Railway service, Stroudley brought his 'improved engine green' with him and from thereon locomotive livery at Brighton never looked back; indeed, it was to blossom into a fine art.

Only Stroudley's sense of diplomacy and powers of persuasion could possibly have induced the LB&SCR Board to concur with his proposal to lavish golden yellow paint and equally flamboyant decoration on 50 small tank engines, most of which would spend their working days in some of London's grimiest localities. Over the years occasional extramural attacks from such

as F. W. Webb, of LNWR fame, on grounds of unnecessary expense were deftly, but sharply, rebuffed. So, too, was one Brighton director who complained in October 1880 of excessive locomotive cleaning costs. Stroudley's response was typically unrepentant. Immaculate livery, he reminded the Board, was the best possible public advertisement the Company could seek and its continuance was well worth an extra £5,000 a year. Needless to say, locomotive and cleaning staff backed him to the hilt.

Stroudley, of course, knew as well as anyone that costs were important; particularly as on the LB&SCR and elsewhere, the gap between income and expenditure was beginning to close during the last quarter of the 19th Century. It was *false* economies he set his face against. Yet, despite his rapidly growing prestige, he still had to face critics. As early as 1877, queries were being raised within the Board as to why domestic locomotive building costs should exceed those of many other companies. Stroudley stonewalled awhile, then delivered a devastating reply in 1885, when he was called upon to deliver a paper to the Institution of Civil Engineers. Between the years 1873 and 1884, he pointed out, LB&SCR annual locomotive mileage had risen to 9,690,000, an increase of 56%. Coal consumption had only risen by 24%. Ergo, the potential saving of £27,000 on coal more than balanced the LB&SCR's increased capital expenditure and clearly justified the great care with which locomotives were designed and built at Brighton. The equation, he might well have added, was further enhanced by the pains he took to instruct train crews in the art of economic firing. If proof was needed, the South London line offered ample evidence: there 'Terriers' worked a full nine hour day, yet coal consumption rarely rose above an average 22¾ lbs per mile. Suburban tanks carrying out similar duties on the SER were consuming 31½ lbs.

Table 1 lists all 50 'Terriers' which emerged from Brighton Works during 1872 and 1880. In light of experience, however, various modifications were introduced and the locomotives fall

The last eight locomotives of those built in 1877 took matters a stage further by introducing the Westinghouse air brake and appropriate screw couplings. As can be seen from this study of *Piccadilly*, however, wooden brake shoes were still retained. A new steel firebox was tried out on this locomotive in July 1889; but was removed after thorough tests. (*Author's Collection*)

TABLE 1
LIST OF 'TERRIERS' IN ORDER OF BUILDING

No.	Name	Date built	Date to traffic	Surplus listed	Duplicate listed	Rebuilt to Class A1X	Sold (S) or Withdrawn (W)
71	Wapping	Sept 1872	12/9/1872	1898	1901	—	(S) Jan 1905
72	Fenchurch	Sept 1872	9/9/1872	—	—	Apl 1913	(S) June 1898 XX
73	Deptford	Oct 1872	12/10/1872	1898	1901	Feb 1912	(S) Apl 1919
74	Shadwell	Oct 1872	12/10/1872	1898	1901	—	(S) July 1920
70	Poplar	Dec 1872	4/12/1872	1897	—	Apl 1943	(S) May 1901 XX
75	Blackwall	Dec 1872	2/12/1872	1898	—	—	(S) Mch 1899
64	Kemptown	Jun 1874	20/6/1874	1898	1901	—	(W) Jan 1903
69	Peckham	July 1874	9/7/1874	1898	—	Apl 1930	(S) Apl 1900
65	Tooting	Aug 1874	29/8/1874	1898	—	—	(W) Feb 1901
66	Hatcham	Aug 1874	21/8/1874	1898	—	—	(W) Feb 1901
67	Brixton	Aug 1874	6/8/1874	1898	1901	—	(S) Apl 1920
68	Clapham	Aug 1874	5/8/1874	1898	1901	—	(S) Mch 1903
59	Cheam	Oct 1875	16/10/1875	1905	1901	Dec 1921	(W) June 1963
61	Sutton	Oct 1875	27/10/1875	1898	1901	Jan 1912	(W) Apl 1963
62	Martello	Oct 1875	27/10/1875	1898	1901	Dec 1912	(W) Nov 1963 XX
63	Preston	Oct 1875	7/10/1875	1898	1901	May 1913	(W) Mch 1925
56	Shoreditch	Nov 1875	18/11/1875	—	1901	—	(S) Aug 1903
58	Wandle	Nov 1875	11/11/1875	—	1901	—	(W) Feb 1902
60	Ewell	Nov 1875	6/11/1875	1898	1901	—	(W) Dec 1902
53	Ashstead	Dec 1875	8/12/1875	1905	1900	—	(S) Feb 1937
55	Stepney	Dec 1875	21/12/1875	1905	1901	Oct 1912	(S) May 1960 XX
57	Thames	Jan 1876	10/1/1876	—	1901	—	(S) May 1902
52	Surrey	Feb 1876	14/2/1876	—	1900	—	(S) Sept 1902
54	Waddon	Feb 1876	16/2/1876	—	1900	—	(S) Sept 1904 XX
47	Cheapside	Dec 1876	15/12/1876	1905	1901	Jan 1912	(W) Oct 1951
48	Leadenhall	Dec 1876	9/12/1876	—	1901	—	(W) Aug 1901
49	Bishopsgate	Dec 1876	2/12/1876	—	1901	—	(S) June 1902
50	Whitechapel	Dec 1876	14/12/1876	1905	1901	May 1920	(W) Nov 1963 XX
51	Rotherhithe	Dec 1876	14/12/1876	—	—	—	(W) Feb 1901
46	Newington	Jan 1877	10/1/1877	—	1902	Mch 1932	(S) Mch 1903 XX
41	Piccadilly	Jun 1877	2/6/1877	—	—	—	(W) Mch 1902
42	Tulsehill	Jun 1877	20/6/1877	1905	1902	—	(W) May 1925
43	Gipsyhill	Jun 1877	15/6/1877	1905	1902	Sep 1919	(S) Dec 1925
44	Fulham	Jun 1877	14/6/1877	1905	1902	Nov 1912	(W) Apl 1951
45	Merton	Jun 1877	12/6/1877	—	1902	—	(W) Jly 1904
76	Hailsham	Jun 1877	6/6/1877	—	—	—	(W) Apl 1903
40	Brighton	Mch 1878	10/3/1878	—	—	Aug 1918	(S) Jan 1902 XX
37	Southdown	May 1878	6/5/1878	1905	1905	—	(S) Feb 1918
39	Denmark	May 1878	18/5/1878	—	—	—	(S) Jly 1902
35	Morden	Jun 1878	1/6/1878	1905	1908	Apl 1922	(W) Mch 1963
36	Bramley	Jun 1878	8/6/1878	—	—	—	(S) Sept 1902
38	Millwall	Jun 1878	9/6/1878	1905	1905	—	(S) Feb 1918
77	Wonersh	Jly 1880	21/7/1880	1905	1907	Nov 1911	(W) Sep 1959
78	Knowle	Jly 1880	23/7/1880	1905	1907	Nov 1911	(W) Oct 1963 XX
79	Minories	Jly 1880	6/7/1880	1905	1907	Jan 1912	(S) Jan 1918
80	Bookham	Jly 1880	29/7/1880	1905	1909	Apl 1912	(W) Dec 1925
81	Beulah	Jly 1880	19/7/1880	1905	1909	—	(S) Jan 1918
82	Boxhill	Aug 1880	20/8/1880	1905	1911	—	(W) Aug 1946 XX
83	Earlswood	Sep 1880	8/9/1880	1905	1912	—	(S) Jan 1918
84	Crowborough	Sep 1880	8/9/1880	—	—	Jly 1916	(S) Nov 1903

XX = Preserved locomotive.

naturally into three main groups. The first of these, of course, embraced the 'original six', all of which entered service during the last quarter of 1872. At least two features were soon found wanting, and did not reappear on subsequent locomotives. One was a pipe which looped across the front of the cab to connect the side tanks; the other was a small lever on the right-hand side of the smokebox which operated a valve therein. The latter controlled the flow of exhaust steam into the tanks. Meanwhile, in the absence of air brake ordinary link couplings were fitted. Inside the cab only one gauge glass could be seen. The driver's side had to content itself with a pair of test cocks.

The second group consisted of 36 locomotives built between 1874 and 1878. Apart from abandoning the two features already mentioned, they introduced slightly different safety valve columns and tank filler caps. Divided steam ports, as on Stroudley's contemporary D tanks, were also employed, and cylinder cocks were dispensed with.

Tireless as ever in his perfectionism, Stroudley conducted further experiments over what were to be the last five years of his life. On the 'Terriers', sand was fed by gravity from boxes which were attached to the leading splasher. This time-honoured practice worked well enough when locomotives were running forward; but only the right-hand side delivered sand when a 'Terrier' ran bunker-first. Obviously this posed problems amidst the hurly-burly of London suburban life, and in March 1887, Stroudley fitted No.40 *Brighton* with steam sanding gear. In October that year, the same locomotive was retubed with a set of patent iron tubes and six months later, a variable blastpipe was

No.80 *Bookham* was one of the final eight 'Terriers' shopped in 1880. As can be seen, this batch embodied all modifications to date, and added little else but iron brake shoes. Earlier 'Terriers' lacking air brake were so fitted as they re-entered Works, and by 1882 the whole class was Westinghouse-equipped. *(Author's Collection)*

The standard of locomotive cleanliness on the LB&SCR is exemplified by this view of *Beulah*, taken at Brighton about 1900. It also illustrates the thinner style of lettering adopted by R. J. Billinton. The locomotive's condensing gear was removed in 1897. *(Author's Collection)*

installed. After thorough tests, however, these special fittings were removed. So, too, were new steel fireboxes tried out on Nos.41 and 49 in July 1889. 'Terriers' were subsequently given new copper fireboxes as and when their original iron boxes required replacement.

Boilers next received Stroudley's attention. In 1889 he had eighteen 'Terriers' fitted with 154 brass tubes of 1½in diameter, as opposed to the normal complement of 125 × 1¾in iron tubes. The net effect reduced heating surface by 34sq ft; though a

slight recovery to 506⅛sq ft was made by his successor the following year, when a further eight 'Terriers' were given 121 iron tubes, 1¾in diameter and 8ft 2in long. In due course something of a compromise emerged, in that tubes of 1¾in diameter were accepted as standard. From August 1893 onward, however, brass took the place of iron.

'Terriers' began life with 13in cylinders. Some modification was effected in 1874, but no further changes were considered necessary by Stroudley as older engines began to require cylinder replacement from August 1879 onwards. Then came the trauma of Stroudley's death in December 1889. As it happened, the man who succeeded him was a friend and former Brighton colleague; but, sympathetic as he was towards many of Stroudley's practices, R. J. Billinton had his own views as to how the LB&SCR's rapidly increasing traffic responsibilities should be handled. Coming too, as he did, straight from Derby, locomotive changes seemed inevitable.

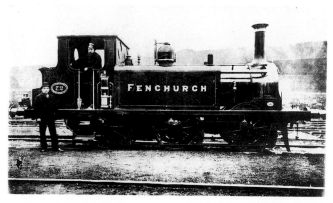

No.72 *Fenchurch*, one of the first two 'Terriers' to enter traffic in 1872, was also the first 'Terrier' to be sold by the LB&SCR, when the Newhaven Harbour Co., sorely pressed for motive power, purchased the locomotive for £350. A South London line veteran of almost 600,000 miles, *Fenchurch*, with only number plates and Westinghouse brake removed, reported for duty at Newhaven Harbour on 27th June 1898. *(Author's Collection)*

The 'inevitable' first affected the 'Terriers' early in 1892, when seven of the class, entering Brighton Works for major repair, were given new cylinders of 14in diameter. Furthermore, these were designed so that the whole of the exhaust steam now passed directly to the blastpipe. Thus, with Stroudley's condensing system rendered redundant, the exhaust pipes which formerly led to the tanks were removed. In most instances, though, the exhaust domes on top of the side tanks were left intact. Forty-one 'Terriers' in all were so treated during the years 1892-1900. Six more were scrapped or sold, still in their original condition and the remaining three were, somewhat belatedly, equipped with 12in cylinders in 1906–8. But, wisely and to the approval of railway staff and travelling public alike, Billinton perceived no need to interfere with the Stroudley tradition of locomotive livery. Passenger yellow and goods green were retained, as was the popular practice of naming locomotives. The only modification was that lettering was thinned a little.

One 'Terrier' left LB&SCR ownership in June 1898, when *Fenchurch* was sold to the Newhaven Harbour Co. This rather special circumstance, however, hardly anticipated a much more sombre decision taken by Brighton's Locomotive Committee seven months later, when it was resolved that the number of working 'Terriers' should be reduced to fifteen over the next three years. Intention was to thin the ranks as locomotives reported for heavy repairs. And here, if you please, was both irony and truth; for the 'Terriers', by being too successful in regenerating London suburban traffic, were now paying the price of being too small to handle longer and heavier trains. For over a decade, Stroudley 0-4-2 D tanks, the most prolific class the LB&SCR ever owned and E Class six-coupled tanks, had been pouring into the London area. Their greater flexibility had all but eclipsed their smaller brethren. As a result, Battersea and New Cross sheds' proud complement of 44 'Terriers' had shrunk by 50%. Sentiment aside, it cannot be denied that the Locomotive Committee had a strong case.

In the event, posterity can thank the Isle of Wight Central Railway for the fact that the proposed near-decimation of the 'Terriers' was halted, or at least postponed long enough to allow other events to take their course. The Brighton Board was strangely apathetic in November 1898 when IWCR first broached the subject of buying 'a suitable small tank'; and only sheer persistence on the minor Company's part forced completion of No.75 *Blackwall*'s sale in March 1899. Finding the 'Terrier' much to its liking, IWCR then proceeded to winkle three

more from Brighton's grasp between the years 1900 and 1903. Each of the four had run well over 500,000 miles, but at prices ranging from £600 to £800, the IWCR saw them as first class bargains. Similar thoughts must have dawned latterly on Billinton; for in due course LB&SCR advertisements began to appear in engineering journals, offering surplus 'Terriers' for sale. A price range of £500–£700 was quoted.

The value of 'Terriers' as secondhand investments was not lost on the railway fraternity and enquiries were even received from as far away as Australia and New Zealand. Once events calmed down, however, such sales as were effected confined themselves within the UK. As Table 2 shows, the LB&SCR disposed of 26 'Terriers', sold or scrapped, between the years 1898 and 1905. Two major railway Companies, one construction

So, exactly five years after the Locomotive Committee's fateful decision of 1899, the 'Terriers' found their numbers reduced by half; though the methods employed had not been quite so draconian as feared. Nevertheless, a second crisis for the species lay not far distant. It duly materialised when once again, unexpected death impinged itself on LB&SCR locomotive affairs. Suddenly, on 7th November 1904 at the comparatively early age of 59, R. J. Billinton died. Reaction to this unkind blow was swift. A meeting of the LB&SCR Board was hurriedly convened, a list of suitable candidates was drawn up, and within less than three weeks, D. E. Marsh moved from Doncaster as Billinton's successor. Interestingly, an application from Dugald Drummond received scant attention from the Board. Obviously Dugald's fire-eating reputation had travelled ahead of him! Still, the undoubted speed with which Marsh was appointed clearly betrayed Brighton's self-recognised need to move towards acquisition of larger and more powerful locomotives. It follows that with a proponent of 'bigger' engines now in the LB&SCR saddle, the future for Stroudley's miniscule six-coupled tanks looked bleaker than ever. Confirmation came when fifteen 'Terriers' appeared in the LB&SCR's withdrawal list for 1905–6.

TABLE 2
A HISTORY OF THE 'TERRIERS'

'Terriers' built by LB&SCR (1872–1880)		50		
LESS				*For individual locomotive histories*
Sold (1898–99)	− 2			
Scrapped (1901–04)	− 11		− 11	See Chapter 4
Sold to Pauling & Co. (1902)	− 5		− 5	See Chapter 4
Various other Sales (1900–05)	− 8	− 26	− 2	See Chapter 5
Sub-Total		− 24		
Sold (1918–22)		− 8	− 8	See Chapter 5
Handed over by LB&SCR to SR at Grouping		− 16		
ADD				
'Terriers' acquired additionally by SR on or after Grouping		− 8 ***		
		24		
LESS				
Sold or withdrawn by SR		− 10***	− 10	See Chapter 6
Handed over by SR to BR on 1st January 1948		− 14	− 14	See Chapters 7 & 8
			50	

*** For convenience sake the return of ex-S&MLR No.9 *Daphne* to Southern Railway stock and its subsequent withdrawal in 1949 have been ignored in the above Table.

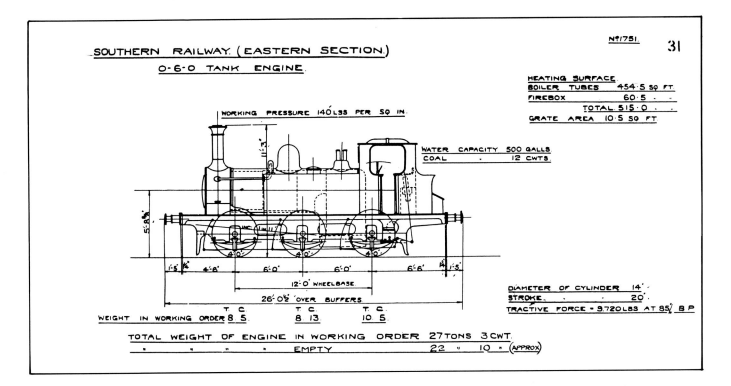

SOUTHERN RAILWAY. (EASTERN SECTION.)
0-6-0 TANK ENGINE.

HEATING SURFACE.
BOILER TUBES   454·5 SQ FT.
FIREBOX   60·5 "   "
          TOTAL 515·0 "   "
GRATE AREA 10·5 SQ FT

WORKING PRESSURE 140 LBS PER SQ IN.

WATER CAPACITY 500 GALLS
COAL   "   12 CWTS.

5'-8"

4'·0"   4'·0"   4'·0"

1'·5" 4'·8"   6'·0"   6'·0"   6'·6" 1'·5"
12'·0" WHEELBASE
26'·0½" OVER BUFFERS

DIAMETER OF CYLINDER 14"
STROKE.   "   20"
TRACTIVE FORCE = 9,720 LBS AT 85% B P

          T. C.   T. C.   T. C.
WEIGHT IN WORKING ORDER 8·5   8·13   10·5

TOTAL WEIGHT OF ENGINE IN WORKING ORDER 27 TONS 3 CWT.
    "   "   "   "   EMPTY   22 " 10 " (APPROX)

This time the Locomotive Committee really meant business; and there can be little doubt that few 'Terriers' would have survived over the next year or two — had not the Brighton Board, equally concerned over ever-spiralling costs of operating short-distance trains, arrived at a quite separate conclusion to experiment with motor-train working. Conventional steam tanks, it was resolved as late as February 1905, should be matched against steam and petrol railcars on short-haul duties. Thus, once again in the nick of time, reprieve came the 'Terriers' way. As the story of their ultimate triumph in the context is told in the next Chapter, suffice it to say for the moment that, ironically enough, Stroudley's original feed water heating arrangements found their way back into favour. Over the years 1906–9, in fact, 22 of the little tanks were so re-equipped as part of their motor-work modification. Motor-train working on LB&SCR had taken off with a vengeance.

Marsh, however, was a much more clinically minded man than Stroudley, and his tolerance of the latter's practices extended little beyond feed water heating. At a Locomotive Committee meeting in April 1905, he chose to express disapproval of both yellow paint and locomotive names and, rather to his surprise, found his ardent advocacy of greater economy struck an agreeable chord with a powerful minority of Directors. The upshot was that six months later, on 13th October 1905, twelve locomotives, dressed in a variety of goods and passenger liveries, were placed on inspection at London Bridge: *Boxhill*, representing the 'Terriers', was turned out in Stroudley 'green', with black and gold lining. After due consideration of colours, costs, and aesthetics the Directors retired to make their final choice — which was that, in future, umber livery would be employed for passenger locomotives; and deep glossy black for goods engines. Stroudley's ghost must have writhed at the solemn respect with which relative expense was examined that afternoon! Yet it must be conceded that Marsh ultimately made his point. Umber paint, it was found, wore just as well, and was easier to keep clean.

Nevertheless, the very human habit Brighton men had of referring to their charges by name was not so easily extinguished. Even 50 years later BR, when erecting a new restriction board along the ballast siding which led from Newhaven Harbour along Bishopstone Beach, saw nothing unusual in spelling out its message thus: NO ENGINES OTHER THAN THE A1X FENCHURCH CLASS TO PASS THIS BOARD.

The 'Terrier' designation A1X was first applied in 1911, and was, in fact, a logical development of the LB&SCR's original system of classifying locomotives. Stroudley started the process in the 1870s, when he introduced his standard locomotive types and grouped them alphabetically according to their ability to perform certain duties. Over the years he employed letters 'A' to 'G'. This method had its shortcomings, however, in that tender and tank engines were sometimes obliged to share the same letter. Class 'D', for instance, earmarked for 'secondary passenger engines', embraced both 'Lyons' class 0-4-2 tender locomotive and 0-4-2 tanks. Class 'B', reserved for 'main line express locomotives', offered an equally confusing miscellany of two and four-coupled types. The 'Terriers' were fortunate in retaining exclusive use of letter 'A' ie 'suburban passenger tanks'; and this state of affairs persisted whilst R. J. Billinton was in charge. But once Marsh, with his Doncaster background, arrived little time was lost in introducing a much more specific system of locomotive classification. The 'Terriers' duly surfaced as Class A1. Subsequent rebuilds of any class on the LB&SCR automatically attracted the suffix 'X'; and, such was the logic of it all, neither the Southern Railway nor British Railways saw fit to interfere in later years.

Had it not been for the facility with which 'Terriers' took to motor-working the question of rebuilding the class would doubtless never have arisen. As it was, re-boilering was considered in 1906; but action was deferred until 1911–3, when twelve 'Terriers', half those remaining on LB&SCR books, were given new boilers of Marsh design. As the latter were constructed in one ring, as opposed to Stroudley's use of three rings, the dome and safety valves of the A1Xs, as the rebuilds were known, had perforce to move forward an inch or two. There were, too, other distinctive changes. A new type of smokebox, circular in section, jutted further ahead and was supported by a saddle. Smokebox wingplates and sand boxes were removed and new leading sand boxes, operated by steam, appeared below the run-

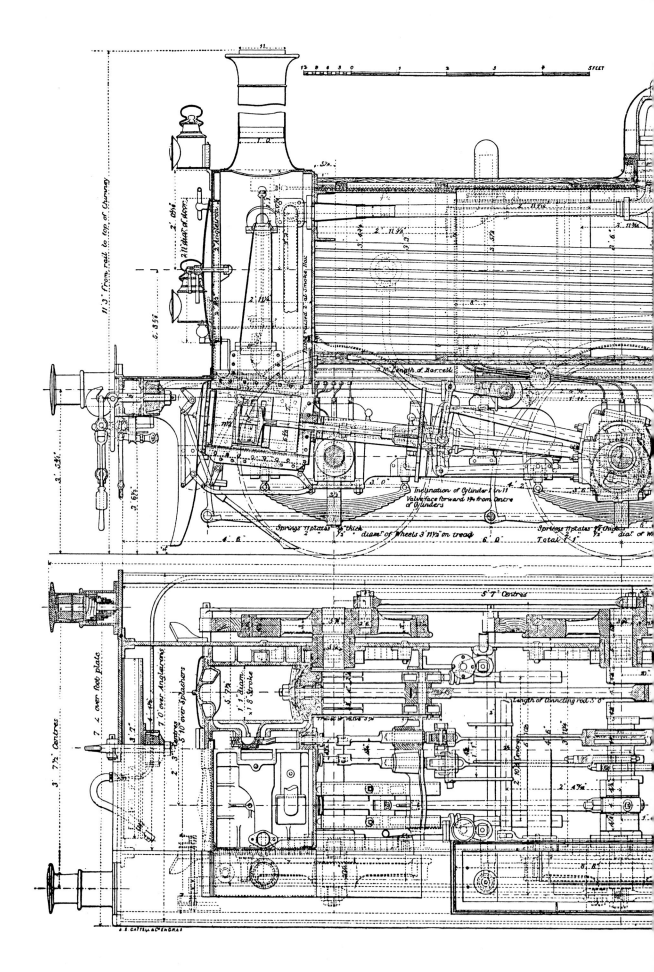

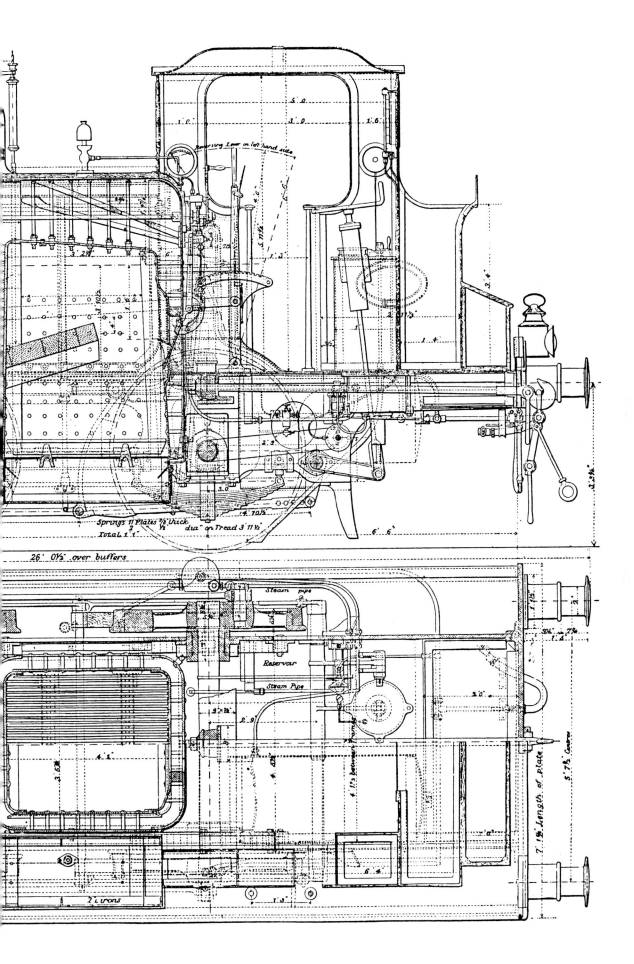

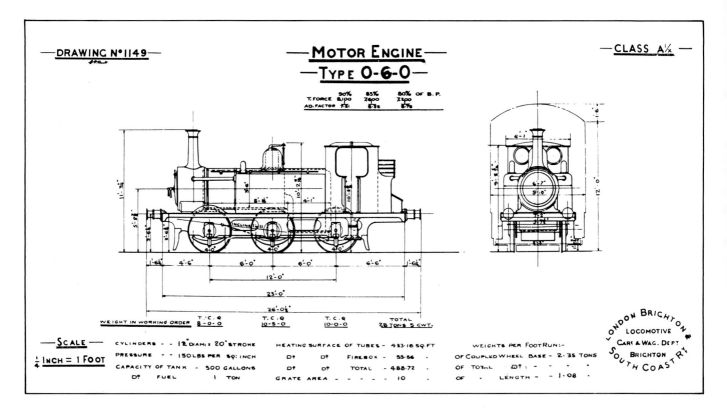

DRAWING Nº 1149 — **MOTOR ENGINE — TYPE 0-6-0** — **CLASS A1X**

LONDON BRIGHTON & SOUTH COAST RY LOCOMOTIVE CARR. & WAG. DEPT. BRIGHTON

SCALE ¼ INCH = 1 FOOT

CYLINDERS - - 12" DIAM.× 20" STROKE
PRESSURE - - 150 LBS PER SQ. INCH
CAPACITY OF TANK - 500 GALLONS
Dº FUEL 1 TON

HEATING SURFACE OF TUBES - 433·16 SQ.FT
Dº Dº FIREBOX - 55·56 "
Dº Dº TOTAL - 488·72 "
GRATE AREA - - - - - 10 "

WEIGHTS PER FOOT RUN:-
OF COUPLED WHEEL BASE - 2·35 TONS
OF TOTAL Dº - - - -
OF LENGTH - - 1·08 "

ning plate. In many instances the copper-capped chimney survived; but some 'Terriers' reappeared bearing handsome new cast iron chimneys. These were designed by B. K. Field, Marsh's chief draughtsman. Opportunity was also taken to replace the wooden brake blocks of any pre-1880 'Terriers' with cast iron ones. Dimensional changes are shown in Table 3.

After this initial flurry the next locomotive to receive A1X treatment was *Fenchurch*, in April 1913 at the Newhaven Harbour Co.'s behest. A brace of IWC 'Terriers' followed suit in March 1916 and May 1918. Then the LB&SCR rounded off the process by rebuilding another four of its own between September 1919 and April 1922. After Grouping, three more rebuilds were effected: two Isle of Wight locomotives by the SR in 1930 and 1932, plus Kent & East Sussex Railway No.3 in April 1943. This brought the final count of A1X 'Terriers' to 22. Meanwhile, as can be seen from Table 2, eight more 'Terriers' were sold by the LB&SCR during and immediately after World War I. Five (four A1s and an A1X) went to the Admiralty in 1918, two (one of each class) were sold to Edge Hill Light Railway in 1919–20, and A1 No.667, after being sold into private hands in April 1920, finished its days on colliery service. A1X or not, most 'Terriers' sold by the LB&SCR were subjected to minor domestic alteration by their new owners sooner or later. The net result was that once the dust settled on the SR's post-Grouping inheritance of 24 'Terriers' no two were found to be alike. The 'mix' consisted of four A1s, seventeen A1X, and an odd trio which had been given non-standard boilers by the SE&CR and LSWR, but were otherwise unrebuilt. British Railways' lot in 1948 was a mite simpler in that the Southern Railway contributed one A1 and 14 A1X, and another A1X came from the GWR. Nevertheless, the additional acquisition of K&ESR No.3 in February of that year succeeded in adding one more variety to BR's collection!

Running Numbers

The compact block of numbers (35–84) Stroudley allotted his 'Terriers' was first disturbed in 1898, when No.72 *Fenchurch* was stripped of its number plate before being delivered to the

Newhaven Harbour Co. Then it happened again, when No.69 *Peckham* left to become No.10 on the IWCR. After that the pace of events quickened and the next half-century witnessed such a maze of scrappings, sales and ultimate returns to the parent fold that, of 50 'Terriers' only five contrived to pursue an uninterrupted career through LB&SCR, SR, and BR ownership. *Martello*'s experience can be taken as typical of this rare species:

No.62	As built by LB&SCR in 1875
662	600 added when locomotive Duplicate Listed in June 1901.
B662	Prefix 'B', identifying LB&SCR locomotives, added by SR at Grouping, 1st January 1923.
2662	2000 added to all ex-LB&SCR locomotive numbers under SR's 1931 Scheme.
32662	30000 added to all ex-SR numbers (except for a few IOW engines) after BR was formed in 1948.

Other variations on the renumbering theme will be found in the locomotive biographies which follow.

Yet another source of number dislocation arose as and when odd 'Terriers' were removed from general stock and given employment with Brighton and Battersea Locomotive Departments. The, as often as not, running numbers temporarily disappeared. 'Terriers', however, which were placed in Service Stock at Lancing Carriage & Wagon Works were given new numbers, plus the suffix 'S'. Later, under BR management, such locomotives were restyled Department Stock, and the prefix 'DS' supplanted the former letter 'S'.

Names

Stroudley's enthusiasm for bestowing place names on secondary duty tank engines found a ready echo in his successor; for, of a total of 282 locomotives designed by R. J. Billinton, no less than 165 fell into the same category. The assiduity with which both men combed their Gazetteers was well matched; though Billinton's feat, perhaps, in avoiding plagiarism deserves the greater credit. Searching through 'Brighton' territory for place

Under Marsh's aegis the dashing air of the 'Terriers' was toned down considerably. Multi-coloured lining gave way to less expensive yellow, number plates were abandoned latterly in favour of neat transfer numerals and, with names removed as locomotives paid routine Works visits, side tanks now bore the legend 'LB&SCR' in large gilt block letters. No.643, formerly *Gipsyhill*, is seen here at Kemp Town Station a few years after the locomotive was Duplicate Listed. *(Derek Brough Collection)*

Below — No.644, formerly *Fulham*, seen here at Brighton, offers a clear display of A1X 'Terrier' characteristics. Condensing pipes are in evidence, sand boxes have been repositioned for steam sanding and coal rails have been reinforced by metal sheeting. Note, too, how tankside inscriptions were reduced to 'LBSC' once L. B. Billinton succeeded D. E. Marsh in office in January 1912. *(Author's Collection)*

names that Stroudley had not already exploited must have been quite a task!

It is, therefore, all the more intriguing to note that Billinton chose to revive at least five former 'Terrier' names in the early 1900s. Motives no doubt varied. When, for instance, he selected No.296, one of Stroudley's D1 tanks, to be renamed *Peckham* in December 1901, he obviously coveted the locomotive's original name, *Osborne*, for inclusion in the altogether grander list of names he had in mind for his new B4 4-4-0s. But the same logic cannot apply when, two years later, he elected to name two of his newly built E5 tanks *Crowborough* and *Brighton*, after a brace of 'Terriers' which had quite recently gone to IWCR. Rather neatly, the Southern Railway returned the compliment later by employing two former Billinton E5 names, *Carisbrooke* and *Freshwater*, when it named its Isle of Wight 'Terriers' in 1928. Lastly, a particularly generous gesture occurred when Billinton's last two *named* locomotives, E6 Nos.413 and 414, left Brighton Works in 1905 bearing proud 'Terrier' names. The arrival of D. E. Marsh may well have ensured that four subsequent E6s were shopped nameless — but at least the name *Piccadilly* lived on to November 1909, and that of *Fenchurch* until August 1911.

Duplicate Lists

LB&SCR running numbers were always something of a mess; for the Company steadfastly declined to follow normal railway practice of keeping Duplicate numbers well away from those on capital stock. The first Duplicate List on the Brighton line was introduced by Stroudley in January 1871. His aim was to segregate locomotives whose book value had fallen below £502, yet whose mechanical condition still offered a working life of up to three years. A prime requisite, of course, was that all locomotives concerned should be surplus to traffic requirements. During his term of office Stroudley had to resort, in the event, to four successive Duplicate Lists; for most were far too prescribed numerically to last very long. R. J. Billinton introduced two more Lists, and it was the sixth and last, begun in 1899, which eventually encompassed the 'Terriers'. It also sufficed until Grouping arrived in 1923.

First 'Terrier' casualties came in 1900–2, when the introduction of new B4 4-4-0s, numberd 42–74, saw 27 of the little tanks placed on the Duplicate List. Their running numbers were accordingly increased by 600. Nos.37 and 38 suffered likewise in 1905, when the first Marsh Atlantics appeared. Next, truly indicative of Brighton's random numbering system, 'Terrier' No.35 had to give way on its own to a Class I2 tank in 1908.

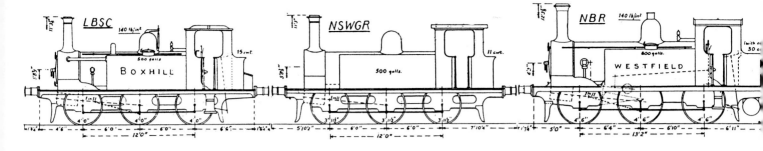

TABLE 3
COMPARATIVE DIMENSIONS — 'TERRIERS' AND THE LIKE

	Proposed Stroudly 0-6-0T 1870	Class A1 'Terrier' 1872	Class A1X 'Terrier' 1911	New South Wales 0-6-0T Class 67 1875	Drummond NBR 0-6-0T 1875
Cylinders (2)	11in × 18in	13in × 20in	12in × 20in	13in × 20in	15in × 22in
Coupled Wheels	3ft 10½in	3ft 11½in	4ft 0in	4ft 0in	4ft 6in
Wheelbase	11ft	12ft	12ft	12ft	13ft 2in
Boiler: Diameter	3ft 6in	3ft 6in	3ft 6in	3ft 6in	3ft 10in
Length	7ft 3in	7ft 10in	8ft 1¼in	7ft 10in	8ft 8½in
Firebox Length	3ft 7in	4ft 1in	4ft 1in	3ft 6in	4ft 8¼in
Heating Surface	482sq ft	528sq ft	488½sq ft	524sq ft	666sq ft
Working Pressure	140 lb	140 lb	150 lb	120 lb	140 lb
Grate Area	8.5sq ft	10.3sq ft	10sq ft	10sq ft	13.75sq ft
Tank Capacity	360 gallons	500 gallons	500 gallons	500 gallons	600 gallons
Bunker Capacity	10cwt	10cwt	20cwt	11cwt	30cwt
Length over Buffers		26ft 0½in	26ft 0½in	26ft 0½in	28ft 6½in
Fully Laden Weight		26t 17cwt	28t 5cwt	28 tons	36 tons
Tractive Effort		7,650 lb	10,695 lb	7,400 lb	10,908 lb

Finally, the seven remaining 'Terriers', Nos.77–83, had 600 added, perforce, to their numbers, as Class I3 Atlantic tanks emerged from Brighton Works in 1909–12. The only 'Terriers', therefore, to escape Duplicate Listing were thirteen which were sold, or scrapped, during the years 1898–1903. The problem of replacing number plates after Duplicate Listing was tackled in various ways. One 'Terrier', No.653, was given new brass plates and at least nine others received wooden plates with numerals inscribed in white or gold. The remainder variously received roughly painted numerals on the cabside, gold numerals painted on a grey background, or, at best, quite tidy transfer numerals in gold leaf.

It should be remembered, of course, that not all renumbering was a direct product of Duplicate Listing. During the years 1880–3, for instance, Stroudley's first eight Class C 0-6-0s, a mere seven years old, were renumbered 401–08 to make way for newly built 'Terriers' Nos.77–84. The remaining Class Cs followed suit later when Stroudley E1 tanks Nos.85–96 again encroached on their territory.

Surplus Lists

The Surplus List was a very different kettle of fish. With a sharp eye cocked towards the Company's Profit & Loss Account and Balance Sheet, it took care of locomotives which, though taken out of service, still remained *in situ* at major running sheds and were still capable of doing 'odd jobs'. In practice quite a number of Surplus Listed locomotives lived on to give many more years of service.

Stroudley initiated the Surplus List in June 1883. 'Terriers', however, were not affected until 1897, when, surprisingly, No.70 *Poplar* was added to what was at the time a very short list indeed. In December 1898, fourteen more 'Terriers' were added to the Surplus List; and at this stage one might well pause to consider their ultimate fate. Four of them were scrapped in 1901–3, eight found buyers between the years 1899 and 1920, and two were withdrawn by the Southern Railway in 1925 and 1963 respectively. *Martello*, meanwhile, hung on long enough to be sold to Butlin's holiday camp empire in 1964. Not a bad record, surely, for surplus (1898 vintage) locomotives!

By December 1905, all 24 surviving 'Terriers' reached the Surplus List. A revised List issued in 1911, however, dropped No.637, which by then was operating as 'Locomotive Department. Battersea'; and under a new arrangement the 23 'Terriers' now listed were given a book value of £125 each. Immediately prior to Grouping, however, Surplus List valuation became less specific. Of the sixteen 'Terriers' handed over to the Southern by the LB&SCR, one, Class A1 No.642 *Tulsehill*, lately 'Locomotive Dept. Battersea', was declared to have 'no monetary value'. Conversely, fourteen A1X class locomotives were styled as having 'monetary value' — though no actual amount was specified. The missing link, No.682, formerly *Boxhill*, currently 'Loco Dept Brighton', was completely ignored. The Southern Railway retained this Surplus List until 30th June 1930. Then it vanished for evermore.

28

Chapter 3
ALLOCATIONS AND PERFORMANCE

DESPITE THE EAST LONDON district names they carried, all six first-built Class A 0-6-0Ts were concentrated in the main on the South London line. No.72 *Fenchurch* reported for duty to Battersea depot on 7th September 1872; then, not quite in the order in which they were built, the other five entered traffic variously at Battersea and New Cross between 12th October and 4th December. Their impact on the South London line was quite momentous and few custom-built locomotives in the history of steam can have received such immediate and unequivocal acclaim from railway men and transport Press alike. *The Engineer* of 17th January 1873, waxing enthusiastically on the 'wiry and lively nature' of the little tanks, promptly dubbed them 'Terriers'. Brighton men, witness to similar stirring developments on the East London line, preferred to style their charges 'Rooters' or 'Pups'. 'Terrier', however, was the nickname which withstood the test of time and passed into railway legend.

As it happened, *The Engineer* was at that time campaigning vigorously against the employment of large and over-heavy locomotives on London metropolitan and suburban services. Few of the major railway companies were innocent in this respect and certainly, LB&SCR engines which had previously worked the South London line weighed half as much again as a 'Terrier'. Craven's last 0-4-4T had a wheelbase almost double that of Stroudley's machine and an adhesion weight of 26 tons. Coal consumption and operational inconvenience were commensurate. It follows that when, during their first ten months of service, Stroudley's six 'Terriers' consumed 1,163 fewer tons of coal than their predecessors, the whole railway fraternity sat up and took notice. In 1878 *The Engineer*, while correcting an earlier over-eulogistic report, was nevertheless able to report that the 32 'Terriers' in service by then were averaging 25,232 train miles each per annum. Total class mileage to date was 2½ million, coal consumption averaged 20.15 lb per mile, and repair costs emerged at the ridiculously low figure of 0.052 pence per train mile. Stroudley's policy of standardisation was indeed paying rich dividends.

In the meantime, Stroudley had carried his standardisation policy a stage further by introducing sets of new specially designed four-wheeled carriages for use on the South London line. Close coupled and centrally buffered, these pioneer vehicles were unusually lightweight in construction, yet each could seat up to 50 passengers, depending, of course, on class. One block train, as the sets were styled, was deemed to consist of ten coaches, and orders for six such units were placed on 7th February 1872 at a total cost of £18,000. From the LB&SCR's point of view, the investment was an enormous success; for the combination of the block trains' remarkably low tare weight of 2¼cwt per passenger and the 'Terriers' miserly fuel consumption added real bite to the Company's drive for South and East London traffic. It is not difficult to imagine how, as 1873 dawned, the mere glimpse of an immaculately groomed 'Terrier' fussing patiently at the head of a train of uniformly designed 26ft long coaches must have lifted the hearts of LB&SCR suburban passengers, long inured to travelling to and fro in comparative dog kennels.

As far as the 'Terriers' were concerned, the ten-coach formula for block trains mattered little. Quite often, off peak, they could be seen toying with eight coaches; but, come mornings and evenings, the same locomotives addressed themselves with sheer relish to the task of hauling ten or twelve, all tightly packed with commuters. Even as early as January 1873, records vouch that No.46 *Wapping* in course of a day's work ran 141 miles and spent over nine hours on trains. Six more miles were run light, 172 stops were made, and the locomotive was absent from shed for seventeen hours. Coal consumed during this extraordinary performance, including lighting up, consistently averaged 20½ lb per mile and during a day's work, the bunker was refuelled twice at London Bridge. Regardless of load, the nine mile journey between London Bridge and Victoria was accomplished in an average time of 35mins. Eleven stops made each trip were by hand brake only. Nor was life any easier on the East London line. There, six intermediate stops on the 3 miles 66 chains which separated New Cross and Shoreditch, plus tough gradients on either side of the Thames, were enough to deter thoughts of similar schedules. Sixteen minutes, therefore, was the order of the day.

As more 'Terriers' were built, London's quota increased steadily and by September 1880, when the 50th locomotive was completed, all but six could be found in the metropolitan area. Of those which escaped, Brighton claimed three, (Nos.41, 63 and 64) Guildford two, (Nos.36 and 37) and Hailsham (No.76). Meanwhile, London traffic boomed commensurately, and by 1881 the average South London line train load had increased from nine coaches to eleven. The 'Terriers' willingly tackled such other suburban duties as came their way and soon the class was running 1 million miles a year. Statistics relating to the first six in London service alone offer classic evidence of the little locomotives' consistency:

Loco	Average miles per *working* day – 1873	Coal burnt per mile 1873	Miles run 1873	Total miles at 30/6/1881	Average yearly mileage 1874–1881
No.70	94	22½ lb	28,673	261,205	31,000
No.71	105	21¾ lb	33,009	275,480	33,400
No.72	111	22¼ lb	34,647	279,794	33,600
No.73	97	22¼ lb	31,744	246,476	28,000
No.74	78	22¾ lb	25,487	253,549	29,000
No.75	97	22½ lb	29,906	226,927	26,250

Yet, ironically, though the 'Terriers' did so much to stimulate LB&SCR London suburban traffic, they could not, in themselves, cope with the results. As Stroudley explained to his Board:

"This railway system offers some peculiarities, when compared with its neighbours, in having less than 90 miles within the metropolitan area, 15 of those having three or four lines of rails. Some of the lines have very heavy gradients, and curves as small as 6½ and 7 chains radius. There are 94 junctions and twenty terminal stations, and, from some of the latter, the line rises with gradients of from 1:64 to 1:80. These features, together with a crowded passenger traffic moving at irregular intervals over about 20 hours out of the 24, cause the working to be very difficult. Some of the engines are attached to as many as sixteen trains in one day; the loss of time in running on and off, and in standing waiting, tends to increase the cost of working, as compared to those railways having more continuous lines."

Gallant though the 'Terriers' were, the limited power, coal and water capacity which had been built into their design began, only too soon, to tell against them as vastly improved suburban services induced more and more LB&SCR clientele to move out of Town. One thing was certain: more powerful tanks were going to be needed. Stroudley, percipient as always, had, in fact, begun tackling the problem in 1873, and between then and 1887 now fewer than 125 Class D 0-4-2Ts and 72 E class 0-6-0Ts were shopped new from Brighton Works and elsewhere.

Their effect on the London locomotive scene is readily apparent from allocations as at April 1887:

Depot	'D' Tanks	'E' Tanks	'Terriers'
Battersea	46	19	17
New Cross	36	28	14

Despite this influx of dangerous competition, the 'Terriers' clung grimly to their monopoly of inner London suburban traffic. East London line activity had shrunk somewhat as other lessees began, from 1884, to assume their share of working traffic under the Thames. Nevertheless, the 'Terriers' major work schedule for January 1887 shows how easily half a million miles a year could be accounted for:

TABLE 4A
'TERRIER' WORKINGS ON THE SOUTH & EAST LONDON LINES — JANUARY 1887

Number of return trips per day				Between	Distance (Return)		Total mileage per week
Mon–Friday	Saturday	Sunday	Total		Miles	Chains	
37	38	27	250	**SOUTH LONDON LINE** London Bridge & Victoria	17	22	4,318
2	2	—	12	London Bridge & Peckham Rye	6	68	82
6	7	—	37	London Bridge & Loughborough Park	10	20	379
27	25	—	160	London Bridge & Battersea Park	14	44	2,328
15	15	12	102	**EAST LONDON LINE** Shoreditch & Peckham Rye	7	40	765
15	15	14	104	Shoreditch & New Cross	7	52	795
Totals — 102 (× 5)	102	53	665	**TOTAL WEEKLY MILEAGE —**			**8,667**

When *Boxhill* was converted for motor-work in 1905, buffers were raised 1¾in, cylinders were reduced in diameter to 9in, working pressure was correspondingly lowered to 130lb, and No.82's leading coupled wheels were replaced by a 3ft pair from a Class D3 engine's bogie. A higher pitched whistle was also introduced, for safety reasons. Note how the sand pipe was positioned in *front* of the small leading wheels. This arrangement soon posed problems once running trials commenced on 3rd June 1905. (*Author's Collection*)

30

TABLE 4 B
THE SOUTH LONDON LINE

DOWN				UP		
Normal Schedule Minutes	Distance between Stations		Stations	Distance between Stations		Normal Schedule Minutes
	Miles	Chains		Miles	Chains	
—	0	0	London Bridge	1	44	5
5	1	44	South Bermondsey	0	72	3
4	0	72	Old Kent Road	0	23	2
2	0	23	Queen's Road	0	55	3
3	0	55	Peckham Rye	0	70	4
3	0	70	Denmark Hill	0	66	3
4	0	66	Loughborough Park	1	12	4
4	1	12	Clapham	0	32	2
2	0	32	Wandsworth Road	0	48	3
3	0	48	Battersea Park	0	51	2
3	0	51	Grosvenor Road	0	58	4
3	0	58	Victoria	0	0	—
Totals — 36*	8	51		8	51	35†

Fast Trains

* The 12.15 midnight Down ran the total distance in 33 minutes by omitting stops at Clapham and Wandsworth.

† The 11.53am Up ran the total distance in 32 minutes by omitting stops at Grosvenor Road and Queen's Road.

New sanding arrangements are clearly seen in this slightly later view of *Boxhill.* The resumed trials were much more successful now that sand was being deflected to the driving wheels rather than to the smaller leading wheels; and once they concluded on 11th June 1905 the 'Terrier' was deemed fit to be handed over to Running Department on 18th July.

It was the turn of the century which marked the real sea-change in 'Terrier' affairs. As will be seen from the individual locomotive biographies which follow, increasing numbers of 'Terriers' were being forced out of London; and certainly the Locomotive Committee's gloomy decision of January 1899 to reduce the class to fifteen added salt to the wounds. Fortunately, sundry sales and disposals up to 1905 kept surgery to reasonable proportions, and a second resolve to scrap fifteen more 'Terriers' during 1905–6 was successfully thwarted by the Brighton

Board's more immediate concern over increasing electric tramway competition. Efforts to mitigate the severe damage to business which tramways had wrought to date in inner London, had already begun in 1902, when the LB&SCR obtained an Act giving it powers to electrify the South London line. Meanwhile, much nearer home, a rival enterprise was proposing to link Brighton and London by fast electric railway. Thus, in February 1905, was born the LB&SCR Board's resolve to combat the enemy by instituting motor-train service, initially between Brighton and Worthing/Kemp Town *Boxhill* was one of two 'Terriers' selected for conversion.

Anxious to leave no stone unturned, the LB&SCR Board, meanwhile, had also ordered two steam and two internal combustion railcars, for comparative tests between Eastbourne and St Leonards. The contest commenced in September 1905 and

31

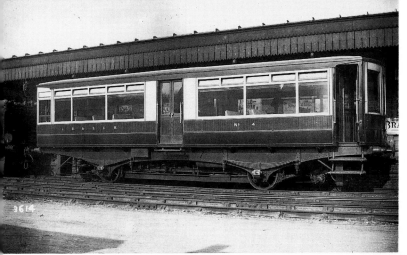

No.4 was one of two petrol railcars supplied to LB&SCR in August 1905 by Dick Kerr & Co. and Daimler Car Co. to run trials between Eastbourne and St Leonards against steam railcars, 'Terriers', and Class D tanks. Over a period of three months, No.4's availability for traffic was only 43%, as opposed to the 95% availability of the two 'Terriers'. Costs per mile were 3.19d and 2.90d respectively. *(Author's Collection)*

Below

Sometimes 'Terriers' ran sandwiched between one of Marsh's 'balloons' and an ordinary six-wheeler. Here 'balloon' No.34 leads as a motor-train passes Balham Intermediate Box. *(Author's Collection)*

TABLE 5
'TERRIER' SHED ALLOCATIONS (1882–1922)

December 1882	April 1887	Mid-1890s	SHED (and CODE)	1900	March 1912	December 1916	31st December 1922
21	17	13	Battersea (B)	—	1	1	1
23	14	15	New Cross (N+)	14	—	—	—
44	**31**	**28**	**Sub-Totals (LONDON)**	**23**	**1**	**1**	**1**
—	1	—	Bognor (BOG)	—	3	2	—
3	5	12	Brighton (BTON)	14	6	7	7
—	—	—	Coulsdon (COULS)	—	1	2	—
—	5	3	Eastbourne (E)	1	—	—	—
—	—	2	Fratton)F)	4	3	1	3
2	—	—	Guildford (GFORD)	—	—	—	—
1	—	—	Hailsham	—	—	—	—
—	—	2	Horsham (HORS)	2	2	2	2
—	1	1	Littlehampton (LTON)	1	—	2	1
—	2	1	Midhurst (MID)	1	—	—	—
—	2	1	Newhaven (N)	1	—	—	—
—	—	—	Tunbridge Wells (T-W)	1	4	3	2
—	3	—	West Croydon (W-C)	—	4	4	—
50	**50**	**50**	**TOTALS**	**48***	**24†**	**25**	**16‡**

* Two 'Terriers' sold (1898–99).
† 24 sold or scrapped (1900–05).
‡ 8 sold (1918–20)
Shed Codes, introduced by Stroudley in January 1884, were painted in white on both sides of the angle iron by the front buffer beam. The practice tended to taper off during Marsh's regime, and it disappeared entirely once Southern Railway took over in 1923.

statistics soon revealed that the 'Terriers' were superior both in cost and service. In the first three months alone, *Boxhill* ran 17,217 miles at an average cost of 2.91d (1.5p) per train mile. Coal consumption hovered consistently below 15 lb per mile; some 7 lb less, incidentally, than that on the South London line.

Faced with such clear evidence, the Brighton Board had no hesitation in modifying a further twenty 'Terriers' for motor-work. One engine, No.642, was given 10in diameter cylinders, but in all other cases 12in cylinders and 150 lb working pressure were adopted as standard. The locomotives were refitted with condensing pipes as an additional economy measure. Brighton motor gear worked well enough, particularly *vis-à-vis* the LSWR system, and such minor idiosyncrasies as existed were finally eliminated in 1912, when L. B. Billinton, successor to Marsh, adopted the use of compressed air from the Westinghouse pump. Early in 1906, the LB&SCR's Locomotive Committee even reached agreement with train men that a driver and fireman could well handle a motor-train on their own, provided the fireman was compensated for taking over the missing guard's duties. Alas, the Board of Trade would not countenance even a trial of this imaginative proposal. Thus, an important railway 'breakthrough' was lost for evermore. Despite this disappointment, the LB&SCR refused to be deflected from its policy of motor-train expansion and during the years 1906–7, many new station halts were purpose-built. But *six*-coupled 'Terriers' proved the best bet, and Nos.81 and 82 were restored to normal in 1913.

The South London line had, in the meantime, been totally revitalised by electrification. Passenger volume which had

dropped from eight million to three million during 1903–8 had now risen to eight million again by 1910. It follows that all 24 existing 'Terriers' were now available for motor-work in the provinces. In practice, two of them, Nos.637 and 638, shed pilots at Battersea and Brighton respectively, remained unaffected. But the remaining 22 were totally involved during the peak years of motor-working. As the following Table shows, the 'Terriers' moved around considerably in course of these duties..

TABLE 6
ALLOCATION OF MOTOR-WORKING 'TERRIERS'

Shed	March 1912	March 1916
Bognor	635, 680, 683, (3)	650, 680 (2)
Brighton	642, 644, 647, 674, & 681 (5)	642, 643, 644, 647, 674, & 681 (6)
Coulsdon	663 (1)	653 & 683 (2)
Fratton	643, 650, & 679 (3)	663 (1)
Horsham	659 & 678 (2)	659 & 673 (2)
Littlehampton	—	662 & 678 (2)
Tunbridge Wells	667, 673, 677 & 682 (4)	667, 677 & 682 (3)
West Croydon	653, 655, 661 & 662 (4)	635, 655, 661 & 679 (4)

Gradually, as other LB&SCR tanks consolidated their grip on London suburban services, the 'Terriers' concentrated elsewhere. No.661, based on West Croydon, was the last to leave the London area, in August 1920, and the last mainland motor-work expired on the Kemp Town branch early in 1928. Thereafter, service locomotives apart, working 'Terriers' could only be found on the Hayling Island branch, at Newhaven Harbour, on the Isle of Wight, or on loan to K&ESR. Each of these distinctive localities has its own story to tell of long association with 'Terriers'.

The Hayling Island Branch

This 4½ mile single line between Havant and South Hayling, opened by the Hayling Railway on 17th July 1867, was worked

Havant Station, opened around 1867, was twice reconstructed: once, during 1889–94 by the LB&SCR and again by the SR in 1937–38. But at all times Hayling Island trains were confined to a bay platform on the down side of the station. In this pre-Grouping scene No.655, formerly *Stepney*, having brought a branch train in, is released and is moving on to the loop line to stand by for further service. The signal box and level-crossing gates just visible in the right background were demolished during the major alterations of 1937. *(Author's Collection)*

The new Havant Station nears completion in 1938. The former up platform has been set back to permit introduction of a four-track layout and, new experience, a London-bound electric train pauses to pick up passengers. Typical of contemporary SR station construction, white concrete and metal windows have been used extensively. Meanwhile, little has changed on the 430ft long Hayling Island bay. A 'Terrier', No.2661, formerly *Sutton*, still heads the branch train and the sister engine it has relieved will be on the loop line, somewhere in the rear.
(*R. Stumpf Collection*)

In this July 1962 scene at Hayling Island Station, No.32646, ex-*Newington*, having run round its train, waits to set off once more for Havant. Traditionally, when summer traffic was at its height and two trains were pressed into use, the bay on the right was used to facilitate spontaneous arrivals and departures at Hayling Island.
(*Author's Collection*)

by contractor's locomotives up to 31st December 1871, when the line was leased to the LB&SCR at £2,000 per annum. The Hayling Railway Co. remained independent until November 1922, when it was finally absorbed by the Brighton company. Initially, the LB&SCR used small elderly tanks on the branch, for the spidery wooden bridge which linked the mainland with the Island at Langstone imposed severe weight restrictions. These were never relaxed during the 96-year life of the branch, hence the continued use of 'Terriers' from 1889 onwards.

At the outset, South Hayling station (later renamed Hayling Island) had a small locomotive shed, where the branch engine was kept. Then, in 1894, economic considerations intervened. The shed was demolished and the local 'Terrier's' welfare was entrusted to Fratton. The latter had just replaced a very cramped shed at Portsmouth. By 1900 Fratton's allocation of 'Terriers' had risen to four, all fully employed on Hayling and Southsea branch work. Motor-train working arrived to enliven the scene in January 1907, and Nos.643 and 673 were fitted accordingly. By 1919, however, it was agreed that one 'Balloon' carriage was insufficient to cope with summer demands, and the branch reverted to normal haulage.

From the start of its tenancy, the LB&SCR, it must be said, made commendable efforts to develop the branch; partly in local interests and partly in coping with the increasing flow of holiday makers which materialised from 1900 onwards. The rotting timbers of Langstone Bridge, however, presented a vexing and recurring problem.

Renewed by the LB&SCR in 1903, the timbers again required major attention from the SR in 1928. In 1931, the Southern went so far as to install new wooden trestles, built on concrete bases. Meanwhile, electrification between London and Portsmouth in 1937 encouraged even greater number of summer visitors, and for the next twenty years, the Hayling Island branch and its 'Terriers' lived through a golden period.

Even in 1961 BR was still running fifteen trains each way on summer weekdays, with 24 return trips on Saturdays and twenty on Sundays. Weekend schedules were very tight indeed.

Yet, ominous clouds were gathering behind this industrious scene. The opening of a new road bridge between Langstone and Hayling Island in 1958 promptly released a flood of competition from private cars and Southdown bus services. This, coupled with BR's stark assessment that both rolling stock and fixed assets were deteriorating at a rate which greatly outweighed potential traffic (Langstone viaduct alone called for renewed investment of £400,000), marked the beginning of the end.

In 1962, BR proposed closure of the branch. Local objection was vociferous but, despite that, the axe finally fell on 2nd November 1963. On the last day 'Terriers' Nos.32650, 32662 and 32670 worked like Trojans to accommodate a veritable host of local inhabitants and visitors who turned out to pay their respects. Subsequent plans by enthusiasts to reopen the branch as an electric tramway proved abortive. Rails were lifted in 1966 — and now all that remains of Langstone Bridge is a pier on either side, left to mark the channel for shipping.

The classic Langstone Bridge scene still obtains on 4th August 1962, as No.32678 ferries its train across to the Island. The concrete piers installed by the Southern Railway in 1931 are clearly visible, even at high tide. Behind the train can be seen the notorious swing bridge and signal cabin. The railway companies' obligatory recognition of navigation rights proved to be a thorn in their flesh all through the years — particularly in the latter period when British Railways was striving to match manpower costs with rapidly diminishing traffic returns. *(J. W. Aston)*

Newhaven Harbour

The Harbour's association with 'Terriers' commenced in 1898, and remained linked with two of them, *Fenchurch* and *Cheapside*, until August 1963, when the West Quay lines were closed. See under *Fenchurch* for further details.

Isle of Wight

The first Isle of Wight railway opened between Cowes and Newport on 16th June 1862. Typical of the times, seven more companies entered the fray over the years to 1898. After sundry amalgamations, however, the twentieth century dawned with four companies in charge of the island's railway system. These were the Isle of Wight Railway, Isle of Wight Central Railway, Freshwater, Yarmouth & Newport Railway, and the LSWR/LB&SCR Joint Committee. The latter, by opening up a rail link in 1880 between Ryde Pier and Ryde (St John's) station, played a significant role in stimulating holiday traffic. At Grouping the island's 55½ miles of track came under Southern Railway control. Later when Nationalisation was effected, BR's Southern Region assumed control.

The 'Terriers'' 50-year-old connection with the Isle of Wight stemmed simply from the fact that track on many of the smaller IOW Companies was not laid to main line standards. Ergo, such a versatile and light-footed creature as the 'Terrier' proved to be a valuable acquisition — particularly if picked up at secondhand price. As Table 7 shows, two IOW Companies were happy so to indulge. Employment of Stroudley's little tanks was still neces-

TABLE 7
THE ISLE OF WIGHT 'TERRIERS'

'Terrier'	Arrived on IOW	Became	Introduced or acquired by SR as	Returned to Mainland
75 *Blackwall*	March 1899	IWCR No.9	W9	April 1927*
69 *Peckham*	April 1900	IWCR No.10	W10 *Cowes*	May 1936
40 *Brighton*	Jan 1902	IWCR No.11	W11 *Newport*	Feb 1947
84 *Crowborough*	Nov 1903	IWCR No.12	W12 *Ventnor*	May 1936
646 *Newington*	June 1913	LSWR No.734 FY&NR No.2	W2/W8 *Freshwater*	April 1949
677 *Wonersh*	May 1927	—	W3/W13 *Carisbrooke*	April 1949
678 *Knowle*	May 1929	—	W4/W14 *Bembridge*	May 1936
650 *Whitechapel*	May 1930	—	W9 *Fishbourne*	May 1936

* Scrapped on the Island

sary throughout Southern Railway years; and only when modernisation of track and equipment was finally completed did the last two 'Terriers' bid farewell, in April 1949.

As can be seen from Table 7, eight 'Terriers' put in a total of 211 working years on Isle of Wight service, with *Brighton*, now happily preserved on its old stamping ground, topping the list at 45 years. *Newington*, still working for a living under similar auspices, continues to add to its earlier 36 years of public service.

A typical 1910 scene on the Isle of Wight Central Railway as IWCR No.11 (formerly *Brighton*), having run round its five coach train, prepares to leave Newport Station again on the 11.00am for Cowes. Coal rails have been added to the bunker but the 'Terrier' has not yet been rebuilt in A1X form. *(Locomotive Publishing Co.)*

Kent & East Sussex Railway

'Terrier' links with this venerable institution were almost as tenuous and for much the same reasons as those on the Isle of Wight: the K&ESR's lightly laid 13½ mile section between Tenterden and Robertsbridge imposed severe locomotive weight restrictions. In any case, Colonel Stephens, never averse to a good secondhand bargain, had a particularly weak spot for 'Terriers'. As a result, his light railway empire acquired *nine* in due course!

Rother Valley Railway/Kent & East Sussex's pair, *Poplar* and *Wapping*, were bought from the LB&SCR in 1901 and 1905 respectively, and became K&ESR No.3 *Bodiam* and No. 5 *Rolvenden*. Both seemed to have completed their working lives by 1931 but, miraculously, No.3, fortified by spare parts from the other, returned to service in 1933 — and even survived to be taken into BR stock in 1948.

Colonel Stephens' death in 1931 might well have seen the end of the K&ESR, but, fortunately, his successor, W. H. Austen, was able to nurse the line along until it was Nationalised in 1948. Prudent interim economies, though, precluded the purchase of further motive power and in 1936, the K&ESR initiated a policy of hiring locomotives from the SR as required. The hop-picking season certainly made extra-mural demands. Thus, at least four more 'Terriers' are known to have trodden K&ESR metals between 1936 and 1947.

Under BR aegis, the line was operated in two sections as before. Class 01 0-6-0 tender engines ran north of Tenterden and 'Terriers' continued to monopolise the southern section. Double-heading was still not permitted on the latter, and the K&ESR section's famous 'fore and aft' procedure became something of a legend amongst railway enthusiasts. In the end, declining traffic receipts saw a last passenger public train run between Robertsbridge and Headcorn on Saturday, 2nd January 1954. 'Terriers' Nos.32655 and 32678, true to tradition, handled it as far as Rolvenden. Thenceforth Rolvenden shed was closed, and freight-only traffic between Robertsbridge and Tenterden was manned from St Leonards shed. Three 'Terriers' were usually kept there for the purpose. Occasional passenger 'specials' still ventured up the line, with two 'Terriers' doing the honours. The last of these ran on 12 July 1961 and, with the exception of minor traffic to and from Hodson's mill, near Robertsbridge, all traffic ceased from there on.

The eventual resuscitation of the line between Tenterden and Northiam by the Kent & East Sussex Railway Association is described under *Poplar* and *Whitechapel* in the pages which follow. Suffice it to record that two 'Terriers' operate once more on thoroughly familiar metals.

Kemp Town Branch

This branch, only one mile 32 chains long, from the east end of London Road tunnel on the Brighton–Lewes line, also deserves mention in any list of 'Terrier' haunts. Its remarkably short course contained a seventeen chain long viaduct and a tunnel, 1024yds in length, gave immediate access to Kemp Town Station. The branch opened in August 1869, using an old Sharp 2-4-0T in the main; and it must have been quite a proud day when 'Terrier' No.64 *Kemptown* arrived new from Brighton Works to take over in June 1874. *Preston* and *Piccadilly* followed in October 1875 and June 1877 respectively, and all three 'Terriers' shared Seaford and Kemp Town branch work for many years. During the 1900s motor-train phase, Kemp Town workings consisted of a 'Terrier' and one 'balloon' coach.

Built as a purely suburban branch, with high hopes on the LB&SCR's part, the line fell sadly short of expectations — and certainly never justified the substantial station and sidings complex which were provided at the Kemp Town end. Ultimately

Kemp Town, 31st July 1926, and No.647, formerly *Cheapside*, one of two 'regulars' at the time, waits with its 'balloon' to leave for Brighton. The advertised time for the journey was ten minutes, with three of those allowed for stops at two intermediate stations. On the Kemp Town branch, motor-working ceased early in 1928 and passenger services were ultimately withdrawn on 2nd January 1933. (*H. C. Casserley*)

Another view at Kemp Town, showing the 1,024yd long tunnel which gave direct access to the station. The Brighton Works 'Terrier', No.377S, is arriving on 23rd June 1956, with a two-coach Special filled with Stephenson Locomotive Society members. (*R. Stumpf Collection*)

fierce tram, then bus, competition led to the withdrawal of passenger services. Kemp Town carried on as a Goods Depot, before finally closing on 14th June 1971. Meanwhile, despite passenger closure in 1933, the branch was used for occasional Sunday School excursions up to 1939. In post-World War II years, thanks to the enthusiasm of Britain's two largest Railway Societies, 'Terriers' again put in appearances on both Kemp Town and Seaford branches. *Fenchurch*, in October 1952, and *Morden*, in June 1956, handled Kemp Town specials. *Fenchurch*, again, tackled the Seaford branch in October 1962.

Chapter 4
EARLY CASUALTIES

This picture of *Thames* was taken after the engine was modified by Billinton in 1894 but before it was Duplicate Listed in 1901. The shed code 'N+' remained until May 1902 when, after having run 498,935 miles, the 'Terrier' was sold to Pauling & Co. When further sold in 1909, the 33-year-old locomotive survived emigration to South America and is believed to have finished its days on La Plate Tramways. Whilst in Pauling & Co. employment, it carried running number 64.
(Author's Collection)

NYONE VISITING THE Bluebell Railway today, and witnessing *Fenchurch* or *Stepney* clamber its way at the head of two or three heavy coaches up and into Horsted Keynes, could be forgiven for doubting the theory that the 'Terriers' were in all probability built to last 25 years. For fact it is that, even allowing for accountancy influences in this over-pessimistic choice of life span, no class of locomotive ever thumbed its nose with greater élan at the rules which normally govern locomotive survival. Had one 'Terrier' contrived to reach the haven of our national locomotive collection, justice might indeed have been seen to be done. But the fact that *ten* of the species, some active, some not, have calmly completed their centenary is an extraordinary re-manifestation of the affection and regard which never deserted Stroudley's little masterpieces from the moment they left Brighton Works. Conversely, some perished by the wayside ere they reached their allotted span; it is these 'early casualties' which fall to be considered in this Chapter.

A period of less than seven years from 1898 onwards saw a remarkable exodus of 'Terriers' from LB&SCR stock. Once *Fenchurch* was quietly sold for £350 in 1898 the pace quickened. So, too, did the price; for, commencing with *Blackwall*'s departure to IWCR in March 1899, fourteen subsequent sales fetched on average £655 each. Significantly, this average leapt to £1,319 when eight more were sold in 1918–20; though it relapsed to nearer £800 when two more 'Terriers' went to Colonel Stephens *after Grouping*. Typical of the complexity of 'Terrier' history, however, only five of the 23 engines sold by the LB&SCR were destined to disappear, completely and comparatively quickly, from the mainstream of British railway life. These were the 'Terriers' sold to Pauling & Co. in 1902.

Pauling & Co. was at the time engaged on construction of the GCR's Northolt–High Wycombe extension and no doubt delighted to add the power of five pugnacious little tanks to its elbow. Even the sprightliest of them had already completed

500,000 miles; but, tough and serviceable, they were a good speculative buy at £670 apiece. Though delivered with LB&SCR livery and names intact, the additional legend 'PAULING & CO' and new running numbers were soon superimposed on the tank sides. Before commencing employment under their new master, the 'Terriers' were also fitted with dumb buffers and wheel rim washing equipment. Guard irons were consequently removed, as was the Westinghouse brake, and, as an insurance whilst working on rather primitive construction lines, a jack was carried on the running plate. In the event three of the Pauling 'Terriers' were sold for scrap in October 1909 and the remaining pair are believed to have escaped to South America. Whatever, each has its own story to tell.

(6)57 THAMES — Built January 1876

A New Cross engine from birth, *Thames* often enjoyed the welcome task of working the up portion of the Newhaven Continental from East Croydon, where the Victoria portion parted company, to London Bridge. This 10½ miles stretch, scheduled to be covered in seventeen minutes start-to-stop, offered footplate men a thrilling momentary reprieve from East London line duties, and in the cool of an evening speeds of up to 60mph were often recorded. It is worth reflecting that at speeds of this nature, a 'Terrier's' modest driving wheels would have to revolve at the rate of 420 times a minute ie *seven* times per second!

(6)52 SURREY — Built February 1876

Also part of New Cross shed's original complement, No.52 was one of few 'Terriers' denied new 14in cylinders during the R. J. Billinton regime. Such was its gradual deterioration, it could only find regular employment as a shed pilot by the late 1890s; which convenient factor probably kept it off the 1898 Surplus

Duplicate Listed in January 1900, No.652, shed pilot at New Cross pauses during the brief spell which elapsed before it was sold to Pauling & Co. in 1902. Because of *Surrey*'s poor mechanical condition, condensing pipes and 13in cylinders were left untouched. *(Author's Collection)*

List. Purchased by Paulings with a cumulative mileage of 626,328 (highest of the five) in September 1902 and renumbered 90, it, too, is thought to have been disposed of to La Plate Tramways in 1909.

(6)49 BISHOPSGATE — Built December 1876

A New Cross engine all its LB&SCR working life, *Bishopsgate* was given a steel firebox experimentally in July 1889; but the experiment was short-lived, and copper became the accepted medium. Then, having run up 540,699 miles in East London service, it went to Pauling & Co. in June 1902, whence it was renumbered 79. The locomotive was eventually sold for scrap in October 1909.

39 DENMARK — Built May 1878

One of the first batch of 'Terriers' to be shopped with Westinghouse brake, *Denmark* went straight to Battersea shed, and remained there for the rest of its Company life, running 620,681 miles in the process. Most of these were comparatively uneventful; though a partial derailment near Bermondsey on 17th February 1883 offered insight into 'Terrier' firing technique. Some youths had placed a sleeper across the track. *Denmark*'s driver was otherwise preoccupied but, fortunately, the vigilance of the fireman averted a potentially nasty accident. Subsequent enquiry revealed that 'Terriers' rode so unsteadily on other than main line metals that firemen on London suburban duties only attempted to fire them when station stops were made.

Seen here in its prime, *Denmark* was never Duplicate Listed. Thus the engine still bore its original number when it was sold to Pauling & Co. in July 1902. Renumbered 87 by Pauling, it eventually went for scrap in October 1909. *(Author's Collection)*

Bishopsgate still retains its name, but the tankside inscription 'P & Co. Ltd. No.79' reminds us of the change of ownership in 1902. Dumb buffers have been fitted, wooden brake blocks have been restored and tyre-washing pipes lead down behind the trainman standing on the footplate. An interesting aspect of this study lies in the fact that the Manning Wardle saddle tank behind, Pauling's No.56 *Northolt*, was sold to the Freshwater, Yarmouth & Newport Rly for £725 on 4th June 1913. Within weeks it resumed old time 'Terrier' association when LSWR No.734, ex-*Newington*, arrived on the Island. *(Author's Collection)*

36 BRAMLEY — Built June 1878

Also equipped initially with Westinghouse brake, No.36 was sent first to the town of Bramley, where it worked services to Guildford. When Bramley shed closed, it and sister engine *Wonersh* found weekday refuge at the LSWR's Guildford shed and paid Sunday visits to Horsham for maintenance purposes. By April 1887, however, *Bramley* had moved to West Croydon, where unseasonable conditions caused it to come a cropper on 4th July 1895, when heading the 6.05pm Wimbledon–Croydon. As West Croydon station was approached speed was duly reduced to 20mph by use of the hand brake. Nearer the station, the hand brake was again applied. It failed, however, to grip on greasy rails and, despite urgent application of the Westinghouse brake, the 'Terrier' slid on to hit the buffer stops. Fortunately, little damage was done.

Shortest lived 'Terriers' of all, however, were eleven which, despite Billinton's belated advertising campaign, failed to excite the interest of buyers. The reason was not far to seek. Most had already been laid aside with defective boilers or fireboxes, and as no minor railway concern was in a position to take on *that* kind of investment, the eleven 'Terriers' remained stubbornly 'on the shelf'. The bulk of them were also occupying storage space at various assembly points and LB&SCR, long accustomed to dealing with scrap merchants, solved the problem by disposing of them in bulk to George Cohen & Co. at a scrap value of £125 each. Cohen, handling them piecemeal over the years 1901–4, duly dismantled the locomotives as they were delivered at the end of a long siding at Redhill.

Their life stories are brief, but not uneventful.

Bramley bore the West Croydon shed code when this photograph was taken. But shortly after the accident mentioned in the text — and completely against the trend of events, for by now 'Terriers' were being obliged to leave London — No.36 was transferred to New Cross. From there, with a cumulative mileage of 607,661, it was sold to Pauling & Co. in September 1902. Duly renumbered 88, it perished in 1909. *(Author's Collection)*

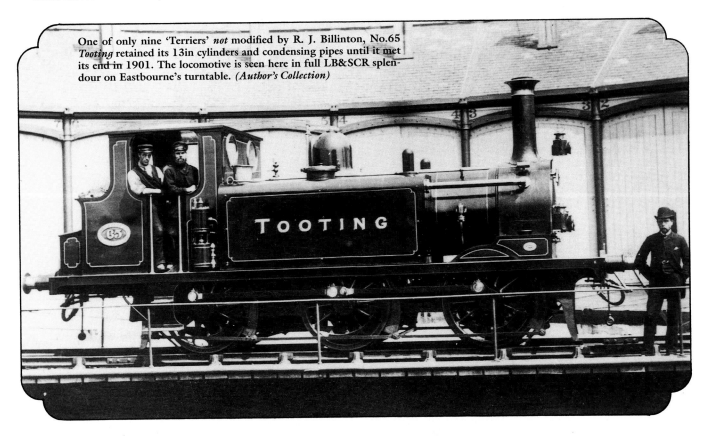

One of only nine 'Terriers' *not* modified by R. J. Billinton, No.65 *Tooting* retained its 13in cylinders and condensing pipes until it met its end in 1901. The locomotive is seen here in full LB&SCR splendour on Eastbourne's turntable. *(Author's Collection)*

65 TOOTING — Built August 1874

Sent to New Cross when new, No.65 was one of four transferred to Eastbourne in the mid-1880s, when New Cross 'Terriers' were being thinned out. A decade later it moved to Brighton, whose allocation of 'Terriers' was increasing rapidly. Then, after a brief return to Eastbourne, it found itself at Littlehampton. Featured in the 1898 Surplus List and still retaining its 13in cylinders, the locomotive finally went to Cohens in February 1901.

Hatcham formed part of Eastbourne's 'Terrier' allocation when this photograph was taken in the late 1890s. After a brief subsequent sojourn at Brighton it became one of the first three 'Terriers' to be withdrawn. *(Author's Collection)*

Most of *Rotherhithe's* life was spent at New Cross; but even when the locomotive was moved to Brighton its 13in cylinders were never modified by R. J. Billinton. The locomotive still bore its original number when it was scrapped in 1901. *(Author's Collection)*

66 HATCHAM — Built August 1874

Hatcham's story was very similar: New Cross in 1874 and Brighton in the mid-1880s. During the 1890s it was transferred to Eastbourne, where local services to Hailsham and Lewes kept it busy. The turn of the century, however, found the locomotive back at Brighton, from where it was sold in February 1901. It had already been Surplus Listed in 1898.

51 ROTHERHITHE — Built December 1876

No.51 lasted rather longer at New Cross and was not obliged to leave until the mid-1890s, when it was transferred to Brighton. Surplus Listed in 1898, it was withdrawn in February 1901.

(6)48 LEADENHALL — Built December 1876

Again a familiar pattern: New Cross when new, Eastbourne *circa* 1887, and Portsmouth in 1890. There, apart from sampling East Southsea branch work, No.48 carved its own niche in LB&SCR locomotive lore by being one of the first 'Terriers' to be regularly employed on Hayling Island branch. Despite being renumbered in June 1901, to make room for Billinton's new B4s, a bleak future lay ahead for the locomotive: in August that same year it returned to Brighton — and was sold on to Cohens.

41 PICCADILLY — Built June 1877

One of the only six 'Terriers' to escape initial London service, *Piccadilly* was allocated to Brighton shed in 1877. Its iron fire-box was replaced by one of steel in July 1889, but the experiment was not a success. Then, on 4th February 1901, came an incident which was to highlight the already known weakness of Stroudley's feed pump system. *Piccadilly* was running light that morning between Newhaven and Seaford, when its driver found the pumps would not work. Working his way along the footplate in time-honoured fashion, ie while the locomotive was still in motion, he duly persuaded the pump to function and was clambering back to his cab when a sudden lurch threw him on to the trackside. Luckily, he escaped with severe concussion, but the Board of Trade enquiry which followed took a very poor view of the incident. As a consequence R. J. Billinton immediately instructed Brighton Works that all engines so fitted should be modified as they entered the shops for attention.

For a period in 1901-2 No.41 was lent to Coulsdon as a pumping engine. Then, not long after returning to base at Brighton, it was withdrawn in June 1902. It was one of six 'Terriers' which were sold, or scrapped, still carrying 13in cylinders.

(6)58 WANDLE — Built November 1875

As New Cross's allocation of 'Terriers' shrank from its peak of 23 to fourteen between the years 1882 and 1887, *Wandle* was one of those which did not budge until it was withdrawn from service in February 1902.

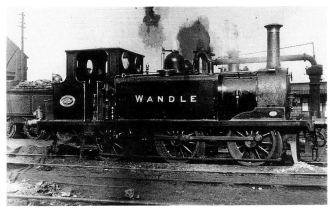

No.58 *Wandle*, built at Brighton Works in November 1875, remained faithful to New Cross shed throughout its comparatively brief life. There, a considerable variety of duties, eg piloting at London Bridge, working on the East London line and local yard shunting, offered full employment. Placed on the Duplicate List in June 1901, its continuing poor mechanical condition, however, saw it taken out of service eight months later. *(Pendragon Collection)*

Piccadilly and *Wandle* head a sad line of condemned Class C goods engines at Redhill siding in 1902. Despite its name, *Piccadilly* never participated in London suburban work. *Wandle* served New Cross shed faithfully up to the turn of the century, when, unable to attract a buyer because of its poor mechanical condition, it, too, went for scrap. *(National Railway Museum)*

Leadenhall received new 14in cylinders and lost its condensing gear in 1892. Two years later it became the first regular 'Terrier' to work the Hayling Island branch, when it replaced the saddle tank *Bognor. Leadenhall* remained on this service until it was withdrawn in July 1901. In the above study the white-painted roof of Stroudley's stylish cab adds a final touch to an elegant Portsmouth grouping. *(Author's Collection)*

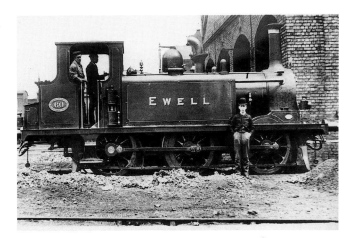

Ewell is seen here at New Cross shed, where it was to spend the first 25 years of its comparatively short existence. It, too, finished up at Redhill siding early in 1903. *(Author's Collection)*

(6)60 EWELL — Built November 1875

'Terriers' Nos.49–62 all went to New Cross when new; and No.60 remained there until the end of the century, when it was transferred to Brighton. Despite receiving new 14in cylinders in 1894 it appeared on the 1898 Surplus List. Duplicate Listing in June 1901 implied a further reprieve; but it was a short one, for *Ewell* was duly withdrawn in December 1902.

(6)64 KEMPTOWN — Built June 1874

As befitted its name, *Kemptown* was sent new to Brighton and remained there for a long time to come. In 1890 it was one of eight 'Terriers' to have its boiler tubes reduced in number to 121, and their length shortened to 8ft 2in. Iron tubes were used at first, though brass later became obligatory. Some years later, the locomotive became Brighton Paint Shop Pilot; but that duty terminated in 1900, when a D1 tank arrived in replacement. *Kemptown* thereafter shared in Hayling Island duties, until it was withdrawn in January 1903.

Kemptown, one of few 'Terriers' to escape London service, entered traffic at Brighton on 20th June 1874 and is seen here, looking very smart, in the mid-1890s. Although renumbered 664 in 1901, it was scrapped less than two years later by LB&SCR. *(Author's Collection)*

Chimneyless and forlorn, *Hailsham* is seen here at Redhill sidings early in 1903. Someone has chalked No.676 on her bunker side; but the locomotive was never, in fact, Duplicate Listed. *(National Railway Museum)*

76 HAILSHAM — Built June 1877

When built, No.76 also went to its namesake town and at Hailsham it replaced an old Craven tank. By 1887, however, it had become part of Eastbourne shed's 'Terrier' allocation. Built in the same batch as Nos.41–45, No.76 was not only numbered out of sequence, but somehow contrived to go through life carrying a works plate dated 1875. Though it successfully avoided the Duplicate List *Hailsham* perished, none the less, in April 1903.

(6)56 SHOREDITCH — Built November 1875

Another New Cross veteran, *Shoreditch*, entered traffic there on 18th November 1875 and working some 25,000 miles a year, as New Cross 'Terriers' were wont, it was still there when it was withdrawn in August 1903.

(6)45 MERTON — Built June 1877

Merton also went straight to New Cross from Brighton Works; but it was one of those which were dislodged in the mid-1880s, whence it moved to Midhurst. Littlehampton claimed it briefly in 1903. In April 1904, the locomotive was inspected by Isle of Wight Central Railway representatives, who were seeking additional motive power. *Merton* was turned down; ostensibly because of its poor mechanical condition — though quite possibly IWCR's newfound interest in steam/petrol railcars (see under *Brighton*) influenced the decision considerably. Whatever, *Merton* moved on to the breakers' yard in 1904, when it incurred the melancholy distinction of becoming the last 'Terrier' to be withdrawn by LB&SCR..

Another sad casualty from New Cross after a lifetime of hard work on the East London line. Demolition was well under way at Redhill when this photograph was taken on 5th December 1903 and the name *Shoreditch* is barely legible. Note the sale markings on the smokebox: 'No.656 — '30-3-03'. *(Author's Collection)*

TABLE 8
EARLY 'TERRIER' CASUALTIES

'Terriers' withdrawn					Running number taken over by		
No.	Name	Date withdrawn	Surplus listed	Duplicate listed	Class	Name	Date built
65	*Tooting*	February 1901	1898	—	B4	*Sandringham*	August 1901
66	*Hatcham*	February 1901	1898	—	B4	*Balmoral*	August 1901
51	*Rotherhithe*	February 1901	—	—	B4	*Wolferton*	July 1901
648	*Leadenhall*	July 1901	—	1901	B4	*Australia*	July 1901
658	*Wandle*	February 1902	—	1901	B4	*Kitchener*	August 1901
657	*Thames*	May 1902	—	1901	B4	*Buller*	August 1901
41	*Piccadilly*	June 1902	—	—	H1	4-4-2	February 1906
649	*Bishopsgate*	June 1902	—	1901	B4	*Queensland*	July 1901
39	*Denmark*	July 1902	—	—	H1	4-4-2	January 1906
652	*Surrey*	September 1902	—	1900	B4	*Siemens*	December 1899
36	*Bramley*	September 1902	—	—	A1X	*Fenchurch* (1927)	—
660	*Ewell*	December 1902	1898	1901	B4	*Kimberley*	August 1901
664	*Kemptown*	January 1903	1898	1901	B4	*Windsor*	August 1901
76	*Hailsham*	April 1903	—	—	I3	4-4-2T	March 1910
656	*Shoreditch*	August 1903	—	1901	B4	*Roberts*	July 1901
645	*Merton*	July 1904	—	1902	B4	*Bessborough*	June 1902

When *Merton* was Duplicate Listed in April 1902 it was given a flat wooden numberplate, with gold numerals painted on a grey background. In this view, taken earlier, the shed code 'MID' can just be seen by the front buffer beam. *(Author's Collection)*

Thus, sixteen of the 34 'Terriers' parted with by the LB&SCR during the Company's lifetime can be fairly unspectacularly accounted for. Three of them did not even last 25 years. Nevertheless, if the sixteen are listed in order of their departure from LB&SCR duty, they offer an interesting microcosm of the manner in which decks were cleared, numerically speaking, to make room for R. J. Billinton's much needed B4 4-4-0s.

Note from the Table above the names the LB&SCR chose for its powerful new express engines. Stroudley ventured into foreign parts latterly in search of locomotive names — and raised his sights to include political figures and Company Directors where express tender locomotives were concerned. During R. J. Billinton's regime, however, the accession of King Edward VII in 1901, coupled with victory in the South African War, induced such a wave of patriotism within the UK that the imperial-sounding names the B4s were given in no way under-estimated the spirit of the times.

Chapter 5
A COMPLICATED TALE

THE LIFE STORIES of eighteen more 'Terriers' sold during the LB&SCR's lifetime offer in themselves an illuminating illustration of the little tanks' uncanny capacity for surviving sundry crises by being able to adapt. London suburban traffic, motor-train work, service on the Isle of Wight, light railway employment — name your task, it seemed, and it was all in a day's work to a 'Terrier'! So true was this, in fact, that eight of the earliest sales may even be left to a later Chapter; for the locomotives concerned pop up again after Grouping. Half of them teased Fate further by entering BR stock in 1948! Thus, for the moment we may set aside *Fenchurch*, sold to the Newhaven Harbour Co. in 1898, four which were sold to the IWCR in 1899–1903, three which were purchased by the LSWR in 1903, and *Waddon*, bought by the SE&CR in 1904. Even then, one of the remaining ten lives on to this day, working for a living in Kent. We refer, of course, to *Poplar*, sold to the K&ESR in 1901. Because of its pioneer Colonel Stephens connection, however, it fits happily into this Chapter with six other Stephens stalwarts. Note how Stephens' purchases (shown in capital letters in the list below) dominate this section.

Mileage to date	Name	Date sold	Sold to	Later owned by
664,108	*POPLAR*	May 1901	Kent & East Sussex Lt Railway	—
787,145	*WAPPING*	February 1905	Kent & East Sussex Lt Railway	—
986,266	*Minories*	January 1918	Admiralty, Invergordon	—
711,605	*Southdown*	February 1918	Admiralty, Inverness	—
895,107	*BEULAH*	January 1918	Admiralty, Inverness	Shropshire & Montgomeryshire Light Railway
766,474	*EARLSWOOD*	January 1918	Admiralty, Inverness	Shropshire & Montgomeryshire Light Railway
617,185	*MILLWALL*	February 1918	Admiralty, Invergordon	Shropshire & Montgomeryshire Light Railway
989,263	*DEPTFORD*	April 1919	Edge Hill Lt Railway	—
1,165,194	*SHADWELL*	July 1920	Edge Hill Lt Railway	—
1,032,276	*Brixton*	April 1920	Mylon & Smith	—

70 POPLAR — Built December 1872 Later RVR/K&ESR No.3 *Bodiam*, and BR No.32670

Last to enter traffic of the six original 'Terriers', No.70, like its companions, was sent straight to London. There it ran 261,205 miles by 30th June 1881, and 20,915 more miles were added in 1882.

Christmas Eve 1881 saw *Poplar* involved in the first of two accidents when, running light between London Bridge and Battersea Yard in wintry conditions, it collided with the rear of the 11.35pm train from London Bridge. The fogman outside Battersea Park box had apparently given No.70's driver erroneous information. Fortunately, little damage was done. Years later, on the morning of 27th November 1895, equally good fortune attended *Poplar* as it led a local train into London Bridge station. The Westinghouse brake was duly applied, but the locomotive slid along greasy rails and hit the buffer stops. Again, damage was negligible. Shortly after that escape *Poplar* settled down to share Woodside line working, in alternate years, with South Eastern Railway locomotives.

The turn of the century, however, brought an abrupt change of venue; for in May 1901, with 664,108 miles completed, No.70 changed hands for £650, and became No.3 *Bodiam* on the newly formed Rother Valley (Light) Railway, one of Mr H. F. Stephens' more ambitious ventures. It was later joined by a second 'Terrier', both locomotives being repainted blue and fitted with vacuum brake in lieu of Westinghouse at Brighton Works before being despatched to Kent. In June 1904, Stephens' railway went on to assume the more imposing title of 'Kent & East Sussex (Light) Railway'.

Eventually even K&ESR No.3, denamed, incidentally, by the mid-1930s, began to show signs of wear and tear. A crisis arrived when its boiler was condemned in February 1943; whence the Southern Railway came to the rescue by offering an A1X boiler for £725. Major surgery of this nature was, of course, beyond the capability of Rolvenden shed, so two K&ESR fitters attended St Leonards, where the job was completed to everyone's satisfaction on 20th April 1943. No.3 resumed normal duties and even found time early in 1947 to participate in a film entitled 'The Loves of Joanna Godden'. Filming took place at Lydd Town station, and for the occasion the K&ESR tank, lettered 'SECR 3', temporarily assumed the name *Brodnyx*. By now, however, heavy repairs were due, and in May 1947, No.3 entered Brighton Works for complete overhaul. It returned to traffic in July painted dark green, with the Company initials inscribed above the number on the tank sides; K&ESR cast plates on the bunker were retained. One minor contretemps occurred, in that No.3 came back from Brighton facing Headcorn, instead of Robertsbridge, the K&ESR locomotives' usual posture. Presumably, in the absence of turntable facilities it remained so for some time!

When shopped new in 1872, *Poplar* had steam brake only; nearly a decade elapsed before the Westinghouse brake was fitted. Still with wooden brake blocks, the 'Terrier' is seen heading a train of vintage stock at Selsdon Road station shortly afterwards. *(Derek Brough Collection)*

Still carrying wooden brake blocks, the former *Poplar*, now Kent & East Susex Railway No.3 *Bodiam*, looks very smart in its new blue livery as it poses at Rolvenden. The first of H. F. Stephens' many 'Terrier' acquisitions, its purchase price was arranged by Barclays Bank loan. *(F. Moore)*

A later version of K&ESR livery; it is rather less flamboyant, but at least *Bodiam* has acquired a nameplate. The year is 1921 and the hop baskets on Tenterden Town station platform are only too typical of the K&ESR's traffic at the time. Both 'Terriers' led active lives on this system, but of the two, No.3 lasted much longer. This was achieved by judicious removal of spare parts from companion locomotive No.5 as the latter lay inert in Rolvenden yard — plus, it is suggested, occasional cannibalisation from two of the Shropshire & Montgomeryshire Railway's 'Terriers'. Rumour has it that *Bodiam's* latterday side tanks came from S&MR No.7 *Hecate*. *(Author's Collection)*

Right

Tenterden Station's newly painted white canopy shows to advantage in this study, as K&ESR No.3, rather optimistically equipped with express headlamps, waits on 27th March 1937, to take its one-coach train on to Robertsbridge. The 'Terrier's' ex-LSWR bogie brake will be augmented by sundry goods vehicles ere it reaches its destination. *(F. C. Le Manquais)*

What seemed likely to be No.32670's last appearance on ex-K&ESR metals came on 11th June 1961, one day before the line finally closed. On that occasion an enthusiasts' special of seven heavily laden coaches laboured from Robertsbridge to Tenterden with No.32662 at one end and No.32670 at the other. In this view, the latter is preparing to bank at the rear as the 'South Eastern Limited' leaves Robertsbridge. (Steamchest)

Grouping in 1923 had ignored such small railways as the K&ESR. Twenty-five years later, however, Nationalisation offered No.3 a new lease of life. It entered BR Southern Region stock on 2nd February 1948 and received its new number, 32670, at Ashford in September 1949. Meanwhile, the presence of 'foreign' 'Terriers' at Rolvenden enabled it to be released on 12th October 1951 to take over Brighton Works Pilot duties whilst the regular engine, No.377S, was undergoing extensive boiler repairs. A month later No.32670 itself was given a boiler inspection in Brighton shed and it, too, finished up by going into the Works for attention. It had hardly returned to normal duties when flood damage on 27th November 1952 brought about temporary suspension of all K&ESR line services. No.32670, isolated at Robertsbridge after working a morning train, had to seek refuge at St Leonards.

In March 1954, the engine went back to Brighton Works for extensive repairs. New frames were fitted on this occasion, and it returned to Rolvenden clad in black and lettered 'British Railways'. Next journey abroad came on 15th February 1956, when it was sent to rescue Class B4 0-4-0T No.30084 which had got itself snowbound, complete with train of wagons, at Eastern Docks, Dover. Significantly, an ex-SE&CR P class 0-6-0T had failed in an earlier attempt, through lack of adhesion. Next morning, No.32670 created a distinct precedent at Dover when it worked the daily goods train along the sea front. Weeks later it moved to Ridham Dock in place of Class P No.31178, which had failed completely. What memories the reappearance of a 'Terrier' must have roused in the Sheppey area!

Came 12th May 1956, and No.32670, though still officially attached to St Leonards, was observed at Faversham shed. Two years later it was transferred to Brighton, where regular pilot duties at Newhaven were interspersed by occasional stints of harbour shunting at Littlehampton. The following year, 1959, no 'hop picker' specials ran on the K&ESR line, though one through excursion from Victoria on Sunday, 18th October saw two Class L 4-4-0s arrive at Robertsbridge at the head of ten coaches. Six of these, including a Pullman Buffet Car, were worked on to Tenterden, with 'Terrier' No.DS680 leading and No.32670 assisting at the rear. Both engines remained with the train at Tenterden all afternoon before working back. Next day the branch diesel broke down, and No.32670 was retained at St Leonards to handle the regular goods trip on the branch until the diesel returned.

Nine days elapsed ere it returned to Brighton. Perhaps as a reward for services rendered, No.32670 was taken into Eastleigh Works in May 1960 and was given a general repair and repaint.

The fact that No.32670 had been fairly recently overhauled did not absolve the locomotive in 1963, when, with imminent closure of the Hayling Island branch in mind, BR resolved to withdraw all 'Terriers'. Mercifully, only three finished up in the breakers' yard. Seven found new homes elsewhere and No.32670's fate was particularly apposite; it was sold to the Kent & East Sussex Preservation Society in April 1964. Years passed and after many a struggle, the short stretch of track between Tenterden and Morghew Crossing, half a mile west of Rolvenden, was triumphantly re-opened on 3rd February 1974. Appropriately, the Society's centenarian 'Terrier', rechristened No.3 *Bodiam*, was accorded the honour of heading the first train. One year later, when a special ceremony was held at Rolvenden on 22 March 1975 to commemorate the 75th anniversary of the opening of the original Rother Valley Railway, *Bodiam* was again employed to haul two 'birdcage' coachloads of guests. Period costume was the order of the day.

During its first three years of preserved K&ESR service, *Bodiam* succeeded in running 1,500 miles. Trains, however, were gradually increasing in weight and in 1977 the 'Terrier' was withdrawn to await a complete overhaul. The wait was to be a lengthy one, but this did not preclude *Bodiam* from joining the Canterbury & Whitstable Railway 150th Anniversary Cavalcade at Canterbury on 5th May 1980. The members of the K&ESR Society, meanwhile, were totally engaged in raising funds for *Bodiam*'s overhaul and, on 1st August 1984, their efforts were fully rewarded, when a completely transformed 'Terrier' resumed service as No.32670. Fully lined-out 1950 vintage mixed traffic BR black livery had been applied and the smokebox even carried a St Leonards (74E) shed plate. Resuming work with a will, the revitalised *Bodiam* soon proved itself capable of hauling three coaches up the 1:50 gradient between Rolvenden and Tenterden Town. On the Sundays of October 1984 it joined *Sutton*, bunker to bunker, in handling a very popular mixed train. Then, on the last three Sundays of November, No.32670 alone operated a similar train. It consisted of one coach, three wagons, and a guard's van. Two months earlier the 'Terrier' had been on loan to the GWR Society, Didcot for their 'Enthusiasts' Weekend'.

(6)71 WAPPING — Built September 1872. Later K&ESR No.5 *Rolvenden*

In August 1872, *Wapping* was expected to be the first 'Terrier' in traffic. Unfortunately, cylinder trouble delayed its debut, and it did not enter South London service until the following month. Nevertheless, like most of its companions, it completed over 250,000 miles in its first ten years. Later, on 1st February 1884, it was involved in an accident; leaving London Bridge at the head of the 12.05pm for Victoria, it was fouled by a D1 tank which had moved a shade too far forward in search of water. Two carriages were derailed, but no one was injured. Later still in the 1880s, more D1 tanks arrived to oust further 'Terriers' from London duties and around 1890, *Wapping* was transferred to Portsmouth. Here it shared Hayling Island and Southsea branch work with three other 'Terriers'.

Wapping had received new 14in cylinders and lost its condensing gear by the time this picture was taken at the turn of the century at Brighton. The locomotive, too, had just been Duplicate Listed, and now bore No.671. *(Author's Collection)*

This was a time, too, when the Isle of Wight Central Railway was on the lookout for suitable tank locomotives. Having already obtained three 'Terriers' at what it deemed to be bargain prices, the minor Company had no hesitation in July 1903, in accepting an invitation to inspect *Wapping*. Its poor mechanical condition, however, persuaded IWCR that this 'Terrier' was no knockdown at £700 and interest subsided in favour of another, No.84 *Crowborough*. Meanwhile, with one 'Terrier' already under his belt, Mr H. F. Stephens, of Kent & East Sussex fame, was also on the prowl for a second. *Wapping*, in fact, was no stranger, for it had already been hired at £2 a day by W. Rigby,

The new arrival, Westinghouse brake gear removed, and still carrying wooden brake shoes, swanks in blue livery as K&ESR No.5 *Rolvenden*. Companion locomotive *Bodiam* just edges into the left of this *Rolvenden* photograph. *(Locomotive Publishing Co.)*

Seen again at Rolvenden, No.5 has acquired iron brake blocks as well as a new nameplate. Company initials have been substituted for the full title, and the 'Terrier' is beginning to look a shade careworn. *(O. J. Morris)*

the contractor of the Sheppey Light Railway, another of Stephens' involvements. Thus, still fetching a price of £700 despite an accumulated mileage of 787,145, No.671 duly passed into K&ESR ownership in February 1905. Serviced at Brighton like its predecessor, the tank on arrival in Kent assumed a new identity as K&ESR No.5 *Rolvenden*.

While both 'Terriers' worked robustly enough over the years, it was No.5 which weakened first. By 1932 it could be found in Rolvenden yard, looking increasingly desolate as sundry parts were 'borrowed' to sustain No.3 in working order. Clearly *Rolvenden's* working days were over — and it came as no surprise when, in 1938, anticipating the war boom, her remains fetched a good price as scrap metals.

Quite remarkably, thirteen years elapsed before the next 'Terrier' sales resumed.

(6)79 MINORIES — Built July 1880

Originally one of New Cross shed's generous establishment of 'Terriers', *Minories* moved on to Brighton during the 1880s and lent a hand at Newhaven Harbour in 1888 when the Harbour Company's entire stock of engines was out of commission. By the mid-1890s it could be found working the Seaford branch from Newhaven shed and in February 1905 it graduated as Brighton Works Pilot in place of *Boxhill*. But this employment did not last long, for in 1906 No.79 underwent modification for motor-work. By 11th June that year it was handling Chichester–Portsmouth motor-trains.

When *Minories* was Duplicate Listed in March 1907 it was given a set of wooden number plates. This action proved to be somewhat premature, for the Marsh I3 tank which was to assume number 79 was not, in fact, shopped until November 1910. Equally curiously, *Minories* received new 12in cylinders in 1907, as opposed to the norm of 14in. Then, in January 1912, with a cumulative mileage of 823,265, it was reboilered to A1X

August 1937, and Rolvenden yard is already acquiring that 'junk yard' look which contemporary enthusiasts found so fascinating. Colonel Stephens could never throw anything away! In the foreground stands *Rolvenden*, barely recognisable but for the figure '5' on the front buffer beam. No.3 has its chimney and No.5's side tanks were leaning against the locomotive shed nearby. Other frames and wheels, sole remains of ex-Ilfracombe Goods *Juno* and *Rother*, are tucked in behind. The distinctive kink in *Juno's* frame shows clearly. Came World War II, and everything was cleared for scrap by 1941. *(Bluebell RPS Archives)*

class. Two months later it was working from Fratton shed on Hayling Island motor trains. Only too soon World War I descended and in January 1918, No.679 answered the call, figuratively speaking, by being sold to the Admiralty for £1,200. In later years it was observed in steam at Catterick Camp (May 1919) and Chatham Dockyard (April 1920). Reduced latterly to supplying steam to a compressor near No.2 Graving Dock, it finally perished at Chatham in October 1933.

Minories, one of the last batch of 'Terriers', was fitted with Westinghouse brake and cast iron brake blocks and hangers from the outset. By now, too, a flatter style of works plate was being adopted. The locomotive completed 986,266 miles before being sold in 1918. *(Author's Collection)*

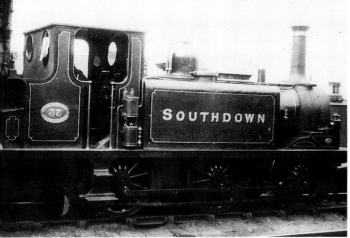

A Battersea 'Terrier' to the core, *Southdown* is seen here on South London line duty shortly after losing its condensing equipment in 1900. Six years later the locomotive was 'written off' with a book value of £200. *(Derek Brough Collection)*

(6)37 SOUTHDOWN — Built May 1878. Later 'Locomotive Department'

One of 21 'Terriers' stationed at Battersea by 1882, No.37 ran 30,236 miles that year alone, and stayed with London suburban duties all through the 1890s while many others were being obliged to leave.

In 1912 the 'Terrier' was offered at £725 to the Freshwater, Yarmouth & Newport Railway, which was badly in need of motive power at the time. In view, however, of the heavy boiler repairs the locomotive would have required, the FY&NR saw fit to decline Brighton's offer. So, the anonymous No.637 soldiered on at Battersea.

The next chapter in *Southdown's* career opened in February 1918 when, with a current mileage of 711,605 and priced now at £1,200, it passed into the hands of the Admiralty. Latterly it was employed at Dalmore Distillery, Invergordon and in one last sad sighting was spotted lying derelict at Ardrossan in June 1920, marked 'Mine Depot, Grangemouth'. Thus, at least one 'Terrier' was known to have perished in Scotland. The engine was cut up in August 1921.

Scheduled for withdrawal in 1906, No.637 was eventually laid up in July 1907 with a mileage of 663,310. Reprieve came one year later when, still in Class A1 form, it took up shed pilot duties at Battersea. As can be seen, the locomotive's running number was dropped, and the legend 'Locomotive Department' was neatly painted on the tank sides. *(Derek Brough Collection)*

Seen here at Kemp Town Station in course of initial motor-train experiments, *Beulah* has been converted to 2-4-0 wheel formation, and sand pipes now lead direct to the driving wheel. This engine and *Boxhill* were the only 'Terriers' fitted with rod-operated motor-train gear. The latter required extra-special service, however, and compressed air gear was employed from 1912 onwards. *(Author's Collection)*

(6)81 BEULAH — Built July 1880. Later Shropshire & Montgomeryshire Railway No.7 *Hecate*

Thanks to the influx of Stroudley D tanks in the London area during the 1880s, No.81 was despatched to Newhaven, where it worked the Seaford branch. A decade later it could still be found at Brighton, where, in conjunction with half a dozen other 'Terriers', it ranged the local gamut. Then in 1905 came the LB&SCR's important decision to combat growing electric tramway opposition by introducing motor-working.

The success the two 'Terriers' enjoyed on the Brighton–Worthing/Kemp Town motor-train trials was further consolidated in December 1905, when No.681 and a D class tank were moved to Eastbourne for a few days to compete afresh against steam and petrol cars on the St Leonards route. Again fuel consumption and general reliability tipped the scales convincingly in favour of the motor-fitted 'Terrier'. But as a corollary it was also decided that the said 'Terriers' would function best with their original wheel formation.

The next stage in *Beulah's* chequered career came in January 1918 when, still in Class A1 form, the locomotive was sold to the Admiralty for £1,200. Mileage at that juncture was 895,107. Three years later the 'Terrier' was working at Dalmore Distillery, Invergordon when Colonel Stephens bought it for use on his Shropshire & Montgomeryshire Light Railway. There, named *Hecate*, it was joined in 1923 by two more 'Terriers', *Daphne* and *Dido*. Like *Dido*, however, *Hecate* entered Kinnerley's 'graveyard' in the early 1930s, and, much cannibalised, it finally went for scrap in october 1934.

Restored to six-coupled form in February 1913, No.681 remained at Brighton during early World War I years; though it contrived to spend a few months assisting on the Woolmer Instructional Military Railway (later the Longmoor Military Railway). In this view the locomotive is seen on motor-train work in the Brighton vicinity. In accordance with L. B. Billinton practice, the legend on her side tanks has been shortened to 'LBSC'. *(Locomotive Publishing Co.)*

When the LB&SCR's first proud 'Baltic' tank, No.327 *Charles G Macrae* emerged, still clad in works grey, in March 1914, Brighton Works management could not resist offering this impressive conjunction of dignity and impudence. Twenty-one years later No.327, duly rebuilt in tender form at Eastleigh, re-entered traffic as N15X 4-6-0 No.2327, and carried the name *Trevithick*. It was condemned in January 1956 with a cumulative mileage of 1,210,802. No.681, meanwhile, soldiered on at Brighton until it was sold to the Admiralty for £1,200 in January 1918. *(Pendragon Collection)*

(6)83 EARLSWOOD — Built September 1880.
Later Shropshire & Montgomeryshire Railway
No.9 *Daphne*

The year 1900 saw No.83 posted, appropriately enough, to Earlswood, a sub-shed of Three Bridges. Here it assumed pilot duties at a modest goods yard between Earlswood and Redhill. Although, in fact, the locomotive carried the code 'EARLS' on its frames, it spent its nights in the open air. At weekends it worked light engine to Three Bridges for routine maintenance — the SE&CR having declined this service unless payment was made twelve months in advance! Next, earmarked for withdrawal under the LB&SCR's 1906 programme, *Earlswood* was offered to Isle of Wight Central Railway early in 1908 for £650; IWCR declined. The saga continued when the 'Terrier' was modified for motor-work in 1909. That same year it was involved in a motor-train accident when, approaching Brighton on 4th August on the 6.00am ex-Shoreham, its driver accidentally opened the regulator instead of closing it. *Earlswood* hit the platform buffers, and nineteen resultant casualties required medical attention

After leaving London for Eastbourne in 1887, *Earlswood* spent seven years at Brighton, during which time it was provided with 13in cylinders and its condensing equipment was removed, all in 1896. It is seen here at Brighton. *(National Railway Museum)*

Duplicate Listed in 1912, No.683 became part of Bognor's allocation that year. Then it passed to Coulsdon, whence it handled Crystal Palace motor trains. By now World War I was well under way and in January 1918, the 'Terrier' was sold to the Admiralty for £1,200. After serving in Invergordon naval yard it moved on to Dalmore Distillery, whence the Disposals Board offered it for sale in 1922.

Yet, despite this parlous existence even *Daphne* had a future — of sorts. A few years later, the Southern Railway, also anxious to obtain 'Terrier' spares, bought the little locomotive. It arrived at Eastleigh by goods train on 10th January 1939, and was promptly sent to the Works. Alas, in this instance appearances were deceptive; for, never steamed by SR and certainly denied its new owner's livery, poor *Daphne* languished in Eastleigh Works' outdoor 'dump' for a long time to come. Despite its varied career the locomotive was never rebuilt to A1X.

Snapped up by Colonel Stephens for £470 in November 1923, No.683 next found a home on the Shopshire & Montgomeryshire Light Railway. Named *Daphne*, it was captured here at Kinnerley on 28th August 1926. The saddle tank behind, *Severn*, already nearly 85 years old, worked on until withdrawn in 1931. *Daphne* survived, largely because S&MLR's other two 'Terriers', laid aside in the early 1930s, provided a convenient source of spare parts. *(H. C. Casserley)*

A forlorn sight at Eastleigh locomotive 'dump' on 22nd September 1945, six years after the SR bought *Daphne* ostensibly to yield 'Terrier' spares. Nameplates and Westinghouse pump have been removed, and part of the locomotive's old LB&SCR number, 683, still shows up after years of open air storage. Scrapping did not take place until April 1949. The 'Terrier' on the right of this photograph bears all the hallmarks of Isle of Wight service. *(H. C. Casserley)*

Below

For some reason or other tank locomotives never enjoyed great success on the Shropshire & Montgomeryshire and this procession, as it approaches Kinnerley in 1930, further illustrates the totally secondhand nature of S&M rolling stock. *Pyramus*, a vintage ex-LSWR 'Ilfracombe Goods', leads *Dido*, and the three coaches are a mix of Midland and LSWR four-wheeled stock. Poor *Dido*, laid up latterly at Kinnerley, lost many a 'spare part' before it was scrapped in October 1934. *(Lens of Sutton)*

This study of 'Terrier' No.638, formerly *Millwall*, may well, judging by the makeshift cab blind, have been taken in Scotland around 1920. Whatever, it and fellow 'Terrier' No.683 were sold, as Government Surplus, in November 1923 to the Shropshire & Montgomery Railway, whence they entered a new lease of life as No.8 *Dido* and No.9 *Daphne*. *(Author's Collection)*

(6)38 MILLWALL — Built June 1878. Later Shropshire & Montgomeryshire Railway No.8 *Dido*

Stationed initially at Battersea, where it ran 24,006 miles in 1882 alone, No.38 took part in the later exodus from London and was posted to Horsham shed in the mid-1890s. Here, working the Bognor branch, it, too, was denied the comforts of normal shed life, for it spent its nights in a shoddy old wooden building just outside Bognor station. An ominous spell of steam raising at Epsom, and an even more protracted period of pumping work at Three Bridges from July 1901 onwards, should normally have spelled *finis* by the time it was towed away to Brighton Works in October 1905. But, miraculously, the 'Terrier' was returned to traffic, equipped with new cylinders and wooden number plates. Its Stroudley livery, though, had given way to black with red lining, and tank sides now lettered 'Loco Department' indicated clearly what new duties lay ahead.

Still shed pilot at Brighton in 1918, with 617,185 miles already clocked up, No.638 next moved to the Admiralty that year for a sale price of £1,200. Then, once hostilities ceased, there came a spell at Glen Albin Distillery before the Disposals Board took over. It was observed, still in Brighton livery, at Dalmuir, Dunbartonshire in November 1921.

Two years later, *Millwall*'s fortunes changed, when it was purchased by Colonel Stephens for the munificent sum of £470 and became the property of Shropshire & Montgomeryshire Light Railway. In keeping with Stephens' fondness for classical names it was rechristened *Dido* on that somewhat careworn concern and, together with two 'Terrier' companions, *Dido* served its new masters faithfully enough into the 1930s before being laid up at Kinnerley.

> The next two to be described were *direct* sales to Colonel Stephens.

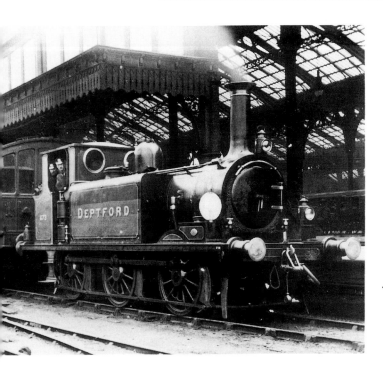

(6)73 DEPTFORD — Built October 1872. Later Edge Hill Light Railway No.1

One of the first six 'Terriers' built, No.73 underwent trials on 10th October 1872, entered traffic two days later, and completed 246,476 miles by 30th June 1881, mostly on South London line service. When the locomotive was Duplicate Listed in 1901 it received unusual treatment, in that its cabside was given transfer numerals *before* a wooden number plate made its appearance. Next, although the 'Terrier' had already featured in the LB&SCR's 1898 Surplus List and was again mentioned in the 1905–6 withdrawal programme, No.673 was, in fact, modified for motor-work in 1906.

From 1906 onwards No.673 spent four years working to and from Hayling Island and by the time it was rebuilt to A1X Class in February 1912, it had completed 917,247 miles. March 1912 saw it stationed at Tunbridge Wells, and it was loaned for several months during World War I to the Woolmer Instructional Military Railway before it proceeded to Horsham in 1916.

As No.673, *Deptford* prepares to leave Brighton Station on a train of four-wheelers for Kemp Town; the transfer numerals on its cabside can be clearly seen. *(Author's Collection)*

Despite a formidable cumulative mileage of 989,263, the 'Terrier' fetched a new high price of £1,300 when it passed from LB&SCR hands to those of Colonel Stephens in April 1919. This time new pastures beckoned, and the locomotive became No.1 on Edge Hill Light Railway. The latter concern, newly created to ferry ironstone from mines at Edge Hill, Oxfordshire, to main line sidings at Burton Dassett, offered *Deptford* and (later) a sister 'Terrier' the comparatively easy task of working wagons some 2¼ miles between the main line sidings and the foot of a 1:9 gradient; cable haulage took over from there. Occasionally the little tanks also worked over Stratford & Midland Junction Railway metals, for the two directorates had close personal connections.

Unfortunately, despite its optimistic launch in 1920, the EHLR soon faltered. Ironstone deposits faded prematurely and mining activity came to a sad end on 27th January 1925, when one last load was cabled down. Thereafter, a strange state of dereliction persisted for many years to come, during which time the two 'Terriers', plus all remaining EHLR rolling stock, silently mouldered away in Edge Hill sidings.

Even when the War Department requisitioned the line during World War II, little happened to alter the situation and *Deptford*'s remains were not removed for scrapping by James Friswell & Co. of Banbury until April 1946. The miracle was that Edge Hill's abandoned stock survived the scrap drives of the Second World War.

A vastly different scene obtains in the late 1930s at Edge Hill, long after iron ore workings ceased on EHLR. Now the two 'Terriers', with No.1 in the background, lie abandoned at the foot of the incline. The brake van, prominently marked 'EHLR', was Great Eastern in origin, and a few four-wheeled mineral wagons are piled carelessly behind. *(Author's Collection)*

Who could guess from this view of Edge Hill Light Railway's neatly groomed 'Terriers' that their working life would end *four* years later! The A1 in the foreground is EHLR No.2, formerly *Shadwell*, while A1X No.1, formerly *Deptford*, brings up the rear. *(Author's Collection)*

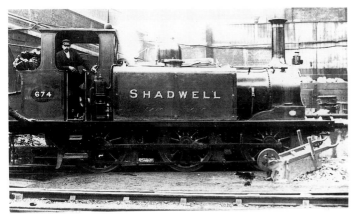

Featured in the LB&SCR's 1898 Surplus List, *Shadwell* was also Duplicate Listed in 1901. Further scheduled for withdrawal in 1906, No.674 eventually emerged motor-fitted from Brighton Works and commenced motor-train duties between Lewes and Seaford in June of that year. By 1912 it was performing similar duties from Brighton shed — still, however, in Class A1 form. *(Author's Collection)*

(6)74 SHADWELL — Built October 1872. Later Edge Hill Light Railway No.2

The life story of *Shadwell*, another of the first six 'Terriers', was similar in many respects to that of *Deptford*. No.74's cylinders gave trouble during initial trials in October 1872, but these were replaced and the engine entered traffic on the 12th of that month.

Came July 1920, and *Shadwell* followed *Deptford* into Edge Hill Light Railway service. This time, thanks to post-war inflation, Colonel Stephens had to pay £1,750 for his 'bargain'. Forty-eight years earlier the locomotive cost only £50 more to build, and it had run 1,165,194 miles since! Despite the smart EHLR livery the 'Terrier' was given, *Shadwell*, like its partner, was doomed to be abandoned in less than five years time. Worse still, two more decades were to elapse ére its remains were removed.

Seen here on South London duty, No.67 *Brixton*, spent the first 32 years of its life as part of Battersea shed's substantial allocation of 'Terriers'. Narrowly missing withdrawal in 1906 it was, in fact, motor-fitted, and completed 1,032,276 miles before being sold in April 1920. *(Author's Collection)*

Lastly, one more 'Terrier' changed hands at 1920 valuation:

(6)67 BRIXTON — Built August 1874

Posted when new to Battersea, No.67 remained there all through the 1890s while many other 'Terriers' were being transferred to country regions. Scheduled for withdrawal in 1906, then motor-fitted the following year, the locomotive moved on to Tunbridge Wells, whence it featured in an odd accident at Oxted Station on 18th March 1912. Having worked in an early morning train, *Brixton*'s driver decided to take water whilst he waited for his London connection. Both platform cranes, however, were frozen and recourse had to be made to a builder's hose in the goods yard. On his return, the driver let the fireman attend to recoupling engine and train. Then, operating from the trailer end, off he went on his return journey. Unfortunately, as the train approached Edenbridge Town Station the driver found his normal brake application was having no effect. As luck would have it the fireman was leaning from the engine cab and, spotting his colleague's anguished signals, he promptly applied the hand brake. Thus, the train stopped safely.

Enquiry revealed a disturbing state of affairs. The fireman, a poor reader, had confused the four motor-train connecting pipes when he recoupled at Oxted. When, eventually, Authority heard of the 'near-miss', arrangements were made to have all such pipes on engines and trailer cars painted distinctive colours and name tabs on the pipes were eliminated.

Still at Tunbridge Wells, No.667's industry was such that 132,898 more miles were notched up during the years 1910 and 1913. In the midst of World War I, it was one of several 'Terriers' which assisted on the Woolmer Instructional Military Railway. Then, with a final LB&SCR tally of 1,032,276 miles, the locomotive was sold to a private firm, Messrs Mylon & Smith of Sheffield, in April 1920 for a consideration of £1,500. Some years later it was resold to Grassmore Colliery, Chesterfield, and there, renamed *Ashgate*, it served its time out. Its remarkable mileage was a true compliment to Stroudley's original A1 design. Even then, the little locomotive was not cut up until 1935.

Duplicate Listed in 1901, but never rebuilt to A1X, No.667 is seen here just before World War I, storming along with its trailer car in approved 'Terrier' fashion. *(Derek Brough Collection)*

Chapter 6
SOUTHERN RAILWAY DISPOSALS

GROUPING ON 1ST JANUARY 1923 brought about an astonishing reunion of Stroudley 'Terriers', for apart from a major contribution of sixteen by the LB&SCR, the newly created Southern Railway also received exiles from the LSWR, SE&CR and two Isle of Wight railways: Isle of Wight Central and Freshwater, Yarmouth & Newport. Four years later, when the SR acquired complete possession of the Newhaven Harbour Company for £383,000, *Fenchurch* also joined the merry throng. Using the original names by which 'Terriers' will always be known, the SR's complement of 24 can be summarised as given in Table 9. Those shown in capital letters were subsequently withdrawn or sold, by the SR, and, as such, they form the substance of this Chapter.

The first 'Terriers' to be scrapped by the SR were three of those received direct from the LB&SCR in 1923. All three went in 1925.

When *Preston* went on the Duplicate List in June 1901, its Stroudley number plates were replaced by simple wooden ones with the new number, 663, painted in gilt. The style of figuring was later adopted by Marsh. Was ever a tiny 'Terrier' bunker more tightly packed with coal than in this view, taken when *Preston* was engaged in motor-work in the Eastbourne area? *(Author's Collection)*

(6)63 PRESTON — Built October 1875

Sent new to Brighton shed, *Preston* remained there all through the 1890s. Although it appeared on the LB&SCR's Surplus List of 1898, it, like others, escaped premature extinction by being modified for motor work. Motor-trains were in their time, of course, an unqualified success. But their silent running posed new problems in branch working; witness an accident which occurred on 7th November 1906, when No.663, handling the 5.15pm St Leonards to Eastbourne, ran down and killed two trespassers at a spot near Hampden Park station. When enquiry revealed that part of the line had been used for many years as an unofficial short cut, Brighton drivers, thus alerted, soon began to make more frequent use of their whistles.

By 1912 all but two 'Terriers' were being deployed on motor trains, and No.663, for its part, operated from Coulsdon. A year later, with a total of 735,684 miles to its credit, it was rebuilt as an A1X.

First World War years were comparatively peaceful, however, and *Preston* spent a deal of its time at Fratton, where it became a regular habitué of the Hayling Island branch. Finally, came the last phase, in March 1925, when, still clad in umber livery, No.663 was scrapped. It was, as it happened, the first A1X class locomotive to go.

TABLE 9
SOUTHERN RAILWAY 'TERRIERS'

Received from	Class A1	Class A1X		Non-Standard
LB&SCR (16)	*BOXHILL* *TULSEHILL**	ASHTEAD BOOKHAM Cheam Cheapside* Fulham GIPSYHILL* Knowle	Martello Morden* PRESTON Stepney Sutton Whitechapel Wonersh*	—
LSWR (1)	—	—	—	CLAPHAM
SECR (1)	—	—	—	Waddon
Isle of Wight Central Rly (4)	*BLACKWALL PECKHAM*	Brighton	CROWBOROUGH	—
Freshwater, Yarmouth & Newport Rly (1).	—	—	—	Newington
Newhaven Harbour Co (1)	—	Fenchurch	—	—
Totals	4	17		3

* Five 'Terriers' marked thus had already run over 1,000,000 miles in LB&SCR service. None of the remaining eleven had an individual mileage of less than 850,000.

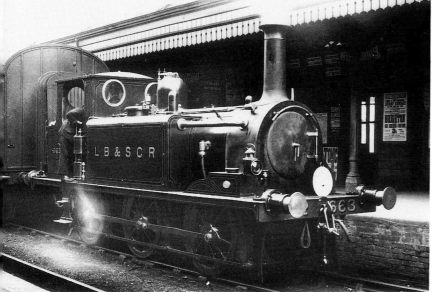

The year is 1914, the scene Barnham Junction and No.663 has just arrived from Bognor, probably bound for Littlehampton. Only the Marsh 'balloon' can be seen, but behind that trailed four six-wheelers and three brake vans: quite a substantial load, even for a willing 'Terrier'. *(O. J. Morris)*

(6)42 TULSEHILL — Built June 1877

Originally a New Cross engine, *Tulsehill*, however, was involved in the 1880s exodus from London and found itself relocated at Littlehampton. Moving on to Brighton a decade later, it next went on to Midhurst, where it worked the Pulborough–Chichester line. Then, fitted for motor work in 1907, it returned to its old haunts at Brighton. Released from there in October 1911, on loan to Longmoor Camp, it did not return until May 1912. The only other variation from normal Brighton duties during World War I years took the form of a short spell at Chatham Dockyard in 1916.

On the eve of Grouping, No.642 was the last LB&SCR 'Terrier' working in original condition. The locomotive's remarkable cumulative mileage of 1,106,848, second highest to date of all 'Terriers', was duly acknowledged when the locomotive appeared in the LB&SCR Surplus Stock List under the heading 'No monetary value'. Content, nevertheless, to ignore this somewhat demeaning accountant's ploy, No.642 soldiered on at Battersea, 'shed-piloting' away until it was withdrawn in May 1925. Vexingly, its replacement, former SE&CR No. 751, proved to be in such poor mechanical condition that it had to be removed again in March 1926.

When *Tulsehill* was fitted for motor-work in 1907, its cylinder diameter was also reduced, for some reason, to 10in, October 1919, however, brought an abrupt change of locale, when No.642 was despatched to Battersea as shed pilot in place of *Southdown*. Duly fitted with steam sanding gear, No.642 began operations bearing only the legend 'Locomotive Department' on its tank sides, though it did regain its running number by June 1922, when this photograph was taken at Battersea. *(LCGB Ken Nunn Collection)*

Seen here at Brighton after losing its condensing gear in 1894, *Bookham* contrived to put in additional service at Littlehampton before it was motor-fitted in 1908. It had previously been offered to the Isle of Wight Central Railway for £650, to no avail. *(F. Moore)*

(6)80 BOOKHAM — Built July 1880

A comparative latecomer to London life, *Bookham* remained a New Cross engine until it was sent to Littlehampton in the late 1880s.

Later developments saw No.680 reboilered to A1X class in April 1912 at a cost of £879. Then, with a cumulative mileage of 740,368 under its belt, the locomotive returned to motor-service at Bognor. It stayed there all through World War I.

In post-World War I years the LB&SCR's interest in a new form of train control, the Angus system, was sufficient to warrant a demonstration being staged and No.680 was one of two 'Terriers' chosen to make test runs over the Dyke branch. The trials, held on 22nd September 1921, were impressive enough in practice, but the LB&SCR declined to place an order. No.680 subsequently reverted to local branch life, and was little troubled until December 1925, when, alas, it was called into Brighton for scrapping.

* * * *

The next SR 'Terriers' to go were three which had seen doughty service in the Isle of Wight. One went to the breakers in 1927. The other two followed twenty years and more later!

75 BLACKWALL — Built December 1872. Later IWCR No.9 and SR No.W9

One of the 'original six' 'Terriers', *Blackwall* ran trials on 1st December 1872, and entered traffic at New Cross the very next day. Having completed 226,927 miles before being fitted with new cylinders in March 1881, it celebrated the event by reeling off an additional 19,463 miles the following year. Battersea then claimed the locomotive in the early 1880s. Within a decade or so, however, it moved to Brighton and there, in addition to working the Kemp Town branch, it occupied itself on station piloting and other local duties. In 1897, under R. J. Billinton's aegis, it acquired new 14in cylinders and lost its condensing gear.

The IWCR's investment proved to be a sound one, albeit financed extraneously by a hire purchase agreement which required monthly payments of £9.8.0d (£9.40) over the next ten years! Duly painted in IWCR red at Brighton, the 'Terrier' reached the Island in March 1899. Its side tanks bore the IWCR garter, within which appeared the legend 'Central Railway' and running number 9. Unloaded with some difficulty from a lighter at Medham Wharf, it eventually made its way, with the aid of temporary track, to the nearby Cowes–Newport line. Unbeknown to all concerned, three more 'Terriers' were to follow the same drill over the next four years.

The time is 1912, and No.680 *Bookham* stands by at Brighton Station, awaiting its next motor-train duty. *(Derek Brough Collection)*

In the meantime a change of livery was effected on the IWCR in May 1901. The crimson colour remained, but the garter was abandoned, and side tanks now bore 'ISLE OF WIGHT' in large letters, with 'CENTRAL RAILWAY' added more modestly beneath. Running numbers were also transferred to the bunker. Always popular with local train crews, No.9 entered Newport workshops seven years later for heavy repair. Its tally to date on Island service amounted to 80,340 miles. Unfortunately, the modest nature of the labour force at Newport inevitably made major locomotive repairs a lengthy and none too incisive process. It came as no surprise, therefore, that, in April 1911, an independent LSWR inspector, having completed an examination of all IWCR locomotives, pronounced No.9 to be in poor condition.

As might be expected, IWCR's 'solution' to the problem was both tardy and makeshift. Minor repairs to No.9 were duly effected, but March 1917 arrived ere a new boiler was forthcoming — and *that* was a Brighton-reconditioned one which had been taken off IWCR No.12 (formerly *Crowborough*) when the latter had been converted to 'A1X' class twelve months earlier. Nevertheless, during the reboilering process, No.9's feed pumps were removed, injectors were fitted, as were new 14in cylinders, and wooden brake blocks were replaced by cast-iron ones. The 'Terrier's somewhat battered copper-capped chimney was also replaced by a locally manufactured cast-iron one.

In 1923, with the advent of Grouping, No.9 took over Freshwater line duties and, one year later, it was repainted SR Maunsell green. The legend 'SOUTHERN' now appeared high on the side tanks, and the prefix 'W' was superimposed above the running number. That sounded as if the SR meant business, but within a year or two, a further influx of 02 tanks into the Island posed ominous overtones for IWCR's older stock. Surely enough, No.W9, already laid up with a faulty firebox, was condemned out of hand in April 1927 and, moved to the Gas Works siding at St Helens, it was sold for scrap and duly demolished. At least it had run 321,669 miles during its 27 years service on the Isle of Wight. That, added to the LB&SCR mainland mileage of 580,982, offered a final total of 902,651 miles — a figure well worthy of 'Terrier' traditions.

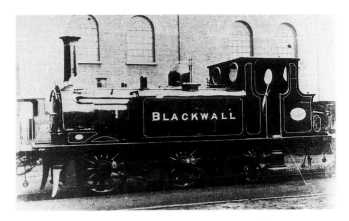

This picture of *Blackwall* was taken before the 'Terrier' lost its condensing gear. A year or two later, enquiries from the Isle of Wight Central Railway for a 'suitable tank locomotive' were given rather cavalier treatment by LB&SCR management. Sheer persistence, however, on the smaller railway's part eventually won the day and in March 1899, *Blackwall*, its mileage increased by now to 580,982, changed hands for £800. The IWCR had been offered a choice of two cheaper 'buys' by the LSWR — an 0-6-0ST at £550 and an 'Ilfracombe Goods' 0-6-0 at £750 — but wisely declined both. *(Author's Collection)*

So popular was the 'Terrier' type on the Isle of Wight, three more (*Peckham*, *Brighton*, and *Crowborough*) passed into IWCR hands by 1903. The four locomotives later became Nos.W9–W12 under Southern Railway auspices. In this view, dated 25th April 1926, No.W9 is about to leave Newport, IOW, on the 4.20pm to Freshwater. Note the extended bunker and locally cast chimney. *(LCGB Ken Nunn Collection)*

69 PECKHAM — Built July 1874. Later IWCR No.10 and SR No.W10 *Cowes*

Also one of Battersea shed's initial complement, *Peckham* was seconded to assist at Newhaven Harbour whilst the Harbour Company's own engines were out of action for two months in 1888. Then, back to London it went and, except for a second brief spell at Newhaven in February 1898, while the purchase of *Fenchurch* was being negotiated, it remained at Battersea all through the 1890s, working suburban passenger traffic as to the manner born. In April 1899, new 14in cylinders came its way and condensing pipes were removed. Next, some months later, the Isle of Wight Central Railway Board, pleased with *Blackwall's* performance on the Island, invited the LB&SCR to sell them another 'Terrier'. Thus, *Peckham*, with 576,292 miles already behind it, passed into IWCR possession on 18th April 1900. The purchase price of £700 was again subsidised on the IWCR's part, by recourse to a Finance Company and, as with *Blackwall*, general repair and a repaint in Island livery were carried out at Brighton before the 'Terrier' left the mainland.

IWCR's second 'Terrier' continued to give its new owners every satisfaction, and during the immediate pre-World War I years it was duly modified in typical IWCR 'Terrier' style — ie its coal bunker was enlarged to take 1½ tons and wooden brake blocks were replaced by cast-iron ones. It also fell heir to a locally made Wheeler & Hurst tapered chimney. New 14in cylinders followed in June 1915, and injectors took the place of feed pumps. Contrary to Brighton practice, however, the leading sandboxes, combined with splasher and gravity sand feed, were retained. The next development, the advent of Grouping, saw

Life for *Peckham* on the Isle of Wight proved to be little less hectic than that at Battersea, for during its first three years the newly acquired 'Terrier', numbered IWCR 10, ran 71,632 miles. When this photograph was taken at Newport the Company title on the side tanks had been shortened to 'IWC', and crimson-lake livery had given way to glossy black. *(Author's Collection)*

the 'Terrier' taken into Southern Railway stock on 1st February 1923, but two more years elapsed before it received Maunsell green livery and SR running No.W10. Then, in February 1926, it and two other Island 'Terriers' were fitted with 'push-pull' gear of a type which was now being used on the Ventnor West branch. A spell of duty on the Freshwater line followed, and carriage heating equipment was fitted to No.W10 in October 1927. The latter refinement was a direct repercussion of the fact that the IWCR's earlier use of custom-built steam rail cars had proved disastrous.

In October 1928, in accordance with the SR's new policy, No.W10 was allocated the name *Cowes*. April 1930 arrived, however, before appropriate bronze nameplates were affixed. By that time the 'Terrier's' A1 boiler had been condemned; and a visit to Ryde Works saw it fitted with an A1X boiler, taken off W12 *Ventnor*, and a Marsh chimney. The engine then resumed duties on the Ventnor West line until May 1936, when, rather ominously, it was recalled to the mainland From there on, the locomotive's existence was something of a quiet agony. Stored in Eastleigh Work's paint shop until 8 April 1940, it was then moved to the works dump; and there it lay, robbed of spare parts from time to time, until demolition finally came its way at the end of March 1949.

Stripped of their nameplates when they were returned to the mainland in 1936, Nos.W10, W14, and W9 lie awaiting their fate at Eastleigh. No.W10, after being stored awhile in Eastleigh Paint Shop, mouldered in the Works for nearly nine years before it was finally scrapped in March 1949. The other two 'Terriers' were fortunate enough to escape the breaker's torch. *(Railway Photographs)*

84 CROWBOROUGH — Built September 1880. Later IWCR No.12 and SR No.W12 *Ventnor*

The last 'Terrier' to be built, *Crowborough* went first to New Cross shed, then followed up with a move to Newhaven in the mid-1880s. It remained there, working the Seaford branch, until 7th November 1903 when, after some initial haggling as to price, it was sold to the Isle of Wight Central Railway for £725. Thus far, it had run 614,090 miles.

In this Newhaven study of *Crowborough*, the shed code 'N' can just be seen by the front buffer beam. *(W. G. Tilling)*

On the Island, numbered IWCR 12, it ran 17,500 more miles during its first twelve months. By April 1911, however, an independent inspector decided that the 'Terrier' was in very poor condition, and recommended a complete overhaul. At that time No.12 was engaged mainly on shunting duties between Newport and Medina Wharf; the IWCR management was extremely reluctant to invest in a new boiler. The matter then dragged until July 1916 when, at last, No.12 was fitted with a brand new 'A1X' boiler at Newport. Total cost was £1,195, and the 'Terrier's' cumulative mileage now stood at 897,589. 14in cylinders were also fitted, but the original sanding arrangements remained. Cast-iron brake blocks, a new locally made chimney and an extended coal bunker also made their appearance at this time. Locomotive livery, too, was changed from crimson-lake to glossy black, with vermilion panelling and white lining. The side tanks now bore the lettering 'IWC' in gilt, with gold shading, with the number 12 superimposed on the bunker. Meanwhile, in the interests of 'waste not, want not', No.12's old boiler, a product of 1880, was sent back to Brighton for reconditioning and, having spent £184 on this luxury, IWCR management lavished the rebuilt boiler on No.9 in March 1917.

1st February 1923 marked the official date when Isle of Wight railway services were taken over by the Southern Railway. In practice, however, a further month elapsed ere IWCR locomotives entered SR stock. Indeed, two more years passed before No.12, in course of heavy repairs at Newport Works, received its new Maunsell green livery and the prefix 'W'. Nine months later, in February 1926, motor-gear was fitted to enable the 'Terrier' to handle 'push-pull' services on the Ventnor West branch. Carriage heating equipment followed in October 1927

In 1927 No.W12 was given temporary employment on the Bembridge branch. October 1928 saw the locomotive allocated the name *Ventnor* and, six months later, confirmation came in the form of bronze nameplates. A reconditioned 'A1X' boiler, formerly carried by No.W11, came as a bonus in December 1929, as did the fitting of a Drummond chimney in 1932. Alas, the transfer of more O2 tanks to the Island, now that the Freshwater and Vembridge lines had been upgraded, enabled No.W12 to be laid aside in October 1935. Sent back to the mainland in May 1936, it lingered in Eastleigh paint shop until October 1940, when it was transferred to the Works' 'dump'. As with No.W10, exile was long and painful. Spare parts were progressively abstracted, and the end did not come until 1949.

A typical Isle of Wight 'A1X' rebuild, No.W12 is seen here at Freshwater on 13th August 1925, a few months after receiving its new SR livery. *(Author's Collection)*

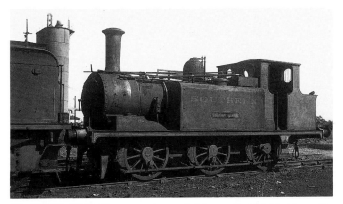

'Terrier' No.W12 *Ventnor* made a sad sight on Eastleigh's 'dump' in the mid-1940s; it gradually disintegrated until it finally disappeared in March 1949. *(S. J. Rhodes)*

The last 'Terrier' to be *scrapped* by the Southern Railway had an even more engaging history, for it was one of two sold to the LSWR by the LB&SCR in 1903 — only to return to SR safekeeping at Grouping.

Clapham, portrayed here on South London line service at the turn of the century, remained at Battersea until 1903, when an LSWR inspection party were sufficiently impressed by its performance to recommend its purchase for work on the LSWR's new Lyme Regis branch. The 'Terrier' was delivered, in full LB&SCR regalia, to Nine Elms on 12th March that year. *(Author's Collection)*

(6)68 CLAPHAM — Built August 1874. Later LSWR No.735 and SR No.E735

Sent to Battersea when new, *Clapham* settled down to vigorous employment on the South London line. It ran 20,041 miles in the year 1881 alone, and was still there at the turn of the century, albeit that it featured in the Surplus List of 1898. Although ignored when Billinton lavished 14in cylinders on most 'Terriers' during 1892–1900, No.68, however, was destined to leave LB&SCR ownership under surprising and highly complimentary circumstances.

The events of 1903 were interesting. The London & South Western Railway, having constructed a 6¾ mile branch line between Axminster and Lyme Regis, anticipated opening the line early that year. What with sharp curves, severe gradients and light railway construction, it was found that this modest branch made unexpected demands on motive power. Suffice it to say that the Class '0330' saddle tanks which LSWR management had envisaged would work the branch, proved woefully inadequate in practice; a much lighter axle loading was required. Dugald Drummond then contemplated building two small 0-4-4Ts for the purpose. This solution was abandoned, however, in January 1903, when an inspection party from the LSWR was allowed to sample the work of *Clapham* as it propelled a train of seven bogie coaches between Victoria Station and Stoat's Nest. The manner in which the heavily laden 'Terrier' tacked formidable gradients that morning clinched matters. Drummond was given a favourable report and on 4th March 1903, he recommended purchase not only of *Clapham*, but of No.646 *Newington* as well. A price of £500 apiece was agreed, and both engines were delivered to Nine Elms. *Clapham* had run 611,070 miles to date.

After spending six weeks on local piloting duties at Guildford, No.735 moved on to Bournemouth for a month's stint on Poole Quay tramway. Next, the Lyme Regis branch became available for trial runs and on 24th August 1903, both 'Terriers' were present to enhance the opening ceremony. Coupled together, they spent the whole day working between Axminster and Lyme Regis. Thus far things seemed satisfactory — but as time went on a new difficulty emerged. Winter traffic, it was found, was light enough to justify use of only one engine; but summer months so taxed the 'Terriers' that a Class O2 tank had to be called in from Exmouth Junction to assist from time to time. And here was more trouble. The O2, because of its increased axle load *vis-à-vis* the 'Terrier', had to work with partially filled side tanks and bunker. This so complicated locomen's

March 1903, and No.668 *Clapham* is duly delivered to Nine Elms once a purchase price of £500 had been agreed. *(Author's Collection)*

work that latterly an O2 tank reported for duty early in 1906, with side tank maximum levels clearly marked. The strategy worked, and from thereon O2s took pride of place on Lyme Regis traffic, with No.735 assisting in a secondary capacity. In any case it had long been apparent that the 'Terrier's' six-coupled wheels were experiencing undue tyre wear on the branch's sharp curves. Logic took its course, and in May 1907, Class O2s took complete command of the branch. No.735 was relegated to steam piloting at Exeter.

That duty did not last long, for by early 1908, No.735 moved to Exmouth for local shunting duties. By October, Bournemouth claimed it, also for light duties. Ultimately, in December 1911, the 'Terrier' was laid aside for reboilering. Eastleigh Works took charge in June 1912, whence No.735 received a new boiler, complete with Drummond-type direct-loaded safety valves. Time was to show, incidentally, that the older Stroudley-type boiler was much the freer steamer. Meanwhile, Eastleigh also provided steam heating apparatus, and

2nd May 1903 and *Clapham* appears in a new guise outside Nine Elms Works. Brighton works plates and Westinghouse gear have gone and the locomotive, still bearing its copper-clad chimney, shines now in full LSWR passenger livery. The 'Terrier's' 13in cylinders and feedwater heating apparatus were left untouched. Only a hand brake obtained now on the engine, though vacuum ejectors were provided for braking the rolling stock. From LSWR's point of view, the pity was that the 'Terrier' did not take kindly to the sharp curves of Lyme Regis branch. *(Author's Collection)*

No.735's feed water heating gear was removed. Over the next few months the locomotive found employment on the Chard branch. Then, after some weeks working between Yeovil Town and Junction stations, it was fitted with LSWR pulley and wire motor-train gear, whence it reported for duty on the Lee-on-Solent Light Railway. It stayed there all through World War I, but received so little mechanical attention during that period that when it entered Eastleigh late in 1919 it was deemed to be fit only for withdrawal.

In due course No.735 entered SR stock, was painted green, and was given number E735 in May 1925. It returned to Lee-on-Solent, but could only find intermittent work there; by now two other 'Terriers', Nos.B655 and B661, both equipped with LSWR auto-train gear, were more highly esteemed by the Running Department. A need for light repairs sent No.E735 back to Eastleigh in January 1927. Alas, its firebox was found to be in such bad shape that a mere patching-up process was carried out. Hardly surprisingly, 15th February 1930 saw it back in the shops. This time the locomotive's Drummond boiler was replaced by an A1X version off *Wandle*. No.E735, however, was *not* rebuilt. Thus, its stove pipe chimney and roof top motor-train fittings remained with it for the rest of its none too active life.

Fortunately, second thoughts at Eastleigh in 1919 enabled No.735 to escape withdrawal by a hairbreadth. The price paid, however — that of being fobbed off with an unsightly welded stove pipe chimney ere it left Eastleigh — was a bitter one to Brighton observers. Traces of LSWR pulley and wire-operated motor-train gear can still be seen on the cab roof in the above study, taken at Ashford, where No.E735 alternated between acting as Works pilot and working on hire at a local colliery from 1930 until it was scrapped in 1936. *(Author's Collection)*

The engine moved to Ashford in May 1930 as Carriage & Wagon Works pilot and there, with the exception of odd loan trips to Chislet Colliery nearby, it remained until it was withdrawn in December 1936. Final mileage was 807,664, and the A1X boiler it had earlier inherited was passed on to 'Terrier' No.680S in February 1937.

Whatever our old friend H. F. Stephens may have lacked in the way of liquid resources, he could never be accused of lacking enthusiasm for his light railway empire. Nor was he easily deflected from his own concept of locomotive standardisation. Already, during the years 1901–23, he had bought seven 'Terriers' and 1925 found him back again, this time on the SR's doorstep. Thus, one more 'Terrier' passed under his jurisdiction. A second which followed in 1937 was, in fact, the last 'Terrier' to be sold by the Southern Railway. Their stories have typically sad Stephens overtones.

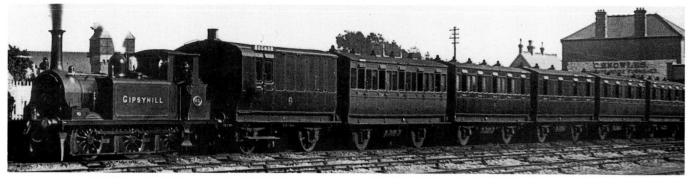

(6)43 GIPSYHILL — Built June 1877. Later SR No.B643, WC&PLR No.2 *Portishead*, and GWR No.5

After being stationed at Battersea for a number of years, No.43 was eventually ousted and it moved to Brighton shed by 1890. Next it went to Portsmouth shed, where it joined an already established 'Terrier' trio which worked the Hayling island and Southsea branches.

Converted for motor-train work at Brighton Works in 1908, *Gipsyhill*, now No.643, returned to its old haunts at Hayling Island, and was shedded at Fratton until 1916, when it moved back to Brighton. In September 1919, having accumulated a massive mileage of 1,083,604, it was given a new Brighton-built boiler, thereby qualifying as Class A1X. A further compliment came in September 1921, when it joined *Bookham* in Angus train control system trials at Dyke. Came Grouping and with it a new number, B643. Gross mileage by now was 1,105,698.

Freed at last from the exertions of London suburban traffic, Gipsyhill is seen here at Bognor station in 1900, ready to transport its train of four-wheelers to Barnham Junction. (Derek Brough Collection)

The next stage in No.B643's career was much more traumatic, for, at the instigation of Colonel Stephens, it was purchased in December 1925 by the Weston, Clevedon & Portishead Light Railway; the price was £785. Earlier that year, WC&PLR representatives had inspected No.B647, formerly *Cheapside*, which was then employed on Kemp Town duties, but turned it down in favour of B643. The latter, painted unlined black by the SR, was duly despatched to Clevedon. There it became WC&PLR No.2 and, third locomotive to bear the name, cast iron plates inscribed *Portishead* were affixed to its tank sides. The previous owner of the name, a Manning Wardle 0-6-0ST, was disposed of to a Bristol firm early in 1926.

Duplicate Listed in 1902, No.643, formerly Gipsyhill, is seen at Kemp Town on motor-train duty a year or two before it was rebuilt as Class A1X in 1919. Despite the massive mileage it had already run it was sold to the Weston, Clevedon & Portishead Light Railway in December 1925. (Author's Collection)

WC&PLR No.2 *Portishead*, the former *Gipsyhill*, is seen here leaving Portishead, *circa* 1935, on a typical WC&PLR train of two ex-Metropolitan Railway coaches. The latter, made redundant in London by electrification, now worked close-coupled in pairs, and were fitted with steps to facilitate passenger access at several platformless WC&PLR halts. *(Author's Collection)*

Typical of many Stephens enterprises, the WC&PLR fought a long, but losing, battle for survival. Internal combustion vehicles were introduced in post-World War I years while a second 'Terrier' was even bought in 1937; but the outbreak of war in 1939 defeated even Colonel Stephens' ingenuity. Inclusion under Ministry of Transport control during World War II *might* have saved the day. But such was not to be; thus the little railway luched on briefly, until a last train was run on 18th May 1940. The GWR, asked to rescue the light railway as a public amenity, declined that formidable task — then later relented sufficiently to buy the system for £10,000 from Excess Insurance Co., the WC&PLR's sole creditor. Intention was to use the line for coal wagon storage but in the event, precious few wagons ever found their way there. Meanwhile, appropriate legal proceedings had granted the GWR sole possession of the WC&PLR's locomotives and rolling stock. They made a sorry lot, and the GWR condemned everything except the two 'Terriers'.

In December 1948, No.5, by now the property of BR Western Region, moved to Taunton, where it was employed in the Civil Engineer's Department Yard. For some reason it carried the word 'Paris' beneath its right-hand nameplate. Newton Abbot was the next move, in mid-January 1950. Here occasional employment as shed pilot kept it occupied for a month or two before the locomotive was finally called in to Swindon and eventual withdrawal.

Life might have been very different for the old warrior. In 1953, Weston-super-Mare Borough Council was asked by the Bristol Railway Circle to buy the locomotive with a view to preserving it as a local attraction. The Council, alas, could not see its way to invest £400 in this manner, and the opportunity went by the board.

Portishead and partner, now Nos.5 and 6 in GWR stock, were lent awhile to Ministry of Works to assist in rail recovery. Then No.5 proceeded to Swindon Works, where it was overhauled and repainted in GWR livery. Given GWR numberplates, and still retaining the name *Portishead*, the 'Terrier' re-entered traffic carrying steam brake and GWR injectors. It carried out minor duties in the West country for ten years before being called into Swindon Stock Shed early in 1950, No.5 lay thus at Swindon for four years before being scrapped by BR Western Region in March 1954. *(Real Photographs)*

Ashstead, seen at Sutton Junction at the turn of the century, carries the Epsom shed code. Even after rebuild to A1X in 1912, it remained in the Greater London area, and only moved to Brighton just before Grouping in January 1923. *(Author's Collection)*

(6)53 ASHSTEAD — Built December 1875. Later SR No.B653 & 2653, WC&PLR No.4, and GWR No.6

No.53's story is similar to that of *Gipsyhill*, but for the fact that *Ashstead* spent its formative years at New Cross. It survived the thinning process which affected London 'Terriers' in the mid-1880s and was still there at the turn of the century. Placed on the Duplicate List in January 1900 it received unique treatment by being given a new set of brass number plates. Then, almost inevitably included in the LB&SCR's 1905–6 withdrawal programme, it escaped by undergoing modification for motor-work in 1908.

In May 1912, with current mileage of 735,419, the 'Terrier' was reboilered to A1X Class and, based on West Croydon shed, assumed motor-train duties that year. World War I had little effect on 'Terriers', other than to see a few more transferred from London to country regions, and December 1916 found No.653 resident at Coulsdon, where it and a companion locomotive shared Crystal Palace motor-train service. Their roster also included morning and evening trips between Crystal Palace and West Croydon stations. Grouping in 1923 found *Ashstead* with a total mileage to date of 922,408.

Renumbered 2653, the 'Terrier' ran a further 8,217 miles, and was wharf shunter at Littlehampton, when Nemesis, in the shape of Colonel Stephens, caught up with it. Fate in this instance consisted of sale to Weston Clevedon & Portishead Light Railway for £800. The bargain was struck in April 1937, nearly twelve years after Stephens had captured his earlier 'Terrier'. This time, however, *Ashstead* was delivered to Clevedon still bearing its green SR livery, with lettering and numerals blacked out.

Weston Clevedon's sad fate has already been mentioned. No.4 at least had the privilege of handling the last train on 18th

Looking quite spruce, despite having completed nearly 950,000 miles, *Ashstead* is now SR No.B653. The locomotive entered Eastleigh Paint Shop in May 1934, and lay there, devoid of wheels and chimney, for over a year before the Works took a hand and treated it to a complete overhaul. *(Lens of Sutton)*

Under WC&PLR auspices the one-time *Ashstead* was renumbered 4, but not given a name. The locomotive was seen here on 25th June 1938, at Clevedon, where WC&PLR stabled locomotives and carriages alike. *(H. C. Casserley)*

May 1940 and the locomotive was further used by GWR officials two months later to test the bridge over the River Yeo. Such was its mechanical condition, however, it could only manage six wagons. Then, renumbered GWR No.6, it also assisted awhile with rail recovery, before the Ministry of Works found it alternative employment at Nottingham. By 1942 both GWR Nos.5 and 6 had been overhauled at Swindon Works, but, unlike its partner, No.6's final equipment included Westinghouse brake and feed pumps. It, too, was repainted GWR green, and was given the familiar circular monogram and bunkerside cast number plates.

The last 'Terrier' to be described in this Chapter was taken out of Service Stock by Southern Railway in August 1946; but, far from being scrapped, it graduated later as a prize exhibit at Clapham and York Railway Museums. *Boxhill*, therefore, only qualifies nominally as an SR withdrawal — for its removal from active service in 1946 really constituted an act of 'railway pride'. It was to be joined in due course by many others.

After overhaul at Swindon Works in 1942 No.6, still nameless, accompanied its partner *Portishead* to St Philip's Marsh, Bristol. Least successful of the two, No.6 had to be laid aside after eighteen months of local shunting. As seen above, it was subsequently stored for some time until the imminence of rail Nationalisation forced a decision — and No.6 was duly condemned in January 1948. *(Author's Collection)*

Boxhill was functioning as Brighton Works Pilot when this photograph was taken on 4th September 1902. Condensing gear has gone and, three years later, the locomotive was to appear in the LB&SCR's Withdrawal List for 1905–6. It and many other 'Terriers' were only saved by the Brighton Board's decision to experiment with motor-train working between Brighton and Woking. *(LCGB Ken Nunn Collection)*

(6)82 BOXHILL — Built July 1880. Later 'Loco Dept Brighton Works' and SR No.380S

Posted to Battersea when new, *Boxhill* saw a change or two before the nineteenth century drew to a close. West Croydon shed housed it around 1887, but by the 1890s it had moved to Midhurst, where it and two other 'Terriers' coped with Pulborough–Chichester traffic. A transfer to Brighton in July 1898 as Works Pilot then took it out of the mainstream until, rather surprisingly, it was replaced by *Minories* in February 1905. The LB&SCR, it appeared, had other plans for No.82.

The plot thickened in March 1905, when *Boxhill* entered Brighton Works; the LB&SCR was taking its motor-train trials seriously. As already described, *Boxhill* re-emerged in 2-4-0T form and it and *Beulah* scored a distinct triumph in subsequent trials against sundry competition. Strangely, neither 'Terrier' was ever rebuilt to Class A1X. Both, however, were restored to six-coupled wheel formation in 1913, by which time *Boxhill* had spent one more year on shed piloting duty at Brighton, been Duplicate Listed in November 1911 and had completed a further 86,474 miles on motor-train work at Tunbridge Wells. It remained there all through World War I.

The next important event in the life of No.380S occurred in November 1946, when it conceded the task of Brighton Works Pilot to another 'Terrier', No.2635. This was no ordinary transfer, however, for it emanated from a Southern Railway desire to see a 'Terrier' preserved. Accordingly, No.380S reported to

In February 1920, No.682 returned to Brighton as Works Pilot and forfeited its running number in the process. It entered Southern Railway stock in 1923 carrying the legend 'Loco. Dept. Brighton Works', but this was soon changed to 'Loco Works Brighton'; and the attractive LB&SCR crests it bore on its bunker sides were eliminated in favour of the letter 'B', circumscribed by the words 'Southern Railway', as seen here on 20th June 1925. Umber livery was also replaced by plain black. (*Author's Collection*)

A decade later, *Boxhill* was transferred to Service Stock as No.380S. It received a Drummond-type chimney in the process and, as can be seen from this 29th June 1946 study, this completely altered the look of the 'Terrier'. (*H. C. Casserley*)

Lancing Works on 11th November 1946, whence careful repainting in Stroudley livery got under way. By 14th December all extraneous paint had been removed, brasses shone afresh, and one side tank already bore the name *Boxhill*. Then, painting complete, the locomotive was passed on to Brighton Works for mechanical restoration — no wooden brake blocks, though, for No.82, one of the last 'Terriers' built, always sported iron blocks. On 9th June 1947, on which occasion Bulleid Pacific No.21C164 was ceremoniously designated 'The 1000th locomotive to be built at Brighton Works', *Boxhill* was hauled out and positioned beside it for the benefit of the Company's photographer. Three days later the 'Terrier' was again photographed, this time alongside Brighton Works locomotive No.377S, its old friend *Morden*.

Then came the great day when full LB&SCR regalia shone again as *Boxhill* quit Brighton Works on 2nd September 1947. First port of call was Dorking North Station, where the 'Terrier' appeared on three day exhibition with electric locomotive No.CC2. No sooner had it returned to Nine Elms than the SR management decided it should participate in Switzerland's Railway Centenary celebrations. Unfortunately, shipping arrangements fell through. Nevertheless, *Boxhill's* triumphal progress continued. After travelling under its own steam all the way from Nine Elms, *via* Clapham Junction, Wimbledon, Epsom, and Dorking North, it celebrated the centenary of the Three Bridges–Horsham line on 13th February 1948 by going on show at Horsham station with Battle of Britain Pacific No.21C158.

August 1948 found *Boxhill* at Farnham electric carriage shed, ostensibly stored. Yet, on 22nd December that year it travelled to Brighton shed, again under its own steam, and underwent minor repair. Next, for some reason, February 1949 found it back at Brighton, looking extremely grimy, and with guard irons damaged. Happily, BR continued to respect *Boxhill's* privileged status and after minor axlebox attention, repaint, and a finishing varnish, the 'Terrier' re-emerged in familiar pristine condition.

The good years rolled on. Early in 1958 BR sponsored a mobile Transport Treasures Exhibition which toured the Southern Area. Its locomotive section consisted of *Boxhill* and another preserved classic, ex-LSWR Adams Class T3 4-4-0 No.563. Both locomotives appeared at Guildford goods yard on exhibition from 12th to 18th February. *Boxhill*, however, did not reappear when the Exhibition moved on to Salisbury; though a subsequent showing, held at Hove down sidings from 12th to 18th March 1958, saw both veterans reunited. At the conclusion of this display, both engines were returned to Brighton shed, where preparations were made to send them North to Tweedmouth shed for safekeeping. Their long trek began at 8.30am on 27th April, when 'School' class No.30935 *Sevenoaks* coupled up, with every intention of hauling them as far as Stewarts Lane. After some uncoupling trouble in the vicinity of Hassocks, the odd procession reached its destination about midday. London Midland Region took over that evening, and a diesel locomotive, travelling *via* Kensington (Addison Road) and Willesden, took them as far as Canonbury. Less than two months later, ex-SE&CR Wainwright Class 'D' 4-4-0 No.31737 moved up from Ashford, again *via* Stewarts Lane, to join them at Tweedmouth.

Alas, conditions at Tweedmouth proved to be far from ideal and in August 1959, suffering somewhat from lack of attention, all three locomotives were returned back south to Eastleigh yard. The object was to prepare them for permanent exhibition at Clapham, where a former tram depot was being converted into a Transport Museum. A year later, on 3rd August 1960, No.563 was seen by the public at Eastleigh's Open Day. *Boxhill*, deposited in the diesel repair shop, was still in the process of being Museum-prepared. Eventually, however, all restoration was completed and to obviate the risk of damage in transit by road — a necessity thrust upon BR by an inconvenient landslide at Hook — neither of the two locomotives was top-painted until it reached Clapham.

Within a decade it became apparent that a national transport collection warranted more generous display and Clapham Museum closed its doors on 23rd April 1973. London Transport items went to an appropriate Museum at Syon Park. Main line

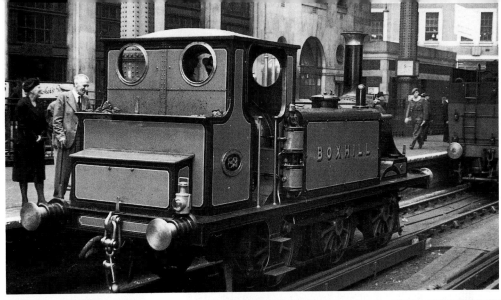

The combined arts of Lancing and Brighton Works were also displayed at Waterloo Station on 14th June 1948, together with a comprehensive display of photographs, documents and models — all part of the Station's Centenary Exhibition. The tender seen on the right of this photograph belongs to fellow exhibit West Country Pacific No.34017 *Ilfracombe*. *Boxhill*, meanwhile, followed up with a second appearance at Waterloo on 23rd June. *(H. C. Casserley)*

The date is 4th July 1959 and, grouped together in the unusual ambience of North Eastern Region's Tweedmouth roundhouse, ex-SR locomotives Nos. 31737, 563, and *Boxhill* await further developments. Ultimately, all found refuge in the National Railway Museum at York. *(Steamchest)*

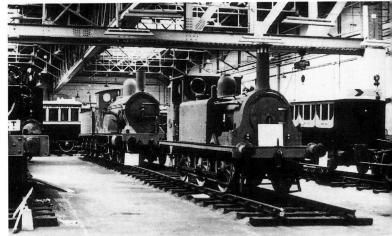

Boxhill was one of many prize exhibits when the Museum of Transport at Clapham opened its doors on 29th March 1961. The locomotive behind in this view is ex-LSWR T3 4-4-0 No.563. Both had been renovated a second time at Eastleigh Works and both, of course, moved to fresh pastures at the National Railway Museum, York in 1975. *(Bluebell RPS Archives)*

exhibits were stored, pending rehousing at York's new National Railway Museum.

The great day came on 9th April 1975, when an extraordinary convoy consisting of *Boxhill* (on a well wagon), *Mallard*, No.563, sundry tenders, and a goods brake van, headed by diesel No.45026, left Clapham and proceeded, *via* Stewarts Lane and Cricklewood, to link up with the old Midland route to York. The rest is history. The Duke of Edinburgh opened York Museum's Main Hall on 27th September 1975, and *Boxhill* took its true place in our priceless national railway heritage.

The historic convoy is caught by the camera in April 1975 as it made its way North to York Railway Museum. *(Author's Collection)*

Chapter 7
SCRAPPED BY BRITISH RAILWAYS

W HEN 'BIG FOUR' resources were pooled on 1st January 1948 the Southern Railway contributed 1,838 steam locomotives to BR stock. They were an interesting 'mix' of which 105 were more than 60 years old and, significantly, 74 of these (70%) were Stroudley engines. Fourteen of the very oldest were 'Terriers'; thus BR acquired one A1 and thirteen A1Xs. One more A1X, No.5 *Portishead* (formerly *Gipsyhill*) came from the GWR and on 2nd February 1948, the last 'Terrier' to be converted to A1X class, K&ESR's No.3 (formerly *Poplar*), also joined BR stock. The age spread of BR's sixteen 'Terriers' makes impressive reading — Table 10.

TABLE 10
'TERRIERS' ACQUIRED BY BR IN 1948

Year built					
1872	2636	*Fenchurch*	2630	*Poplar*	
1875	2659	CHEAM	2661	SUTTON	2662 *Martello*
	2655	*Stepney*	680S	*Waddon* (Class A1)	
1876	2647	CHEAPSIDE	515S	*Whitechapel*	
1877	2644	FULHAM	5	PORTISHEAD	W8 *Freshwater*
1878	377S	MORDEN	2640	*Brighton*	
1880	W13	CARISBROOKE	2678	*Knowle*	

The seven shown in capital letters in Table 10 were scrapped by BR during the years 1951–63. Meanwhile, all but one of the 'Terriers' were classified 'OP' by BR. No.5 *Portishead*, retained within BR's Western Region, was styled 'OF' in light of its West country activities. Its demise in 1954 has already been dealt with in Chapter Six. Of the remaining six 'Terriers', each completed over 1,000,000 miles before bowing the knee.

Fulham still clung to its original 13in cylinders and condensing gear when it left Battersea for Brighton in 1900. In this view it was captured just before it appeared on the 1902 Duplicate List. (*Derek Brough Collection*)

(6)44 FULHAM — Built June 1877. Later SR No.B644/2644, and BR No.32644

A staunch Battersea engine from the outset, *Fulham* withstood the eventual onslaught of new Stroudley tanks and heavier stock in the London suburban area and remained there in case of need right up to the turn of the century, when it was transferred to Brighton.

When *Fulham* acquired its new number 644, in April 1902, it also became one of few 'Terriers' whose number plates were immediately superseded by gold numerals *painted* on a grey oval background. To balance matters, a less complimentary form of selection came along a year or two later, when No.644 found itself earmarked, with fourteen others, for withdrawal under the LB&SCR's 1905-6 programme. Fortunately, the scheme was never implemented.

Meanwhile, the fact that *Fulham* still retained 13in cylinders and condensing gear was to stand it in good stead, for, hot on the heels of the highly successful motor-train experiments of 1905-6, it and two other 'Terriers' were pressed into stopgap operation on single-coach trains. While these offered the public what appeared to be a 'motor-train service', the locomotives, in fact, lacked motor gear and had to run round their trains after each journey. Nevertheless, the gallant trio held the fort until a sufficient number of 'Terriers' could be modified at Brighton Works and fifteen new trailer cars placed in service. The three 'Terriers' were rewarded by being fully equipped for motor-work in 1907 and on that occasion, No.644's cylinders were duly bushed to 12in. Stroudley's original condensing gear stayed put until the locomotive was rebuilt to A1X specification in November 1912. By then *Fulham* had completed 737,873 miles.

Ten years and 200,000 running miles later, No.644 entered SR stock as No.B644. It remained faithful to Brighton shed, where much of its time, and that of B647, was spent on Kemp Town branch service. Indeed, the two were still hard at it when the last 'Terrier' motor-working in the country drew to a close there early in 1928. Then, once the branch closed completely for passenger work on 2nd January 1933, No.2644 moved on to Fratton, the last mainland outpost for 'Terriers'. Here, locomotive weight restrictions on the Hayling Island branch still placed a valuable premium on the little locomotive's services.

In 1942, after a fairly active branch life, No.2644 was 'appointed' shed pilot at Fratton. Then, as the decade advanced, Fratton's need for its increasingly large establishment of 'Terriers' so receded that No.2644 joined the ranks of the unemployed in 1947. The creation of British Railways in January 1948 merely accelerated an already established countrywide practice of withdrawing older locomotives from active service. In the South, ex-LSWR, SE&CR, and LB&SCR types were being stored and, rather ominously, of twenty such engines observed, immobile, at Fratton in March 1948, four, No.2644 again included, were 'Terriers'. Yet, despite the 'writing on the wall', all four contrived to escape in typically Houdini-like fashion. One of them, *Stepney*, is still with us!

Even then No.32644 had barely resumed its old duties as Fratton shed pilot when Fate intervened to introduce one last interesting spiral to its career. The crisis in question occurred on

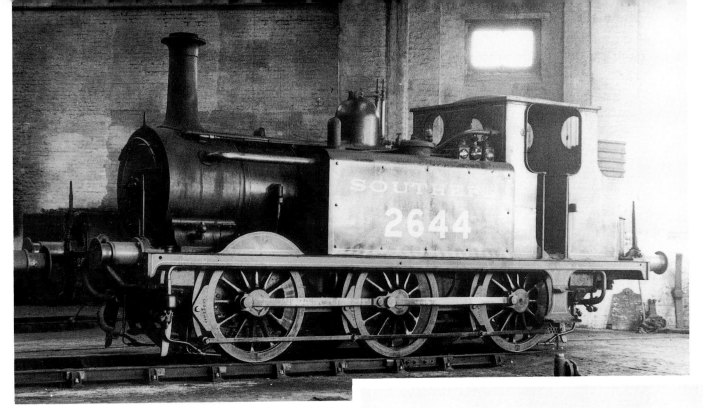

No.2644, formerly *Fulham*, relaxes at Fratton shed in August 1938 from its normal fairly hectic activities on Hayling Island duties. Four years later it 'graduated' as Fratton shed pilot. *(Author's Collection)*

Right
No.2644, formerly *Fulham*, is caught leaving North Hayling with the 3.53pm Havant–Hayling Island train on 29th May 1939. *(LCGB Ken Nunn Collection)*

29th March 1949, when a call for help came from Kent. 'Terrier' No.32678, on loan to the Kent & East Sussex branch, had apparently come a cropper through rail subsidence and was presently lying on its broadside by the trackside at Witterham. Could Fratton help? Fratton could — and did. Within hours, No.32644 was despatched *via* Ashford to act as replacement. It arrived at Rolvenden on the 30th, in good time to share passenger services from the Robertsbridge end on Easter Monday.

With typical 'Terrier' cheek, it was still there on 6th January 1951. But that morning the 11.20am Robertsbridge–Northiam train was reflecting reality by carrying only five passengers, albeit fourteen wagons and vans were dropped off at various points along the line. Coal for Northiam and Tenterden seemed now to form the only visible source of income and understandably, BR was seriously contemplating termination of passenger service. Unfortunately, No.32644 pre-empted that sad event by almost three years: denied BR's rather smart latter-day lined livery to the bitter end, it was officially withdrawn in April 1951. Demolition took place at Ashford and final mileage was 1,252,822.

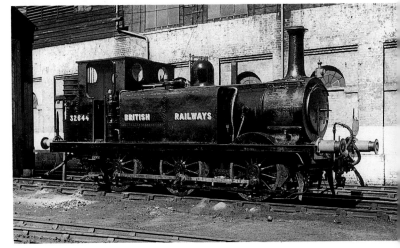

Fulham's 'escape' took the form of a summons to Brighton Works. First 'Terrier' to be repainted by the new regime, it re-emerged, as seen here in July 1948, renumbered 32644 and painted jet black. Its stark unlined side tanks now bore the legend 'British Railways'. How William Stroudley would have disapproved! *(G. W. Sharpe)*

(6)47 CHEAPSIDE — Built December 1876. Later SR No.B647/2647 and BR No.2647

Another Battersea veteran, *Cheapside*, also remained there in reserve until the early 1900s, but, unlike *Fulham*, it entered Brighton Works in 1899 and there it forfeited its condensing gear in exchange for new 14in cylinders. Meanwhile, extensive new sea defence works were upsetting Newhaven Harbour's normal routine; in 1901, probably without great inconvenience, Battersea shed released *Cheapside* to lend a hand for a month or two.

In April 1912 the locomotive was rebuilt to A1X specification. Mileage to date was a very healthy 862,730, but as 'Terriers' were no longer required in Inner London, No.647 was found a new home at Brighton. Here, apart from a few months on loan to the Woolmer Instructional Military Railway, it spent a fairly uneventful World War I.

Still, Brighton shed had a habit of keeping its charges busy and when Grouping arrived, No.647 shared the distinction with four other 'Terriers' of entering Southern Railway stock with more than 1,000,000 miles to its credit. Renumbered B647, the little locomotive remained part of Brighton shed's allocation and continued to work regularly on Kemp Town branch motor service. Indeed, it shared the last rites there with No.B644, when the last 'Terrier'-worked motor-train ran early in 1928.

Meanwhile, an odd little incident had occurred in 1925, when representatives from the Weston Clevedon & Portishead Light Railway examined No.B647 with a view to purchase. Apparently undeceived by its smart copper-capped chimney, they opted latterly to buy No.B643 instead. Why, one wonders? We shall probably never know. But hindsight offers a hint that the WC&PLR spotted something significant, for in stark contrast to the sparkling 25,000 miles *Cheapside* put up annually in LB&SCR days, the locomotive's performance over 29 subsequent years under SR and BR ownership produced a mere 150,000 miles, ie an annual average of only 5,200.

It must be conceded, though, that a transfer to Newhaven shed in 1936, followed by a fifteen year long co-operation with *Fenchurch* on Harbour shunting duties, hardly lent itself to exuberant mileage. Whatever, the partnership of the two engines, both now sporting Drummond-type chimneys and SR black goods livery, remained undisturbed until April 1950, when *Fenchurch* entered Brighton Works. General relief at the reap-

When *Cheapside* featured on the LB&SCR's 1901 Duplicate List, it was given, ostensibly as a temporary measure, wooden number plates with the number 647 painted in white. A few years later the advent of motor-working in the Brighton area rekindled interest in Stroudley's feedwater heating arrangements and condensing gear was duly restored when the locomotive was modified for motor-work in 1907. *(Author's Collection)*

pearance of the latter swelled into positive local pride when *Fenchurch* resumed Harbour duties, renumbered 32636, looking resplendent in lined black livery and carrying BR's new lion and wheel emblem. Less than a year later hopes must have risen when No.2647 received *its* summons to Brighton. Minor repairs were, in fact, carried out, but, disappointingly, British Railway's concern stopped short of livery — and poor old *Cheapside* reported back to Newhaven, still clad in black and with large SR tankside numerals untouched. Clearly its high flying days were over.

Came April 1951 and, probably in a last attempt to squeeze whatever mileage was left in No.2647, BR despatched the locomotive to Fratton. Gentle employment on Hayling Island branch trains, however, proved to be rather more than it could tolerate and a month or two later, the little 'Terrier' earned maximum opprobrium by blocking the Portsmouth main line for many more hours than its crew would care to remember. A crank axle had broken while the locomotive was running light between Havant and Fratton. With some difficulty it was eventually persuaded into a siding and there it lay until the following Sunday, when it was towed into Havant. No.DS681, the Fratton breakdown crane, duly turned out to lift it into a bay and the offending wheel was removed.

The sequel to this mishap was almost inevitable. A visitor to Eastleigh Works in August 1951 would have found both Nos.2647 and 32640, formerly *Brighton*, lying in the yard, obviously awaiting final decision as to their respective fates. Decision came right enough, but of the two, No.2647 fared much the worse: in October that year, still bearing its pre-1939 SR livery, the gallant little 'Terrier' was cut up. Final mileage was 1,231,309.

Changes effected by the SR to 'Terriers' in general included fitment of vacuum ejectors, the removal of motor-train gear and condensing equipment, and substitution of injectors for feed pumps. Newly renumbered 2647, seen above in this form, was also given a Drummond-type chimney. (G. F. Burtt)

Wonersh, seen here at Midhurst shed around 1900, spent ten years of its life, assisted by *Boxhill* and *Tulsehill*, working the LB&SCR's Pulborough–Midhurst–Chichester section, until 1905 came along and saw it put into store with fourteen other 'Terriers'. *(Derek Brough Collection)*

---

(6)77 WONERSH — Built July 1880. Later SR No.B677/W3/W13 CARISBROOKE, and BR No.32677

The 45th 'Terrier' to enter service, *Wonersh*, complete with Westinghouse brake and iron brake shoes, was also one of only six 'Terriers' to escape initial duties in London. The locomotive reported new to Bramley shed, and there, in conjunction with No.36 *Bramley*, it settled down to work Horsham–Guildford services. Later, when Bramley shed closed, the two 'Terriers' moved to the LSWR's depot at Guildford for weekday shelter, and reported to Horsham on Sundays for maintenance. By 1895, when *Wonersh* was given 14in cylinders and lost its condensing gear, the locomotive ventured a little further West to Midhurst shed.

Such an active engine was unlikely, however, to be ignored when the LB&SCR made its bold decision that same year to revitalise the 'Terriers'. Thus, two years later, in addition to being placed on the Duplicate List, No.677 was duly modified for motor-train work. Rendered nameless and painted in Marsh umber brown livery, it was equipped with appropriate 'push-pull' gear. Cylinders were also sleeved down to 12in diameter. Amidst the proliferation of motor services which followed, No.677 eventually found its way to Tunbridge Wells, where it logged an impressive series of annual mileages: 21,358 (1910); 36,124 (1911); 36,151 (1912) and 39,152 (1913). The latter two figures came after the locomotive, already a veteran of 925,078 miles, was reboiled to 'A1X' status in November 1911 at a cost of £898. Subsequent regular employment on Tunbridge Wells, Groombridge, and Oxted motor services produced a commendable coal consumption of 16.41 lb per mile. Weekly mileage was equally commendable at 1,400 miles. Patently No.677 was a 'goer'.

In keeping with this rather hectic record, No.677 was transferred to Horsham towards the end of 1916 whence, in conjunction with 'Terrier' No.673, it took care of Midhurst–Chichester services. At Grouping it entered Southern Railway stock with the highest track record of all LB&SCR 'Terriers' — a grand total of 1,230,531 miles. Probably that explains why September 1925 found it laid aside and stored at Preston Park paint shop with every likelihood of being broken up. Whatever, luck intervened — very late in 1926 — when one 'Terrier' (formerly *Blackwall*) and several Beyer Peacock 2-4-0Ts were withdrawn from Isle of Wight service. This left the Island short of light engines and three 'Terriers' were drafted in as replacement.

Here, at Ryde in early BR years, we see 'Terrier' No.W13 and Class E1 0-6-0T No.4 *Wroxall*. Unlike other IOW 'Terriers', *Carisbrooke* still carries its Stroudley chimney. Unlike other Southern Region locomotives, however, those serving in the Isle of Wight were not renumbered at Nationalisation. Neither did they carry smokebox number plates. *(Author's Collection)*

No.B677 was one of them. It entered Brighton Works for repairs and re-emerged in February 1927 with feed pumps removed, injectors fitted, and bunker extended in IOW tradition. Now liveried in Maunsell green, it also carried the legends 'SOUTHERN' and 'W3' on its side tanks. Three months later it was shipped across the Solent and Ryde Works fitted the requisite motor gear. During 1929–30 two more 'Terriers' crossed from the mainland, by which time No.W3, in accordance with SR 1928 policy, carried the name plate *Carisbrooke*. 1930 saw No.W3 transferred from Newport to Ryde shed, where it was fitted with a hooter for the purpose of working the Bembridge branch. Two years later, in April 1932, its running number was changed to W13. Still allowed to keep its 12in cylinders, its original copper-capped chimney also remained with the engine during its spell on the Island — even when it was reboilered in May 1932 and fitted with front foot steps and hand rails.

By now, track improvements on the Island under SR management were such that ex-LSWR Class O2 tanks were gradually monopolising passenger work. Most goods traffic, however — cement and coal in the main — was still entrusted to 'Terriers'. Yet, despite their ability to handle reasonable loads, the little engines' inadequacies were cruelly exposed in winter months, when divided trains and double-heading frequently became the order of the day. The problem did not escape Waterloo's attention and four E1 class 0-6-0Ts were sent in 1932–33 in an effort to relieve the situation. In practice this ploy upset the Island 'Terriers' much less than might have been expected, for, about the same time, two IWCR 2-4-0Ts and a former Freshwater, Yarmouth & Newport Rly Manning Wardle saddle tank were also taken out of service. The 'Terriers', thankful for small mercies, moved to fill the gap.

A much more serious reverse came in 1936 , when four more O2s arrived at Ryde and four 'Terriers', Nos.W9, W10, W12, and W14, trooped disconsolately back to the mainland. *Carisbrooke* was now one of only three 'Terriers' left on the Island and, as all were already fitted with motor gear, they took over Merstone-Ventnor West services, filling in occasionally with light shunting duties. Three years later, the onset of World War II put paid to heavy holiday traffic for years to come. Many locomotives were laid up at Ryde and by 1942, *Carisbrooke* was the only 'Terrier' active on the Island. Even then, its modest duties consisted largely of piloting at Newport station.

All through the war years, Isle of Wight railway morale remained high and shed staffs at Ryde and Newport kept their near-moribund charges in first class condition. It follows that, once hostilities ceased in Europe, the men voiced a keen desire to catch up with current SR practice. Accordingly, supplies were sent from Eastleigh. Locomotives were soon refurbished and by late November 1945, *Carisbrooke* could be found back on the Ventnor West branch, looking immaculate in SR malachite green. Early in 1947 another 'Terrier' was called back to Eastleigh. Thus, on 1st January 1948, the Island's two remaining 'Terriers', Nos.W8 and W13, entered British Railways stock.

Meanwhile, regardless of whether its locomotives needed repair or not, Ryde Works took the law into its own hands and hand painted the words 'BRITISH RAILWAYS' in shaded characters high on the tank sides, well clear of the name plates. A year later, the Island's two 'Terriers' were still proving themselves perfectly capable of working motor-train services. In the interests of rationalisation, however, it was agreed that there was little point in Ryde Works maintaining spares for a class of only two locomotives. thus, on 13th April 1949, stripped of name plates, the IOW's last two 'Terriers' embarked for the mainland. After some weeks of inactivity at Eastleigh shed they were admitted to the Works, where light repairs were duly effected. Apart from renumbering, however, neither engine was repainted. Then, early in August, still retaining their copper-capped chimneys, both left for Fratton.

In the Autumn of 1952, Hayling Island branch duties being conducted by No.32677 were interrupted by a summons to Brighton Works. Implications seemed ominous, but fortunately, the object of the visit proved to be one of administering light repairs and altering the 'Terrier's' somewhat unconventional green livery to lined black, with BR's lion emblem substituted in lieu of the BRITISH RAILWAYS lettering. A coal rail was also added to its bunker before the 'Terrier' resumed Hayling Island duties. The polished copper chimney top, however, survived.

In this view, taken on 3rd May 1953, *Carisbrooke*, now plain BR No.32677, is heading the 2.35pm train from Havant to Hayling Island. Summer traffic was heavy that year, and August Bank Holiday alone kept Nos.32677 and 32661 on the move all day, running two separate trains each way. Whit Monday 1954 called for even more intensive service and in the course of the day, the two 'Terriers' worked a very heavy excursion forward from Havant to Hayling Island. The return journey was taken over by two other 'Terriers', brought in to assist!
(LCGB Ken Nunn Collection)

June 1957 again found No.32677 awaiting attention at Brighton Works. The visit was a short one, however, for the 'Terrier' was back in circulation at Hayling Island by August. Life ran normally for the next year or so; then came news that Fratton shed was closing in 1959. Its somewhat over-robust complement of 'Terriers' obviously had to be dispersed, particularly as Hayling Island traffic was beginning to feel the pinch of motor competition. In the event, six of Fratton's 'Terriers' were transferred to Eastleigh on 2nd November 1959.

Unfortunately, No.32677 never reached that stage, for it was withdrawn in September 1959. Cumulative mileage was officially assessed at 1,301,612, but quite a number of observers still insist that 1,500,000 miles was, in fact, a truer figure. Whatever, this sturdy 'Terrier' was cut up at Eastleigh in April 1960. Appropriately, it carried its copper-capped chimney right to the bitter end.

This later study, taken at Havant on 26th August 1956, shows the spark arresters which had by now become obligatory on the Hayling Island branch. Presumably this was at the request of local inhabitants, who feared a fire risk. Note, too, that a tool box has also put in an appearance on top of No.32677's right-hand tank.
(Steamchest)

(6)35 MORDEN — Built June 1878. Later SR No.B635/2635/377S and BR No.DS377/32635

One of the first half-dozen 'Terriers' to be fitted with Westinghouse brake when new, *Morden* entered traffic at New Cross on 1st June 1878. Within less than a decade, however, as other Stroudley tanks poured into the London area it was transferred to West Croydon and there it graduated as one of two 'Terriers' in regular charge of the Wimbledon branch;.

Though it featured in the LB&SCR's 1905–6 withdrawal programme, *Morden* escaped in time honoured fashion by being modified for motor-work in 1907. By now, for some reason, wooden number plates had replaced its original brass pattern. The end met the means just the same when the locomotive was Duplicate Listed in November 1908.

At Grouping, *Morden* entered SR stock as No.B635 with a cumulative mileage of 1,053,697 and Fratton shed and Hayling Island service claimed it for a good number of years thereafter. Fratton's quota of 'Terriers' grew steadily as their deployment elsewhere declined and by 1937, *seven* of the little locomotives could be found there, all painted in full passenger green livery. *Morden*, one of the fold, had long since acquired the additional distinction of being the first 'Terrier' to have 2000 added to its running number under the SR's 1931 Scheme. Meanwhile, some light relief to the congestion at Fratton came in the summers of 1936 and 1937, when No.2635 was despatched on loan to the Cordite Factory at Holton Heath, near Hamble. During both spells of duty it fell to Bournemouth Central shed to provide weekend facilities in the way of boiler wash and minor repairs. A spark arrester was also fitted there for use in the factory area. Record has it that Waterloo charged £3 a day when the locomotive was in steam, plus £18 a week for train crew. The winter of 1937 found 2635 back at Fratton; and there it stayed until January 1942, when it added to the war effort by working at Shell Oil Company's Depot at Hamble. Later that year a shortage of Adams dock tanks caused concern at Bournemouth Central, and the 'Terrier' was moved there as shed pilot.

Morden, carrying the West Croydon shed code, was working the Wimbledon branch when this picture was taken in the mid-1890s. The first 'Terrier' to lose its condensing gear, it also received 14in cylinders, under R. J. Billinton's regime, in February 1892. *(Author's Collection)*

For some time to come, motor-work kept *Morden* busy enough and, allocated to Bognor shed in 1912, it moved back to Croydon four years later. Then, the last LB&SCR-owned 'Terrier' to be rebuilt, No.635 duly emerged from Brighton Works in A1X form in April 1922. It has already completed 1,000,000 miles by the time this photograph was taken at Brighton a month or two later. It then moved on to Portsmouth. *(O. J. Morris)*

Right — The really significant turn in No.2635's somewhat peripatetic career came in August 1946, when 'Terrier' No.380S was withdrawn as Brighton Works shunter, to enter a new phase of glory as *Boxhill*, whereupon No.2635 was selected as substitute. The latter's side tanks were promptly inscribed 'Locomotive Works, Brighton', and *Morden*'s new Service Stock number, 377S, was boldly applied, Brighton fashion, high above the tool box behind the bunker. *(Lens of Sutton)*

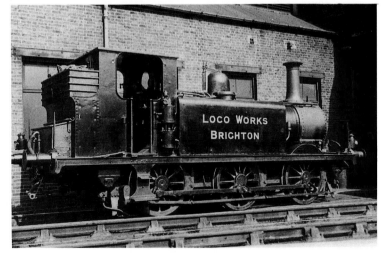

Changing times at Brighton Works circa 1949. Ex-'Terrier' No.377S still occupies centre stage; but the Southern Railway's third Co-Co, No.20003, awaits attention on the left. An 'Austerity' 2-8-0 can also be seen (right). *(Author's Collection)*

In this view, taken at Kemp Town station on 23rd June 1956, No.377S is preparing to return to Brighton with a two-coach Stephenson Locomotive Society Special, crammed to the gunwales with railway enthusiasts. *(Steamchest)*

Almost a year later came a magical moment, when Brighton Works, left with a surplus of yellow paint after restoring *Boxhill*, had the happy inspiration of applying Stroudley livery to its new Works Shunter. As a consequence No.377S became a positive showpiece once it resumed duties in June 1947. Yellow paint apart, its side tanks were now lettered 'Brighton Works', the number 377S was painted on the bunker side, and a new copper cap had been added to enhance its previously plain cast iron chimney. To add a touch of perfection, the locomotive attended Lancing Works for final coats of paint and varnish. Then, almost inevitably, 377S went on public show, together with Pacific No.21C164, Brighton's 'thousandth locomotive', when a group from the Institution of Mechanical Engineers visited Brighton Works on 12th June 1947. Lancing Works, too, was proud of its handiwork; thus, on 7th September 1947, after running light from Brighton, No.377S made a second public appearance, this time alongside electric Pullman car *Iris* at the Lancing Works Flower Show. That done, back to Brighton it went. No doubt it was conspicuously busy when a party from the Institute of Transport visited Brighton Works on 6th March 1948. Certainly, much was going on around it, for construction of a first batch of 'Battle of Britain' Pacifics then on order was well under way and in the Yard outside, quite a number of miscellaneous locomotives were awaiting repair.

By this time, of course, the name 'Southern Railway' had disappeared, and BR had absorbed all three Departmental 'Terriers'. Lancing Service locomotive No.680S received short enough shrift in November 1950, when it was given both unlined black livery and a DS number prefix. Thus, when No.377S was obliged to enter Brighton Works in October 1951 for extensive boiler repairs many must have feared the worst. Happily, fortune smiled, and the Brighton shunter returned to work a month later, unrenumbered and still bearing yellow livery. In August 1953, No.377S again had to enter Brighton Works for attention. By now its yellow livery was fading noticeably and after repair, it ran light to Lancing Works on 2nd September, whence it was treated to a repaint, once more in Stroudley colours. Looking a shade greener than before, it reported back to Brighton on 28th September 1953. Two more 'celebrity' appearances arrived to brighten the year 1956 and are illustrated nearby.

August Bank Holiday 1956 and No.377S, duly adorned to celebrate the Centenary of the Caterham Railway, drifts through East Croydon station. With past bitter feuds long forgotten, the Works 'Terrier' fraternised with the 'enemy' that day by hauling a SE&CR 'birdcage' three-set special train from Purley to Caterham and back. Despite inclement weather public response was healthy. *(Steamchest)*

Despite contemporary edict that all repair work would cease at Brighton Works as from 31st March 1958, Works 'Terrier' No.DS377 was hustled into the Shops on 10th March. Reasons for this precipitate action emerged later, on 12th January 1959, when the locomotive was officially transferred from Service Stock to Motive Power Department. A new number, 32635, duly made its appearance, but the yellow livery and the legend 'Brighton Works' were left alone. Indeed, they remained with the 'Terrier' for the rest of its working days. *(G. W. Sharpe)*

Later that year publication of a Government White Paper on future BR plans caused a frisson of apprehension to run through Brighton Works, for it postulated that total UK construction throughout the year 1957 and early 1958 would be confined to 145 steam locomotives. After that, few more, if any, would be built. By early 1957, fears hardened into reality when announcement was made that Dunsford Tools Ltd. had been granted a long-term lease over part of Brighton Works for the purpose of assembling BMW Isetta cars. Production, it was expected, would commence in May 1957. On 20th March 1957, with a marked absence of ceremony, Class 4 2-6-4T No.80154, the last steam locomotive to be built at Brighton, emerged ex-Works. Subsequent hints that light repairs and scrapping might, after all, continue to occupy Brighton's work-force were rather dampened when the first Brighton-assembled Isetta 'bubble car' made its public debut on 10th May. No.377S , meanwhile, had moved into the shops for repair and came December, 'Terrier' No.32646 arrived to take over as Works Pilot. Rumour now was that No.377S would be repaired, but would probably lose its Stroudley livery.

Fortunately, the early months of 1958 introduced some clarity to an extremely confused situation. No.377S *was* repaired, then despatched to Lancing Works. There it was renumbered DS377 in accordance with BR practice; but at least it had the satisfaction of returning to Brighton on 17th February 1958, looking very smart in fresh Stroudley livery.

One year later derailment *inside* Brighton shed on 22nd March 1960 caused some vexation and ex-SE&CR P Class No.32556 stood in briefly as deputy works shunter while the problem was being resolved. A month later, No.32635 repaid its debt by putting in a fortnight's stint at Newhaven Harbour. Next, one last public appearance came No.32635's way on 7th October 1961, when the Centenary of the Steyning line fell due for celebration. BR had West Grinstead and Steyning stations specially decorated and No.32635, as part of a well arranged

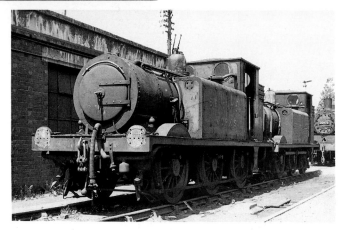

June 1963, and No.32635 joins No.DS681, formerly *Cheam*, as the unfortunate pair await their fate. Time prolonged the agony, and No.32635 was not cut up until September 1963. The USA tank, No.30070, seen behind in this picture, survived to be bought by the Kent & East Sussex Railway in August 1968. *(Steamchest)*

exhibition at the latter, was placed on public view in the goods yard.

Then came the other side of the coin when a sad little event took place at Brighton in January 1963. No.DS680, formerly *Waddon*, now destined for Canada, was given No.32635's copper-capped chimney and it bequeathed, in exchange, a Drummond-type chimney which ill suited Stroudley livery. It came as little surprise to at least one railway observer, when he visited Brighton shed in February 1963, to find No.32635 lying idle with the Drummond fitment slung heedlessly in the pit below. Worse was yet to come, for, still chimneyless and further cannibalised, poor No.32635 was hauled off to Eastleigh on 30th March.

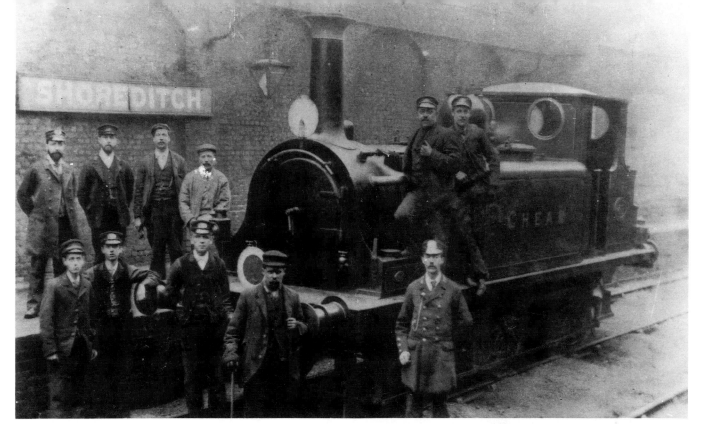

A proud assortment of LB&SCR men surround *Cheam* as the locomotive stands at Shoreditch station. The presence of a foreman-like figure in the foreground suggests the date may not be long after the Wapping–Shoreditch extension was opened in April 1876. *(Bluebell RPS Archives)*

(6)59 CHEAM — Built October 1875. Later SR No.B659/2659 and BR Nos.32659 & DS681

Sent direct to New Cross in 1875, No.59, like others at that august establishment, contrived for years to resist an almost immediate invasion of Stroudley D and E Class tanks. By the mid-1880s, however, the need for such a generous allocation of 'Terriers' at New Cross could no longer be justified and in the midst of a positive flurry of outer region transfers, *Cheam* found itself at Epsom. Some habits, though, tend to die harder than others and early in the 1890s, *Cheam* was called back to New Cross

As the 'Terrier' slipped back easily into old routines at New Cross, however, who could possibly have foreseen that one imminent human error would bring its long industrious association with the East London line to an ignominious close? Fate conspired thus at 3.48pm on Saturday, 7th August 1897. *Cheam*, heading the 3.29pm Shoreditch–New Cross, was approaching New Cross station with its train of close-coupled carriages. Conditions were good, yet, somehow, the driver misread signals, over-ran the Home Down — and paid the penalty by colliding with one of Stroudley's handsome 0-4-2s, No.199 *Samuel Laing*, as the latter emerged from a siding with an empty stock train. Impact was violent, and fifteen people, including two Company employees, were injured. So, too, were the locomotives, for *Cheam* lost its bunker and one side tank and the derailed 'Gladstone' suffered even greater structural damage. All in all, repairs cost £314, quite a considerable sum of money in those days.

Like so many others, *Cheam* was saved from premature extinction in 1905 by the LB&SCR's sudden interest in motor-working and by mid-1906, extension of the practice far beyond Brighton–Worthing confines really got under way..

Cheam entered the motor-work fray at Horsham, where Horsham–Three Bridges–Horley duties sufficed to keep it occupied to 1916. Then the locomotive was transferred to Coulsdon, where, in conjunction with No.653, it handled similar services to Crystal Palace and West Croydon.

Inevitably, in post-Grouping years, the significance of Brighton 'Terriers' narrowed considerably. London had seen the last of them in 1920, and 1928 brought mainland motor-working to a close. It follows that such 'Terriers' as were not preoccupied with special duties tended to congregate around Portsmouth, where Newhaven Harbour and the Hayling Island branch still valued their services. Thus, Fratton shed, long accustomed to sheltering three 'Terriers', suddenly found itself invaded by *seven* in 1937!

It was as well, perhaps, for No.2659, kicking its heels in idleness at Fratton, that the Kent & East Sussex Railway chose about then to combat hard locomotive times by hiring Southern Railway engines to help handle its hop-picking traffic. So, one day in February 1940, *Cheam* was despatched to Rolvenden on short-term loan. Pleasure clouded somewhat, however, when the 'Terrier' turned out to be in such poor mechanical condition that two K&ESR fitters were obliged to devote the best part of a fortnight towards installing spare parts as they were received from Eastleigh! Fortunately, the story had a happy ending.

The Fratton scene when No.2659 returned in 1942 was hardly encouraging. So overwhelmed by now was the Hayling Island branch by spare 'Terriers', that only intermittent work could be found. Indeed, by mid-1947 four of Fratton's six 'Terriers', including No.2659, were lying dead inside the shed. Further indicative of the times, twenty main line locomotives were stored outside. Then No.2659's lot improved in the summer of 1949 and the 'Terrier' got back into circulation on the Hayling Island branch. In Autumn that year it moved to St Leonards and from that unusual base, it worked the former K&ESR line awhile.

The locomotive's next move had an element of mystery about it. On 10th October 1949, Ashford shed, of all places, was found to be sheltering three 'Terriers'. No.2659 was there

Renumbered 659 in 1901, *Cheam* is seen here at Brighton Works in 1908. The 'Terrier' is being modified for motor-working, and it will emerge in due course with cylinders bushed to 12in. *(Derek Brough Collection)*

and so, too, was ex-LSWR B4 0-4-0T *Trouville*, which unlikely coincidence gave rise to local speculation that No.2659 was about to be tried out in lieu of the four-coupled tank on shunting duties at Chislet Colliery. Whatever the truth of the matter, the 'Terrier' was certainly back at Brighton Works by March 1950; there it received its new BR number, 32659, plus lined black livery, before moving on to Rolvenden — the lightly laid section of K&ESR line between Tenterden and Robertsbridge still demanded the nimblefootedness of a 'Terrier'. In May 1951 another 'Terrier' joined No.32659, and No.32670 lay stored, awaiting works. The following year two ex-SECR 'birdcage' brakes arrived to enliven the vintage scene and they were used alternately with the resident LSWR brakes. No.32659 soldiered quietly on, working the Robertsbridge section.

A graphic change of life style came the engine's way in 1953, when it was taken back to Brighton and transferred to Service Stock as No.DS681. The move was hardly a complimentary one, though, for the Lancing 'Terrier' it was to replace, No.DS515, was being restored to Running stock as 'the sounder engine of the two'. Anyhow, No.DS681 duly emerged from Brighton Works on 7th August 1953, painted unlined black and with number and 'C&W Lancing Works' inscribed in yellow on its bunker sides. It functioned awhile as deputy Pilot at Brighton before reporting to Lancing Works in October 1953.

One could hardly describe No.DS681's career from thereon as spectacular. It and No.DS680 worked stolidly in tandem at Lancing for a number of years, with little happening to excite

In December 1921, second-last of sixteen LB&SCR-owned 'Terriers' to be rebuilt to A1X class, No.659 moved on to Brighton shed, with 913,739 miles to its credit. It was to complete another 34,000 miles before entering SR stock as No.B659. This photograph was taken at Eastleigh Works shortly after Grouping in 1923. *(Author's Collection)*

attention until June 1958, when No.32655 (formerly *Stepney*) moved in as second shunter — and No.DS681 found itself at Eastleigh Works. Rather ominously, its future was described as 'uncertain'. Time passed and No.32662 arrived from Brighton, ostensibly for 'shunting duties', though many assumed it was intended as permanent replacement for No.DS681. Fortunately, this plausible theory was confounded in May 1962, when all three 'Terriers' were observed in the Lancing Works precincts.

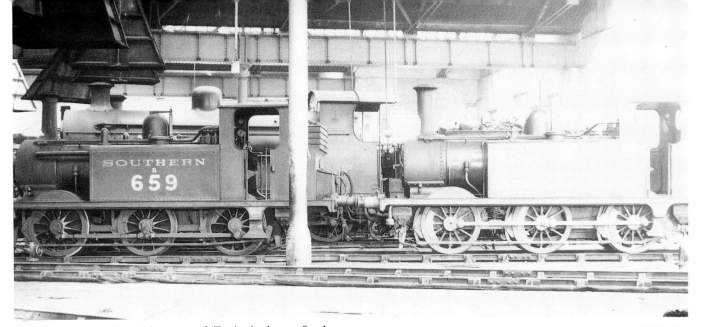

Two of Fratton shed's healthy quota of 'Terriers' relax on Sunday morning, 28th August 1938. On the left we have No.B659, formerly *Cheam*; on the right No.2678, built as *Knowle* in 1880, and later restyled *Bembridge* while on Isle of Wight service. In the event both lasted until 1963. *(Steamchest)*

By the end of that month, however, No.DS680 left for Brighton, and ultimate presentation to the Canada Railway Historical Association.

Patently, events were closing in on the 'Terriers'. In February and March 1961, diesel shunters and USA six-coupled tanks had already been tried out at Lancing, albeit without conspicuous success; the USA tanks were by no means popular with local men. Nevertheless, two of them, clad in malachite green and renumbered Nos.DS235 and DS236, moved to Lancing Works in March and June 1963 respectively. The future of No.DS680 was already assured, but No.DS681 had no such luck and, withdrawn from service, it left Lancing on 8th June on one last trip, dead, behind Class N 2-6-0 No.31289. Duly dumped at Eastleigh Works, it was broken up there on 27th June 1963.

Despite its bad start at Rolvenden early in 1940, once No.2659 was repaired, it proved extremely popular on K&ESR service and October 1942 arrived before the 'Terrier' was sent back to Fratton. The fireman seems to be piling coal rather high in this Rolvenden view! *(Author's Collection)*

(6)61 SUTTON — Built October 1875. Later SR No.B661 & 2661 and BR No.32661

Sutton entered traffic at New Cross on 27th October 1875 and, after an industrious decade of inner London service, was obliged, like many others, to move outwards. Thus, by the mid-1890s it and *Martello* found themselves in full charge of the Wimbledon branch. Surplus Listed in 1898, *Sutton* reappeared on the Duplicate List for June 1901 when, for some reason, it transgressed the usual procedure by receiving transfer numerals first and wooden number plates later.

No.661 was still at West Croydon by December 1916, for World War I years were quiet. The year 1917 brought an element of surprise, however, when, despite its motor-work fittings, *Sutton* was given regular employment ferrying four or five ancient carriages to and from West Croydon and Wimbledon.

Motor-train services did not take over there until 1st November 1918. Thus, Hayling Island work apart, No.661 was the last 'Terrier' to be used on mainland non-motor duties.

A year or two later Nos.B661 and B655 were both fitted with LSWR-pattern motor gear and found new pastures at Lee-on-Solent. Alas, the former light railway was already doomed and it came as no surprise when passenger traffic ceased there in 1931. The line closed completely two years later and metals were lifted. So, devoid of other livelihood, *Sutton*, now No.2661, drifted in the Fratton direction. By 1937, it was one of the family of seven and the tedium of World War II years was only broken briefly in January 1942, when No.2661 was despatched to the War Department at Gosport on short-term loan. An improvised spark arrester was fitted for the purpose. The locomotive's next move was to Brighton Works.

Sutton had moved out of inner London, and had just been renumbered 661 when this photograph was taken. The locomotive worked short trains of ancient four-wheeled carriages on the Wimbledon branch until motor-working was introduced in the early 1900s. *(Author's Collection)*

One of the first half-dozen 'Terriers' to be motor-fitted in 1906, No.661 soon swept into action with its Marsh 'balloon' coach and its own still beautiful Marsh livery. The number plate is wooden; so, too, are the 'Terrier's' brake blocks. A few years later, in January 1912, the locomotive was reboilered to A1X specification at a cost of £1,800 and March of that year found it ensconced at West Croydon shed with three other 'Terriers'. Total mileage to date was 750,000. *(Author's Collection)*

After Brighton Works, there was nowhere else for No.2661 to go but Fratton, where at least it found employment as spare engine in steam. At that time four 'Terriers' were lying dead inside Fratton shed and in March 1948, No.2661, joining the ranks of the unemployed, was also put to store. Luckily, summer traffic in 1949 offered new hope and No.2661 joined three other 'Terriers' in handling heavy Hayling Island traffic that year. As often as not, the little tanks were called upon to cope with heavily laden four-coach trains from Havant but, being

'Terriers', cope they did. A spell at Newhaven Harbour early in 1950, while *Fenchurch* visited Brighton Works, must have seemed comparative bliss to No.2661's crew! In 1st July 1950, the locomotive paused overnight at Brighton shed *en route* once more to Fratton. Less than twelve months later it was repainted black, and given BR No.32661, at Eastleigh Works.

For the remainder of *Sutton's* life, its own welfare and that of the Hayling Island branch were closely linked. Considerable improvements to the $4\frac{1}{2}$ mile single line were effected in the early 1950s, though the continued existence of the old wooden bridge across Langstone Channel guaranteed retention of A1Xs as sole motive power. Goods traffic became virtually non-existent by 1952. Summer passenger traffic, however, still ordained the use of three Fratton 'Terriers'. Despite increasing bus and car competition, the summer of 1953 proved even busier and on August Bank Holiday, two separate trains, one consisting of four coaches, the other three, were run hourly each way for most of the day. Again, No.32661 was deeply involved.

It is April 1919, and No.661 displays the classic A1X outline as it prepares to leave Coulsdon Station. The locomotive had just joined two other 'Terriers' at Coulsdon shed for the joint purpose of working Crystal Palace motor-trains. Then, last 'Terrier' to leave the Greater London area, it moved on to Littlehampton in August 1920. It was still there, with a cumulative mileage of 918,209, when Grouping was effected. *(O. J. Morris)*

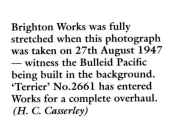

Brighton Works was fully stretched when this photograph was taken on 27th August 1947 — witness the Bulleid Pacific being built in the background. 'Terrier' No.2661 has entered Works for a complete overhaul. *(H. C. Casserley)*

This study of No.32661 was taken at Fratton shed on 27th August 1956. The BR OP classification and spark-arrested chimney are both reminders of the unique demands posed by Hayling Island branch work. Coaling facilities on the branch were primitive; hence the high rails on No.32661's short original bunker. The other four Fratton 'Terriers' had large Isle of Wight-type bunkers which extended to the rear of the frame. *(Steamchest)*

Now it is June 1959, and No.32661, taking a breather from branch shuttle service, relaxes beside Hayling Island's 'coaling stage'. The train crew is not visible but judging by the quantity of hot ash smouldering by the cabside, the fireman, at least, has been busy. *(Steamchest)*

The following year, deterioration of the mainland road bridge affected bus services adversely and BR responded vigorously by inaugurating an intensive regular-interval train service on Saturdays and Sundays all through the summer of 1954. On Whit Monday, a special excursion to Hayling Island had to be intruded, each way, into the normal timetable; and No.32661 joined No.32677 in handling the special on its forward journey from Havant to Hayling Island. Two fresh 'Terriers', working fore and aft, were used for the return trip.

The opening of the new road bridge at Langstone marked the beginning of the end for the Hayling Island 'Terriers', though when Fratton shed closed officially on 2nd November 1959 and its six 'Terriers' allocated to Eastleigh for maintenance purposes, locomotives directly concerned with Hayling Island service continued to be stabled overnight at Fratton. Even in the mid-Summer of 1962, No.32661 and two others could be observed taking turns at working a brace of Hayling Island trains. Traffic was still heavy at each terminus, though intermediate stations, one noted, played no role. On 1st July 1962, a herd of cows chose to evoke traditional country branch memories by straying on the line!

The rest is railway history. Sadly, the mounting pressures of road traffic, plus continued deterioration of the Hayling Island 'Terriers', led inexorably towards complete public closure of the branch on 2nd November 1963. Sadder still for railway lovers, poor old No.32661 was not present to welcome the Locomotive Club of Great Britain when enthusiastic members conducted their 'Hayling Island Farewell' Railtour the following day; sent to Eastleigh six months previously, it had perished at the hands of the breakers in September 1963.

As it happened, No.32661 was the last 'Terrier' to be scrapped by British Rail.

Chapter 8
THE ULTIMATE SURVIVORS

W E COME NOW to the ten 'Terriers' which, miraculously, escaped oblivion to afford us infinite pleasure today. *Boxhill*, the first to be rescued, was a Southern Railway 'disposal' in 1946. The next survivors were *Stepney* and *Waddon*. These found secure homes in May 1960 and June 1962 respectively, and from thereon the ten 'Terriers' which remained in BR harness worked stolidly on towards a very fateful year — 1963.

That was the year when such escape routes as existed for 'Terriers' finally closed. The K&ESR line had already seen its last BR engine in 1961, West Quay, Newhaven bade farewell to its one remaining 'Terrier' in August 1963 and at Lancing Works, USA 0-6-0Ts moved in to dislodge BR Service 'Terriers' Nos.DS680 and 681 in April and June 1963. Then fell the most grievous blow of all when the Hayling Island branch also succumbed to economic pressures in November 1963. The last regular duty for 'Terriers' had gone. Yet, the miracle occurred — and only three BR 'Terriers', *Morden*, *Sutton*, and *Cheam*, went to the breakers that year.

Boxhill, the 1946 withdrawal, has already been featured in Chapter 6 of this book. So, too, in Chapter 5, has the story of *Poplar*, Colonel Stephens' first 'Terrier' acquisition. Our concern to this final Chapter, therefore, is how eight more BR 'Terriers' contrived in their individual ways to escape the breaker's hammer.

		TABLE 11		
		PRESERVED 'TERRIERS'		
No.	Name	Date withdrawn	Left BR	Initial destination
380S	*Boxhill*	Nov 1946	Mch 1961	Museum of Transport, Clapham
32655	*Stepney*	May 1960	May 1960	Bluebell Railway, Sheffield Park
DS680	*Waddon*	Jun 1962	Jun 1962	Canada Railway Historical Association
32662	*Martello*	Nov 1963	May 1964	Butlin's Holiday Camp, Ayr
32640	*Brighton*	Sept 1963	May 1964	Butlin's Holiday Camp, Pwllheli
32678	*Knowle*	Oct 1963	May 1964	Butlin's Holiday Camp, Minehead
32670	*Poplar*	Nov 1963	Apl 1964	K&ESR Preservation Society
32636	*Fenchurch*	Nov 1963	May 1964	Bluebell Railway, Sheffield Park
32650	*Whitechapel*	Nov 1963	Sept 1964	Borough of Sutton & Cheam
32646	*Newington*	Nov 1963	Nov 1964	Sadler Rail Car Company

* * * * *

(6)55 STEPNEY — Built December 1875. Later SR No.B655 & 2655 and BR No.32655. Presently Bluebell Railway No.55 *Stepney*

The years 1875 and 1876 were vintage ones for New Cross, for of seventeen 'Terriers' built over that period fourteen were allocated to the East London shed. The only escapees were No.63 *Preston*, sent new to Brighton, and Nos.47 *Cheapside* and 48 *Leadenhall*, which joined Battersea's already large complement. Thus, *Stepney* started life at New Cross and remained part of the solid core, Nos.49-62, which withstood the initial shrinkage of 'Terrier' East London duties during the 1880s.

Surplus Listing in 1905 led almost inevitably to No.655's appearance in the 1905–6 withdrawal programme. Fortunately, however, these were the years during which steam and petrol railcars competed against two motor-fitted 'Terriers' in LB&SCR's initial motor-train trials. The travelling public soon learned to appreciate the comparative briskness and reliability of 'Terrier' haulage. From a railway management point of view the 'Terriers' also offered economy in fuel consumption; the combination of these factors persuaded the LB&SCR Directorate to

pin its future motor-train faith in 'Terriers'. As a result twenty more of the little tanks were modified for motor-work over the next three years. Meanwhile, purely as an interim measure, three others, including *Stepney*, were hitched to single coaches and employed on pseudo motor-train service. Although this involved a smart run-round after each journey the deception proved efficient enough to satisfy a growing public demand. Reward for services rendered came in 1907, when all three were officially modified. Accordingly, *Stepney*'s 14in cylinders were bushed to 12in and condensing gear was restored.

Six years later, in October 1912, No.655, by then part of West Croydon shed's establishment, was fitted with a new Brighton-built boiler at a cost of £865 and joined the select ban of A1Xs. Thus far it had completed 750,043 miles. Duly returned to West Croydon, it continued to serve local motor-train requirements for another decade. There was only one brief interruption, in 1920, when No.655 went on temporary loan to the Woolmer Instructional Military Railway. By the time Grouping arrived, *Stepney*'s mileage had risen to 926,064 and, based on Fratton, it was one of three 'Terriers' being employed in Hayling Island services.

Posted to New Cross in December 1875, *Stepney* was given new 14in cylinders in 1894, and also lost its condensing equipment, all in line with R. J. Billinton's modest 'new broom' policy. The locomotive was Duplicate Listed in June 1901 and neat gold transfer numerals appeared on its bunker sides. They are barely evident here, when the 'Terrier' was caught being coaled at New Cross on 20th September 1902. *(LCGB Ken Nunn Collection)*

Looking back, one can see now that the odd assortment of 'Terriers' which flocked Southern Railway's way like homing sparrows as a result of Grouping must indeed have presented the parent Company with something of an embarrassment. Finding employment for all was a problem in itself; sorting out the wheat from the chaff was another. Inevitably, resolution of the jigsaw took time and it was hardly surprising that 1925 arrived ere a tentative process of elimination got underway. Even then, casualties were remarkably light; only three 'Terriers' were scrapped and Colonel Stephens obliged by buying one more. Some, like No.B655, were simply laid aside pending future developments.

No.B655's enforced idleness lasted for over a year. Then, towards the end of 1926, Fortune smiled, and the locomotive was taken into Eastleigh Works for thorough overhaul. Even more intriguing prospects followed when it and No.B661 were further equipped with LSWR-pattern auto-gear — and both were despatched to completely new territory, the one-time Lee-on-Solent Light Railway. Whatever misgivings the 'Terrier' crews may have entertained soon vanished; the little locomotives gained immediate popularity with the Running Department, to such extent that Solent's former 'Terrier' incumbent, No.E735, was squeezed out of the picture. Alas, the new arrivals' success was comparatively short-lived, for remorseless erosion of traffic closed the branch to all passenger traffic by January 1931. Left with little option, the two 'Terriers' drifted back towards Fratton. Poor Fratton! More and more 'Terriers' were beginning to seek refuge there, though only two, or three at most, could possibly find day-to-day employment.

Fratton congestion lessened none and, still deemed fit for active service, No.2655 was fortunate enough the following year to be hired by the Kent & East Sussex Railway to assist with hop-picking traffic. So successful was its employment that Rolvenden held on to the 'Terrier' until October 1939. By this time, of course, both World War II and O. V. S. Bulleid had made their respective marks on SR affairs. Amongst other considerations, livery changes were in the air; these overtook the 'Terrier' class for the first time on 21st December 1939, when No.2655 left Eastleigh Works duly clad in dark green paint and lettered in new style sans serif. Times, however, proved unpropitious for such novelties and subsequent 'Terrier' repaints soon conformed to wartime black. All through the early war years, No.2655 functioned quietly as spare engine at Fratton. Then luck began to fade. By late 1942 the locomotive was stored under cover and this situation persisted into post-war years. During the summer of 1949, for instance, Fratton accommodated six 'Terriers'. As the Hayling Island branch, however, only required two 'live' engines, four, including No.2655, lay dead within the roundhouse. There was only just one ray of hope: four of the six had at least been given BR numbers.

By 1952, the Hayling Island branch saw a resumption of fairly healthy holiday traffic. The track was in good order and the future looked reasonably bright for the 4½ mile line. Fortunately for the 'Terriers', Langstone Channel's ageing wooden bridge still required their light-footed services and No.32655 was one of three which currently shared the working of the branch. Yet, shadows were hovering — for the real weakness of the branch still remained: its metals stopped half a mile short of the Island's southern shore. As this was the area most favoured by visitors local bus services were presented with a harvest of passenger traffic they had done little to deserve. Meanwhile, thanks to the glut of 'Terriers' at Fratton, No.32655 found itself placed back in store by September 1953. Fortunately still in good mechanical order, it was restored into action on 2nd January 1954, the fateful day on which the Kent & East Sussex line, now part of BR's Southern Region, ran its last public passenger train.

The ray of hope became positive encouragement for No.2655 in December 1949, when it, too, was given new BR lined black livery. As it happened, it was the first 'Terrier' to receive the British Railways emblem at the hands of Brighton Works. When seen above in July 1950 No.32655 was busy rounding its train at Hayling Island station. *(G. W. Sharpe)*

That day No.32655 and shedmate No.32678, despite the sadness of the occasion, revelled in the full glare of public limelight. During the forenoon No.32655 confined itself to working two-coach trains between Rolvenden and Robertsbridge. Then came the major event, when the 4.15pm Tenterden–Robertsbridge, returning at 5.50pm, ran both ways with the two 'Terriers' attached fore and aft. Their train, made up of six Southern corridor coaches brought specially from Ashford, was probably the most substantial ever seen at Rolvenden. Nor was the drama yet complete. Once the return journey had been accomplished, O1 No.31064, waiting at Rolvenden, backed on to take the coaches on to Headcorn. Rather gallantly, No.32655 remained at the rear and insisted on offering the O1 banking assistance as

far as St Michael's, before dropping off modestly and returning to Rolvenden! That same evening Rolvenden yard was cleared of regular engines and rolling stock and the two 'Terriers' capped their exertions by working the resident ex-SECR 'bird cage' coach all the way to Hastings *via* Robertsbridge. No.32655 lingered on locally and in March 1954, after running light from St Leonards, it relieved yet another O1 by handling a five-vehicle engineers' train between Rolvenden and Robertsbridge. Next day, once the steam crane had been deployed on main line work at Robertsbridge, No.32655 calmly worked the set back to Rolvenden. Again, when 'hop picker' specials resumed on 31st August 1954, it was No.32655 which stood by in case of need at St Leonards. Then came October; No.32655 was transferred to Brighton and within a month it was put to store there.

Typical of the times, Southern Region's Condemnation Programme for 1957 listed 73 locomotives. Yet the 'Terriers' continued to lead a charmed existence. Certainly No.32655 had no cause for complaint. During the months of August and September 1956 it put in several stints at Littlehampton Quay, while the 'Terriers' normally supplied visited Eastleigh. This, too, was about the time that an axle failure on No.32646's part on the Hayling Island branch brought all 'Terriers' under suspicion. Accordingly, No.32640 arrived at Brighton on 24th December 1956 and one week later No.32655 left for inspection at Eastleigh Works. The inspection must have proved satisfactory, for No.32655 was soon back in harness. During the summer of 1958 it replaced No.32670 as second shunter at Lancing Works. Later that year it followed No.32670 west, and the two A1Xs put in several appearances shunting at Littlehampton. A subsequent visit to Eastleigh Works in April 1959 could have been ominous — but, miraculously, No.32655 re-emerged with a new boiler! That Autumn a visitor to Hayling Island would have found local traffic still going strong, and two 'Terriers', Nos.32655 and 32640, coping energetically with four-coach

During the winter of 1960-61, No.32655, though lying in the open, was painstakingly restored to Stroudley livery and soon No.55 *Stepney* was well on the way to becoming a living legend. Certainly the little 'Terrier' looked thoroughly at home as it paused at Sheffield Park to take water during the busy summer of 1961. *(Steamchest)*

trains. Six months later, however, No.32655 was transferred officially to Eastleigh shed, as distinct from being a 'lodger', and No.32636 took its place on the Hayling Island branch. What now, indeed? 1,396,027 miles had been run to date.

The ultimate answer was, in fact, already being forged. On 16th March 1959, exactly one year after the ex-LB&SCR line between Lewes and East Grinstead closed for the second and last time, a meeting of railway enthusiasts resolved to form a Lewes and East Grinstead Preservation Society. Realising that preservation of the whole line was beyond their means, the Society's Committee concentrated on the section between Sheffield Park and Horsted Keynes and tackled British Railways accordingly. The story is a long and heroic one; but suffice it to say that once negotiations reached a realistic stage the Trustees reported back to Society members on 14th June 1959 and on that date the Lewes Society was formally reconstituted as the Bluebell Railway Preservation Society. Money required to realise the Society's aims hovered stubbornly in the region of £34,000.

Again we must short-circuit a fascinating story. Within a year, a requisite Guarantee of £10,000 was raised, Bluebell Railway Limited was created to facilitate granting of a Light Railway Order and a small army of willing volunteers gradually restored order from a weed-ridden Sheffield Park station. Already, time had arrived to think realistically of locomotives and rolling stock. Taking the bull by the horns, the Society's Committee approached BR and was delighted to find the latter not only willing to part with 'Terrier' No.32655, but also prepared to enhance the asking price of £750 by adding two coaches: one ex-LSWR third and a SR composite corridor brake. Needless to say, such a generous offer was too good to be refused and No.32655, after final inspection at Eastleigh Works, was delivered, with coaches, to Sheffield Park on 17th May 1960.

Once the initial excitement and publicity subsided, the Committee chose, wisely, to address itself to future practicalities. Hopes of installing a run-round loop at Horsted Keynes foundered on economic grounds, so the principle of providing a locomotive at each end of the Bluebell Line was finally accepted. BR was again approached, this time on the subject of releasing a second 'Terrier'. Alas, the time was not yet ripe, according to BR, and the Bluebell acquired ex-SECR P class No.31323 instead. Meanwhile, pending the grant of a final Transfer Order, work proceeded steadily towards a Grand Opening Day. The event took place on 7th August 1960, whence Nos.31323 and 32655 spent a glorious day ferrying two packed coaches back and forth between Sheffield Park and Horsted Keynes.

The years which followed were not devoid of disappointment; the Bluebell Railway's sole rail link with the outside world, for instance, BR's Haywards Heath–Horsted Keynes section, closed on 27th October 1963. Despite that body blow, opportunity was taken to run one last special train from Brighton to Sheffield Park and back — and at its head ran two immaculate Bluebell Railway ex-Brighton stalwarts, E4 No.473 *Birch Grove* and A1X No.55 *Stepney*. Since then, endless voluntary work has seen the Bluebell Railway develop, almost beyond recognition, into one of the railway preservation movement's crown jewels. Nowadays a vastly increased variety of locomotives and rolling stock treads its metals. But none continues to excite greater public interest and affection than *Stepney* — and, of course, its eventual companion, *Fenchurch*.

Duplicate Listed in January 1900, *Waddon*, now No.654, is caught by the photographer as it indulges in a spot of shunting at New Cross on 21st September 1901. *(LCGB Ken Nunn Collection)*

(6)54 WADDON — Built February 1876. Later SE&CR No.751, SR No.751 & 680S and BR Nos.680S nd DS680. Presently preserved in Canada as No.54 *Waddon*

Waddon, another New Cross worthy, led a particularly industrious life from the moment it entered traffic on 16th February 1876. The bulk of No.54's energies was expended on East London line work but, held in respect at New Cross shed as 'a good engine', it also occasionally joined the select 'Terrier' link which was entrusted with the daily task of handling the London Bridge portion of the Newhaven Continental boat express (see under *Thames*). At other times its willingness to work saw it deployed on banking heavy goods trains between Willow Walk and Forest Hill.

As it happened, No.654's presence at New Cross in 1901 was quite fortuitous, for in May 1900, at a time when the future of the 'Terriers' as a class was fraught with peril, instructions had been issued for the withdrawal of the locomotive. Total mileage at that stage was 578,421. Fortunately, the order was not immediately implemented, and the engine was still intact by 5th July 1904, the date on which the South Eastern & Chatham Railway enquired as to the possibility of purchasing a light six-coupled tank engine for the purpose of working goods traffic on the Isle of Sheppey Light Railway. Agreement was readily reached that a 'Terrier' would fit the bill and on 26th August 1904, *Waddon* moved into new ownership at Hastings; purchase price was £670. Eighteen months previously, the LSWR had paid £500 apiece for its two 'Terriers'. To ensure delivery in steam, Brighton Works partially retubed the locomotive's boiler, rebored the cylinders and carried out other essential repairs.

Despite these attentions, No.654 was promptly laid aside in store at Hastings for over a month. Then, summoned to Ashford Works in October, it was modified to suit SE&CR requirements. Westinghouse equipment was removed, as were the feed pumps. Vacuum ejectors and SE&CR injectors were fitted and painted in full Brunswick green; the locomotive, now SE&CR No.751, entered traffic on the New Romney branch on 14th February 1905. Less than a week later the crank axle broke and back went the 'Terrier' to Ashford Erecting Shop. Brighton was good enough to supply a spare axle free of charge and once this was fitted, No.751 resumed its interrupted trials. All proved well and the 'Terrier' moved on to Sheerness on 24th May 1905.

The current scene in that locality was interesting. Ever since its inception on 1st August 1901, the Sheppey Light Railway, with its 44 ton fully laden weight restriction, had been in the habit of employing former London, Chatham and Dover Railway (later SE&CR) 2-4-0Ts on goods and passenger trains alike. Then, in 1903, came misgivings on the SE&CR Board anent the soaring costs of branch and short-haul passenger services. No doubt much to the interest of LB&SCR, which was experiencing similar qualms, H. S. Wainwright opted to conduct trials on the Sheppey line with a pair of small petrol-electric railcars, supplied free by Messrs Dick, Kerr & Co. For a variety of reasons the experiment was not a success and the SE&CR turned to steam railcars. Kitson & Co. supplied two, at £2,400 each, early in 1905. These, despite their transparent unpopularity with both enginemen and travelling public, at least offered superior fuel consumption when tested against a 2-4-0T and its conventional branch train. Thus, much encouraged, the SE&CR'S Locomotive Committee decided to order six more Kitson steam cars.

Once No.654 *Waddon* was sold to the SE&CR for £670 in August 1904 it entered Ashford Works two months later and re-emerged, liveried in full Brunswick green, as SE&CR No.751. *(Author's Collection)*

By the time, therefore, that No.751 reported to Sheerness, passenger services on the Isle of Sheppey were already being operated by railcar No.1. The sole remaining task the 'Terrier' could be offered, that of handling the 'daily goods', turned out to involve such a leisurely return journey — 2½ hours, with shunts, between Queensborough and Leysdown — that the 'Terrier' was sorely understretched. So, extra work was found for it, shunting at Sheerness Dockyard; and occasionally it was asked to stand in for the steam car when the latter was indisposed. Meanwhile, a deep well was bored at Leysdown to ensure constant water supply and, thus reassured, the little tank settled down to its miscellaneous duties. Its ubiquitous 'Terrier'-bred versatility guaranteed popularity on the Island, and soon No.751 acquired the affectionate nickname 'Little Tich', after Harry Relph, then all the rage of London music halls as the 'Man of Kent'. In mid-1907 the locomotive paused to attend Ashford Works for heavy repairs, but no repainting was undertaken. The real crunch came on 16th October 1909 when, with 631,433 miles accumulated to date, No.751's boiler was condemned. Other complications existed, in that an acute summer water shortage at Leysdown had already ordained the use of O class 0-6-0s on the daily goods. Thus, much to the consternation of Sheerness shed staff, the 'Terrier's' presence on the Isle of Sheppey was no longer considered necessary. Initial SE&CR instincts were to withdraw No.751. Then, fortunately, second thoughts produced a decision to reboiler the 'Terrier' and add it to an existing nucleus of small Class P motor-fitted locomotives.

No.751's new Wainwright boiler cost £485 and was fitted in time for trials to be run on the New Romney branch on 29th January 1910. All told, the 'Terrier's' basic dimensions were little altered, though provision of a longer firebox and an increase in bunker capacity increased working weight to 27 tons 3 cwt. Cosmetic changes, however, were considerable. The new boiler, made of steel in two rings, was surmounted by a closed dome and Ramsbottom safety valves now sat over the firebox. The original Stroudley chimney was retained and Westinghouse air pump and brake fittings were reinstated. At the same time,

LC&DR six-wheeled carriage No.2101 was converted into a motor-train trailer, and the revitalised 'Terrier' and carriage were linked to provide a unit totalling 62ft 8in in length. A neat triangular bracket on top of No.751's roof supported a cord and lever which actuated the whistle, while rodding and universal joints took care of remote control of the regulator. After brief trials between Appledore and New Romney, the new unit was sent to Dover to handle Sandgate services while railcar No.1 was being repaired at Ashford. Later that year No.751 was transferred to Orpington, where it occupied itself on Beckenham Junction–Norwood Junction shuttle services until the latter were restored to LB&SCR control in 1912. Subsequently transferred to Strood, No.751 and trailer spent more time abroad than at home, acting as relief, as railcars or motor-fitted Class P tanks required Ashford Works' attention. The years 1913 and 1915 saw the unit back again at Beckenham Junction. Then followed a belated return to the Sandgate branch. Symptomatic of the times, No.751's motor-train equipment was removed when the locomotive entered Ashford Works in January 1917 for general repairs. First port of call after that was Richborough. Then the 'Terrier' moved to permanent duties at Folkestone Harbour and was so employed when Grouping was effected in January 1923.

July 1924 saw No.751 transferred to Ashford and there it functioned as Carriage Works shunter until May 1925, when it was called upon to replace 'Terrier' No.642 as Battersea Park shed pilot. Alas, deprived of works attention since 1921, No.751

By the time this photograph was taken at Ashford in 1920, No.751's livery had reverted to wartime grey. The 'Terrier's' Stroudley chimney now bears a spark arrester and a last trace of its former cord and lever controls can still be seen on the cab roof. This livery lasted until 1932, when the locomotive entered Southern Railway Service Stock. *(Photomatic Limited)*

On 18th October 1959, Nos.DS680 and 32670 (formerly K&ESR No.3), jointly handled a six-coach 'Kent & East Sussex Special' each way between Robertsbridge and Tenterden. No.DS680 is seen here at Bodiam on that occasion. Next morning the Works 'Terrier' interrupted its return journey from St Leonards to Lancing long enough to conduct a morning shunt in the wagon scrapyard at Polegate. *(Steamchest)*

soon proved to be mechanically unfit, even for that light duty; ten months later, in March 1926, the locomotive was removed and placed in store at Preston Park paint shop. It was rather fortunate not to have been withdrawn out of hand.

Fate, however, can play some queer tricks. After lying at Preston Park for the best part of three years, the 'Terrier' was suddenly found employment where its weakened condition posed no disadvantage. It was transferred to Eastbourne shed in January 1930 and there it was found a niche — supplying steam at 75lb per sq in to a pulverised coal hopper! The latter had been installed to facilitate fuel trials which were being conducted by U class 2-6-0 No.A629 — hardly the most dignified of tasks for a 'Terrier'! But at least it was a life-saving one; for once the fuel trials ceased, somewhat abortively, in September 1932, No.751, by now the last active SR engine bearing pre-Grouping livery, was rewarded by being given a general repair at Brighton Works.

It was a very different locomotive which quite Brighton's Erecting Shop on 22nd December that year, for, renumbered 680S in the SR's Service Stock, it now sported black livery and a Drummond-pattern chimney had been substituted for its rather more flamboyant Stroudley one. A brief spell as coal stage pilot ensued; then the 'Terrier' embarked on what was to be a quite lengthy association with Lancing Carriage Works. Came January 1937, and No.680S's boiler was once more condemned. This time Brighton Works replaced it with an A1X boiler which had already been borne by 'Terriers' Nos.B678 and E735. Bunker coal rails and iron brake shoes were also fitted. Still carrying its short smokebox, however, the locomotive resumed normal duties at Lancing — very much an odd mixture of classes A1 and A1X.

The 'Terrier's' remaining working life consisted of a series of permutations centred round Lancing Works, Brighton Works,

and Eastleigh. Late in 1949 it entered Brighton Works for retubing, but no repainting was carried out. It then went back to Lancing — and virtual unemployment, for the railway scene was changing rapidly. In the Autumn of 1947 it functioned single-handedly for a brief spell while its Works companion, No.515S, underwent reconversion from oil to coal burning. By February 1948, however, an observer visiting Ashford Works would have found the status quo reversed; No.680S had graduated as Works Pilot, and No.515S lay dead in the Works yard. In November 1950, No.680S visited Brighton Works, whence it was partially repainted black, and its new BR number, DS680, was painted on the sides of the coal bunker only. Side tanks were left plain, but contrary to general expectation, the locomotive's A1X boiler, with its steam dome and spring safety valves, remained intact.

In March 1952, a second visit to Brighton fell due and No.32662 stood in at Lancing Works while No.DS680 was treated to a complete (black) repaint. On this occasion, as with No.DS515, the legend 'C &W Lancing Works' was added below the number on the coal bunker. No.DS680's next appearance at Brighton Works coincided with Open Day at Lancing Works on 21st August 1957 and, in the absence of the normal Works locomotive, Nos.32566 and 32662 attended to carriage shunting duties. One year later, the future of the two Service 'Terriers'

hung in the balance. Meanwhile, No.DS680 was observed at the head of a ballast train in the Works sidings on 6th July 1958.

The latter half of 1960 was less happy for No.DS680, for the locomotive went into long-term unemployment at Eastleigh shed whilst British Railways wrestled with the problem of providing efficient new shunting power at Lancing Works. In the event, diesel trials proved disappointing and, to everyone's surprise, No.DS680 again turned up at Lancing on 22nd February 1961. A USA 0-6-0 tank reported for duty on 5th March, but it was sent back to Southampton less than a week later. Probably more in sorrow than in anger, No.DS680, by now in rather poor mechanical shape, was despatched light to Fratton for valve and piston attention. The 'Terrier' was still active at Lancing Works on 5th May 1962. At the end of that month, however, it was officially withdrawn; and on 4th June 1962 it was formally presented to the Canada Railway Historical Association during a brief ceremony at Brighton Works.

Curiously enough, No.DS680, though withdrawn and now, technically speaking, Canadian property, continued in quasi-service at Lancing pending Works availability in the matter of restoration. Eventually however, on 27th December 1962, the little locomotive made one last journey to Brighton and there, during the following month, shed staff fitted it with a copper-capped chimney off No.32635. After this it was steamed — and employed quite frequently as coal stage pilot. Next, still bearing its new chimney, No.DS680 returned to Lancing on 2nd February; and there it remained until complete overhaul could be arranged. The call came on 23rd February and the 'Terrier' obliged by running light to Eastleigh.

Later in 1963, the fruits of Eastleigh's eventual endeavours were proudly exhibited at the Works Open Day, when No.54 *Waddon*, richly clad in Stroudley yellow livery and with condensing gear restored, appeared publicly with four other historic locomotives. These were West Country Pacific No.34084, Merchant Navy No.35024, BR 4-6-0 No.73029, and Dugald Drummond's classic 4-4-0 No.120. (A. J. Wheeler)

A few days later *Waddon* was loaded on to a well wagon and, protected against the elements by polythene sheeting, it left on the 4.30am Eastleigh–Feltham freight, bound for Tilbury Docks. On 23rd August 1963 it and a 21ft length of LB&SCR rail recovered from a disused siding at Lancing, were loaded aboard at King George V Dock, and the m.v. *Tautra* sailed for Montreal. After initial display by Canadian National Railways in the city itself, the little 'Terrier' was moved on to a welcome and permanent resting place in Canada's National Railway Museum at Delson, fifteen miles south of Montreal.

Now that preservation precedents had been firmly established, one expected further activity. What *was* unexpected, however, was that the next bid should emanate from such an unusual source — to wit, Butlin's Holiday Camps. Early in 1964, rumour was rife that Billy Butlin wanted ten locomotives for public exhibition. Whatever the railway fraternity thought of the rumour it must have been considerably surprised to discover, in April 1964, that *two* 'Terriers' were, in fact, being restored at Eastleigh at Mr Butlin's request. Even more surprising, *Martello*, the doyen of all 'Terriers' where gross mileage was concerned, followed the same course a few months later.

It soon transpired that Butlins cherished very realistic ambitions in their bid to enter the locomotive preservation game. By the end of 1964, the firm salvaged no fewer than eight engines from BR and, already sited at various Holiday Camps, these were being prepared for open air public exhibition.. The eventual pairings were interesting. Minehead Camp received 'Terrier' No.32678 (ex-*Knowle*) and LMS 'Pacific' No.6229 *Duchess of Hamilton*, Pwllheli Camp fell heir to No.32640 (ex-*Brighton*), once of Paris Exhibition fame, and LMS No.6203 *Princess Margaret Rose*. Further East, Skegness Camp's masterstroke in obtaining No.6100 *Royal Scot* was only marginally offset by the additional presence of ex-LSWR 0-4-0T, formerly *Granville*. Up in Scotland, Ayr Holiday Camp did very well by treating itself to

'Terrier' No.32662 (formerly *Martello*) and LMS No.6233, *Duchess of Sutherland*. And so, for the remainder of the decade this luscious selection of locomotives afforded much pleasure and interest to Camp residents. It is a fact, however, that steam engines do not take kindly to prolonged exposure to sun, sea air, and winter gales. Thus, by the late Summer of 1970, conditions were such that Butlins felt obliged to have second thoughts on the subject. The Company's misgivings were two-fold: (1) Maintenance in mechanical order had never entered into the scheme of things and even the most modest prophylactic measures now required to protect paintwork etc were duties that Butlins had neither anticipated, nor welcomed. (2) In the last analysis, the locomotives, it was realised, were only being seen by a comparatively small section of the populace — and that during the few months of the high summer season.

Wisely, and much to the excitement of Britain's rapidly increasing preservation groups, Butlins resolved to seek new pastures for their valuable locomotive collection. Eventual disposal of the larger LMS engines caused quite a furore as various interests clashed in their fight for possession. Fortunately, redisposition of the smaller locomotives, which were more easily transported by road, seemed to generate less heat. None the less, there was plenty of enthusiasm on tap as the three 'Terriers' entered their new homes!

(6)62 MARTELLO — Built October 1875. Later SR Nos.B662 & 2662 and BR No.32662. Now owned by Bressingham Steam Museum

Martello, with its strangely unspectacular life history, was perhaps the most cryptic 'Terrier' of all. In 1923, after 47 years of unblemished service with the LB&SCR, it quietly slipped into Southern Railway ownership. Twenty-five years later, it entered British Railways stock with equal lack of obtrusion. In 1963, it was one of BR's last three 'Terriers' to be withdrawn. Yet, somehow, particularly during the latter half of its existence, it contrived with ease to outstrip all other 'Terriers' in the matter of sheer mileage. One suspects it must have been a particularly good engine.

Certainly, neither it nor *Sutton* was likely to have had much time for dawdling once they reported for duty at New Cross shed on 27th October 1875. Consider the situation: the LB&SCR was working the East London line single-handedly and extension from Wapping to Shoreditch was imminent; it duly materialised in April 1876. South London line traffic, too, was booming as never before. Meanwhile, pilots had to be provided for London Bridge, yards had to be shunted and track ballasting required constant weekend attention. Small wonder it was that New Cross shed, though teeming with Stroudley tanks, was frequently stretched to the hilt! Yet, from the midst of this mêlée came clear evidence that *Martello* was held in particularly high regard. It lay in the consistency with which the locomotive was detailed to handle one of New Cross shed's few prestigious main line duties, the London Bridge portion of the Newhaven Continental express.

This important link operated as far as East Croydon, 10¼ miles distant, where it joined the Victoria portion. The up express, of course, ran *vice versa*. Whatever, New Cross employed 'Terriers' in both directions. No.62 usually fell heir to the down portion and thus faced considerable gradients, including 2¾ miles at 1:100 up New Cross bank, in course of its difficult schedule. Day after day the little 'Terrier' would proceed to London Bridge, and back on to its three coaches and a van. Then, with complete élan, it would speed its complement of Continental-bound passengers on to East Croydon. There,

doubtless oblivious to the railway drama which was being played about them, they and like-minded passengers from Victoria joined forces to proceed South with proper main line decorum. The up train offered an easier task — if such a phrase might be used to describe a still hectic seventeen minutes start to stop schedule. New Cross enginemen, plucked momentarily from the grime and squalor of East London railway life, revelled in it, whichever duty they faced.

These excitements apart, *Martello*'s life at New Cross was as pedestrian as most. It took a full decade for the 'Terriers'' supremacy to be challenged. But challenge did eventually come, in the mid-1880s, when three other major Companies took a hand in the East London game and, more insidiously, within the LB&SCR itself, as more and more Stroudley tanks began to pour into inner London. By April 1887, when New Cross shed alone housed 64 'D' and 'E' class tanks, the need for its large establishment of 'Terriers' became no longer tenable and many were transferred to outer regions. *Martello* was one of those retained. The process, however, continued. Over the next decade more prime duties continued to slip from the New Cross 'Terriers' grasp, and by the mid-1890s both *Martello* and *Sutton* could be found working the Wimbledon branch.

In December 1913, after completing 788,853 miles, No.662 was converted to A1X class. It later joined No.668 at Littlehampton. War years, however, were comparatively quiet, and No.662, stationed by then at Tunbridge Wells, entered Southern Railway stock on 1st January 1923 with a cumulative mileage of 901,273. Although 'push-pull' services had been abandoned on the Hayling Island branch in the early 1920s and normal haulage was now employed, the continuing frailties of Langstone Bridge still warranted use of 'Terriers' by the SR. Motor gear was gradually removed from the locomotives, vacuum ejectors became standard equipment and by 1925, No.B662, one of three A1Xs stationed at Fratton, was intimately involved in what was to be a long spell of Hayling Island service. Fratton, incidentally, was one of only two sheds in Britain to be shared, in pre-Grouping days, by two major Companies — the LB&SCR and LSWR in this instance. The other shed was at Ferryhill, Aberdeen, where Caledonian and North British locomotives once sheltered under the same roof.

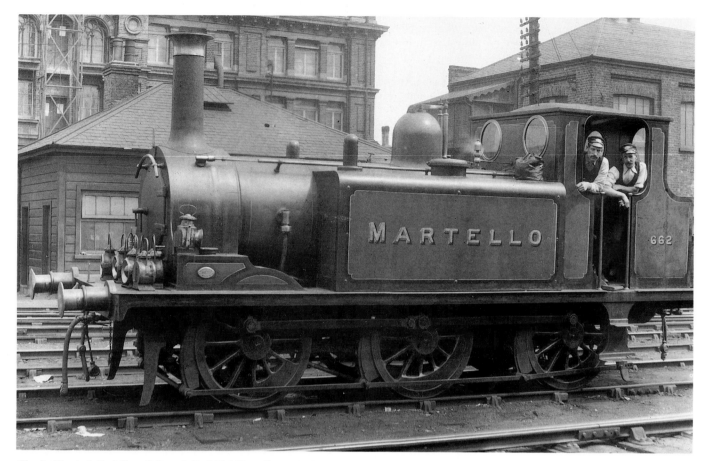

Classic 'Terrier' disciplines followed. In 1894 *Martello* received new 14in cylinders, and duly forfeited its condensing gear. Surplus Listing followed in 1898. So, too, did appearance in the Duplicate List for 1901. Significantly, No.662 escaped the withdrawal programme of June 1901. But modification for motor train work came late in the day, in 1909, whence No.662 moved on to West Croydon. *(Author's Collection)*

In September 1949, instructed to proceed to Brighton, No.2662 received its baptism of fully lined black livery and returned to Fratton bearing its new BR number, 32662. Routine work remained undisturbed, until a request from Lancing Works in April 1952 saw it take over No.DS680's duties while the latter was at Brighton Works. By late summer No.32662 was back in harness, working hard at Fratton. Then followed an intriguing call for help, in the summer of 1953. The Railway Correspondence and Travel Society, having decided to celebrate its 25th Anniversary in style, opted to sponsor a record 380¾ mile rail tour, based on Waterloo–Exeter–Paddington. A trip on the Lyme Regis branch was also envisaged in view of that line's impending 50th anniversary. As ever, the Society's intentions were quite specific. A stop would be made en route at Axminster, to permit a sortie up the branch behind 'Terrier' No.32646 (ex-LSWR No.734), which locomotive had participated in the opening ceremony on 24th August 1903. Alas, like many a best laid plan, this one foundered rather late in the day, when No.32646, currently based on Newhaven, failed to complete the long journey West. No.32662, ever reliable, was hurriedly called in by BR, and on 10th June 1953 it and ex-LSWR 4-4-2T No.30583 were tested over the branch at the head of a five-coach train. On Sunday 28th June, when Society members arrived at Axminster, the branch train was again stepped up to five coaches and, with both veterans at its head, the cavalcade

By mid-1937 Fratton had six 'Terriers' to choose from and competition grew in intensity. Fortunately, *Martello*, now SR No.2662, was able to retain a fair share of branch work, as this Havant photograph shows. *(Author's Collection)*

completed two delightful round trips. At Lyme Regis the special was met, amongst others, by a local 80 year old JP who had served on a 'Terrier' footplate when the branch was opened 50 years earlier.

After that triumph it came as a shock to find No.32662 moved into store at St Leonards for three months. The gloom had hardly lifted when news from Newhaven early in 1954 vouchsafed that No.32662 was still lying there — 'stored amongst some trucks, some distance from the shed'. What

Early in World War II several of Fratton's 'Terriers' were dispersed elsewhere, and No.2662 settled down, no doubt thankfully, as one of two regular Hayling Island branch engines. By October 1947, however, the situation changed again. Of nine 'Terriers' left on the mainland, six elected to invade Fratton! No.2662, however, was largely unaffected, and life went on much as before. The 'Terrier' is seen here at Fratton shed on 21st May 1949, measuring itself for size against a T9 4-4-0. *(Steamchest)*

seemed to be the final blow came on 19th September 1955, when Newhaven shed lost its independent status and became a mere stabling depot. Fortunately, the cloud had a silver lining. No.32662 now came officially under Brighton shed's wing and the latter despatched it to Littlehampton on 12th December 1955, as reserve 'Terrier', when the Southern Section's Civil Engineer pronounced Littlehampton's quayside lines unfit for all but the 'lightest class of tank engine'. In August 1957 came a familiar call and No.32662 again officiated at Lancing Works during No.DS680's absence. One month later it took up duties at Newhaven, and had to be content with occasional visits to Littlehampton.

The next employment Brighton devised for No.32662 involved a disappointingly brief stint on the Kent & East Sussex line. Sent to St Leonards in readiness for the 1958 hop-picking season, it and No.32636 met the human contingent for Bodiam as they arrived at Robertsbridge, ex-London Bridge, on 2nd

No.32662 was able to show off its new livery and bunker on 11th June 1961, when it and No.32670 handled 'The South Eastern Limited', a heavy special train sponsored by the Locomotive Club of Great Britain, between Robertsbridge and Tenterden. The two 'Terriers' are seen here taking water at Robertsbridge prior to hitching up fore and aft. *(Steamchest)*

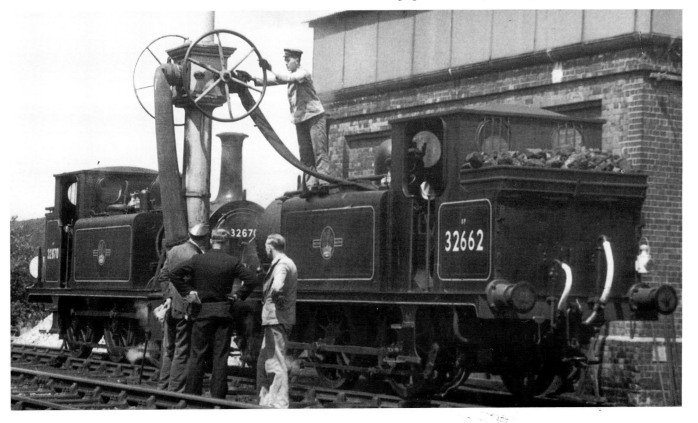

One year later, in 1974, No.32662 came back on public view, immaculate in Marsh livery and in October 1975, Bressingham Steam Museum staged a special opening to mark *Martello's* 100th anniversary. A more recent visit in September 1985 found the 'Terrier' resting quietly, as above, in Bressingham's train shed, gleaming bright in other distinguished locomotive company. *(Steamchest)*

September 1958. The two 'Terriers' then worked the special down the branch in traditional fashion. Alas, whatever pleasure No.32662 may have derived from its change of environment proved to be short-lived, for Brighton recalled the locomotive on the 13th. Routine duties ensued, until 27th March 1960, when, in response to time-honoured request, No.32662, standing in for No.DS681, again carried out shunting duties at Lancing Works. Ten months later it was summoned to Eastleigh for a last repair and repaint; Brighton shed staff must have been agreeably surprised when No.32662 reported back in April 1961, carrying an Isle of Wight type bunker which had once belonged to 'Terrier' No.32677. Patently, there was life in the old dog yet!

Lancing Works, meanwhile, was not shy in restaking its claim. No.32662 was spotted there in May 1962 — and presumably it lingered on — while No.DS680, formerly *Waddon*, underwent formal presentation to its new Canadian owners at Brighton on 4th June. Then, for good measure, No.32662 stood in once more when No.DS680 quit Lancing Works on 23rd February 1963. It was eventually relieved, on 30th April, by the arrival of a USA 0-6-0T from Eastleigh, and normal summer service on the Hayling Island branch followed. But even that moved inexorably to a sad climax as storm clouds gathered over the single-line branch. Thus, on the afternoon of Saturday, 2nd November 1963, No.32662, carrying a funeral wreath, joined two other 'Terriers' in handling a brisk final service of three-coach trains. After that, public passengers were no longer *persona grata* on the Hayling Island branch.

Now that the 'Terriers'' last stronghold had gone, the Winter of 1963 marked the end for the species as far as BR employment was concerned. Eastleigh became the sole Mecca, and No.32662, one of few still left in steam, towed No.32646 there from Fratton on 2nd January 1964. The effort was not unrequited, for word emerged in April that Eastleigh Works was restoring some 'Terriers' for preservation by Messrs Butlins.

Surely enough, Open Day at Eastleigh on 16th August that year afforded a glimpse of No.32662 being reconditioned in the Erecting Shop. Such a fate seemed only right for a veteran of 1,505,955 miles.

Less than a month later, on 2nd September 1964, No.32662, loaded on to a Flatrol, left Eastleigh on the 11.35pm Basingstoke freight. Next morning it slipped North on the 4.15am Basingstoke–Oxley and, later that month, shed staff at Ayr witnessed a strange meeting, not unlike that between Stanley and Dr Livingstone, when No.32662, clad in chocolate brown livery and still bearing its BR number plate, was introduced to its companion-to-be, LMS 'Pacific' No.6233 *Duchess of Sutherland*. Elaborate arrangements made to transfer both locomotives to their new home at Point of Ayr were put into operation on 19th October and lasted one week. The 'Terrier' and the tender of the 'Duchess' travelled first, both being collected by road from Beresford Lye, a convenient spot near Ayr station. The sheer length of the 'Duchess', however, posed formidable problems, and the best efforts of two diesel shunters were required ere the massive locomotive was winched, with some difficulty, on to a 40 ton Pickford trailer at Greenan Castle. In due course the incongruous pair reached their exhibition site, just outside Point of Ayr Holiday Camp.

Time and weather took their toll. Latterly, Butlin's were quite relieved to lend No.32662 to Bressingham Steam Museum and, in February 1971, the 'Terrier' again embarked on a long road journey — this time back South, to Norfolk. Came 1973, and word emerged that the 'Terrier' was being completely overhauled at Bressingham..

Never Duplicate Listed, No.40 is ready at Victoria Station to hoist its South London train up the 1:64 of Grosvenor Road bank. The little locomotive has had a repaint since its glamourous Paris Exhibition days. It also received new 14in cylinders in January 1894.
(Author's Collection)

40 BRIGHTON — Built March 1878. Later IWCR No.11, SR No.W11 *Newport* and 2640, and BR No.32640. Presently Isle of Wight Steam Railway No.11 *Newport*

Whatever else might be said about 'Terriers', none started life more stylishly than *Brighton* — for within weeks of being built the locomotive was despatched under its own steam to Portsmouth, where, on 30th March 1878, it set sail for Dieppe aboard the LB&SCR steamer *Honfleur*. This was the happy consequence of a recommendation to the Board by the Company's General Manager J. P. Knight, two months earlier, that an example of the 'Terrier' class, of which they were so proud, should be exhibited at the Paris International Exhibition. Certainly, a more brightly burnished engine never left Brighton Works! Once safely across the Channel, the 'Terrier' availed itself of coal and water supplies which had been placed conveniently by the quayside at Dieppe. Then, with steam raised afresh and paintwork given a final rub down, off set *Brighton* — running light for Paris with the LB&SCR's chosen driver, George Aylwin, at the helm, accompanied by a French fireman and pilotman. No doubt that strange minuscule yellow-green object raised many an eyebrow as it scuttled across northern France!

At Paris, the Chemin de Fer de l'Ouest provided overnight accommodation in a running shed near its St Lazare terminus. Next morning, *Brighton* ran briskly to the Exhibition site — only to find it was fully a week ahead of schedule. Many of the Exhibition stands, including the British, were still incomplete. The Westinghouse Brake Co. of America, meanwhile, having equipped a complete French train with its air brake to no great promotional advantage, gladly seized on the delay to arrange the transfer of its demonstration train to the care of *Brighton*. Thus, to the satisfaction of all concerned, the 'Terrier' was able to

make quite a number of highly publicised runs in and around Paris. French officials, we are told, were particularly impressed by the Westinghouse brake. *Brighton*, of course, was the only 'Terrier' to carry Stroudley's patent speed indicator, a simple device employing a water gauge; but posterity, alas, does not record any specific native reaction thereto. Whatever, *Brighton* was duly accorded its place in the Machinery Hall at Paris, and the Exhibition was publicly opened on 1st May 1878.

Proud as he was inventive, Stroudley instinctively seized the opportunity the Paris Exhibition offered to display his sheer versatility. The 'Terrier' it was which won the Gold Medal; but a secondary exhibit, that of motion taken from a sister engine after 185,446 miles service and seen to be hardly worn, lent striking credence to the durability and precision of locomotive construction at Brighton Works. A third exhibit, often overlooked, was a beautiful scale model of *Brighton*, LB&SCR's latest sea-going vessel. Its advanced design, too, owed much to the indefatigable energies of this remarkable man.

The Paris Exhibition closed in November that year and no sooner had the 'Terrier' and its (by now) celebrated creator returned to England, than their joint success was further advertised by the addition of a celebratory 'Gold Medal' legend on *Brighton*'s tanksides. Possibly even something of an aura of visiting Royalty hovered over Battersea shed on the day the 'Terrier' eventually reported for public service. Life on the South London line, though, left little room for romancing and it is reassuring to note that during 1882 alone, *Brighton*'s mileage of 29,126 was well above the batting average for Battersea's 21 'Terriers'.

Coal consumption, too, at 22.5 lb per mile fell comfortably within the general figure. *Brighton*, it appeared, was a 'good engine'.

It would seem, too, that *Brighton* continued to occupy a warm spot in William Stroudley's heart, for it was used quite frequently to test various experimental devices. Steam sanding gear was fitted in March 1887, a set of patent iron tubes followed in October, and in May 1888 a variable blast pipe was tried out. No single experiment, however, set the heather on fire and all special fittings were later removed. In 1889, still subject to experimentation during what were to be the last weeks of Stroudley's life, No.40 was one of eighteen 'Terriers' which were given sets of 1½in diameter brass tubes. Results were again inconclusive, and 1¾in brass tubes were later adopted as standard. In 1894, under R. J. Billinton's aegis, *Brighton*, in common with many others, forfeited its condensing gear and seven years later, when sea defence work dislocated normal Harbour routine at Newhaven, it was one of several Battersea 'Terriers' which were hired out briefly to lend a hand. By now, of course, both major London sheds were being obliged to shed their substantial quotas of 'Terriers'. Coincidentally, the Isle of Wight Central Railway management was pressing hard to be allowed to add to the two 'Terriers' it already possessed. It came as no real surprise, therefore, when *Brighton*, by now a veteran of 522,583 miles, passed into IWCR hands in January 1902 for a consideration of £600. As a condition of sale, the locomotive was fitted with a secondhand pair of 13in cylinders before it left Brighton Works. The IWCR, an 1887 amalgam of three Isle of Wight railways, traditionally painted its locomotives metallic crimson lake, with gold lining and, like its two 'Terrier' predecessors, *Brighton* was reliveried thus ere it entered Island traffic, unnamed, as IWCR No.11.

Latterly, the erstwhile *Brighton* received the same treatment at Newport Works as the other IOW 'Terriers' — ie the rear tool box was removed and the bunker, now unrailed, was extended to accommodate 1½ tons of coal. Later still, as each 'Terrier' Stroudley chimney gave up the ghost it was replaced by a cast-iron chimney of local manufacture. Meanwhile, No.84 *Crowborough* also arrived on the Isle of Wight scene, as IWCR No.12, and all four 'Terriers' soldiered on to give admirable local service. By October 1904, when bunker rails were again added, No.11 had already completed 78,000 miles on the Island. Even more significantly, 1904 was the year when railway companies throughout the UK were dabbling in the use of steam and/or petrol-engined railcars in an earnest search for branch line economies. Faced with the same problem, the IWCR soon succumbed to the current craze. A delegation visited Swindon, Basingstoke — even Rolvenden (!) — in mid-1904, and, apparently impressed by what they saw, they recommended the adoption of rail cars.

IWCR steam car No.1, a product of Hurst Nelson, duly arrived on the Island on 4th October 1906; and had no sooner entered Ventnor Town branch service than it was tested against 'Terrier' No.11, with its traditional train of three four-wheeled coaches plus brake van. Rather surprisingly, the rail car emerged a clear winner where fuel economy was concerned. IWCR management's immediate reaction was to order a second steam car.

Shortly after receiving its new A1X boiler in July 1918, IWCR No.11, formerly *Brighton*, was photographed as it headed a Sandown train into Newport station's up platform. The locomotive's Stroudley chimney looks as though it has been battered back into shape not once but many times . . ! Unlike Brighton Works normal rebuilds, however, No.11 still retains its combined front splashers and gravity fed sand boxes. It has also received new 13in cylinders. The latter cost the IWCR £50. *(Author's Collection)*

'Terrier' No.W11, formerly *Brighton*, and rebuilt to Class A1X specification in 1918, was captured at Ventnor West Station in the late 1920s. A year or two later bronze plates bearing the name *Newport* came its way at Ryde Works. *(Pendragon Collection)*

This, however, proved to be too expensive a proposition and Newport Works compromised by converting 0-4-2T No.3 into a rail motor of sorts. Somewhat overshadowed by these events, the 'Terriers' soldiered quietly on.

Typical of the times, the early 1900s also saw economies enforced in the matter of IWCR locomotive livery. The Company crest disappeared, and tanksides began to bear the inscription 'Isle of Wight Central Railway', with the running number resited on the bunker. Came 1906 and tankside inscriptions were reduced to 'IWCR'. Then, by 1913 or thereabouts, the rail-motor phase exhausted itself in rather dismal circumstances and attention re-focused itself on the merits of the 'Terriers'. July 1916 saw the last of IWCR's crimson lake, and when No.11 was fitted with a new Brighton-built A1X boiler in July 1918 the locomotive, now with 739,282 miles behind it, resumed work clad in deep glossy black, with vermilion panelling and fine white lining. The inscription on the tanksides had shrunk to 'IWC'.

The next event on the Island was Grouping, when all nine surviving IWCR engines entered Southern Railway stock, officially from 1st February 1923. Hardly surprisingly, new management brought about operational changes. As all IOW railways were absorbed within the SR's Western Region and the latter was dominated by ex-LSWR influence, Eastleigh, perforce, acquired complete control over the Island's locomotive destinies. Evidence was soon forthcoming of future intent, when two Class O2 0-4-4Ts were shipped from the mainland in April 1923. These, liveried in Maunsell green, proved highly accept-

able and four more followed by early 1925. Thus, the 'Terriers', which had resumed work on Ventnor West services after the demise of the rail-motors, were themselves superseded in April 1925 by motor-equipped O2s and SE&CR bogie carriages. Fortunately for the Brighton engines, this arrangement proved somewhat over-powered and less than a year later, once all four 'Terriers' had been fitted with the requisite train control equipment, No.W11 and company resumed their former duties. Carriage steam heating gear followed in October 1927. Then, in September 1928, came a decision to allot local names to all IOW engines and in June 1930, bronze plates bearing the name *Newport* were eventually affixed to No.W11's side tanks at Ryde Works. In the meantime, the withdrawal of several ex-IWCR tanks in 1926/27 had created a shortage of light engines. As a consequence, three more 'Terriers' were imported from Eastleigh over the period from May 1927 to May 1930. In the consequent reshuffle of duties, No.W11 *Newport* settled down to work the Bembridge branch. A Drummond chimney came its way in 1932. A boiler change was effected in July 1933 and, three years later, whilst at Ryde Works for repair, *Newport* was fitted with footsteps and handrails at the leading edge of her side tanks.

Eastleigh's first act in 1947 was to remove *Newport*'s nameplates and transfer them to O2 tank No.W34. Then, mercifully, after spending several months at the back of Eastleigh shed, the 'Terrier' was sent to the Works for repair. Still retaining its Isle of Wight bunker and cast-iron chimney, and repainted unlined black, it re-entered traffic in July 1947 and, after a week's shunting at Winchester, travelled light to Fratton. *(Author's Collection)*

Once the Freshwater and Bembridge lines were upgraded, however, the noose began to tighten around the 'Terriers', and by 1937 only three remained on the Island. By then No.W11 was sharing duties on the Merston–Ventnor branch with two others and putting in occasional light stints on Medina Wharf. June 1939 witnessed another overhaul and boiler change at Ryde Works. Then came World War II. The effect on holiday traffic within the Island was as instantaneous as it was dramatic. Many locomotives were laid up and in September 1939, No.W11, for its part, found itself stored at Ventnor. By late 1942, however, a measure of rationality had returned to Island rail services and No.W11 was back handling Ventnor West motor-trains. Heavy holiday making resumed after D-Day and soon there was full employment for every locomotive the Island could summon. Time, however, was drawing short for *Newport* and 22nd April 1946 saw it taken out of service in poor condition to be stored at Newport. Ten months later, a floating crane arrived from Southampton Docks, bearing a new IOW recruit, ex-LB&SCR E4 class 0-6-2T No.2510. On its return journey the crane left Medina Wharf carrying two 'old soldiers', Nos.W11 *Newport* and O2 tank No.W29 *Alverstone* back to the mainland.

At Fratton the 'Terrier's' capacious bunker earned the locomotive a particularly warm welcome from Hayling Island train-men. Alas, the honeymoon proved to be a brief one; for, much to local chagrin, No.2640 was summoned to the Kent & East Sussex line during the summer of 1948 — ostensibly to 'stand in' whilst the resident 'Terrier', No.2678, attended Ashford Works for repairs. Again, No.2640 must have proved a popular import, for the summer of 1949 found it still working between Tenterden and Robertsbridge. Even one year later, when the season's first hop-pickers special was being worked forward to Bodiam, an observer had occasion to remark at the unusual simultaneous presence of *three* 'Terriers' at Robertsbridge. One of them, No.2640, was described as being 'dirty black' . . .

Early in 1952, No.32640 was moved to store at Fratton. But Brighton Works Centenary celebrations were also imminent: hence, during October 1952 No.32640 basked in public display at Brighton running shed with two other engines which were associated with the name *Brighton* — Class E5 No.32587 and

'Schools' class No.30915. Life at Fratton must have seemed tame after that! Nevertheless, rail traffic to and from Hayling Island continued to blossom as road conditions deteriorated and on Whit Monday 1954, No.32640 and three other 'Terriers' were stretched to the limit in coping with public demand. In 1956 spark arresters became *de rigeur* on Hayling Island and over Christmas that year, No.32640 was attached temporarily to Brighton shed while No.32655 went into Eastleigh Works. A second 'Terrier' arrived from Fratton early in January to take its place.

By 1958, the plethora of 'Terriers' resident at Fratton was such that little difficulty was experienced in releasing No.32640 on 17th July for a day's filming at Midhurst at the request of Boulting Bros. That must have evoked happy memories locally; seventy years previously, Midhurst shed had housed two 'Terriers' of its own. Then, back to Fratton and Hayling Island service went No.32640. By September 1959, business was so brisk that two 'Terriers' at a time were employed to handle four-coach trains. Ironically, Fratton shed lost its independent status from 2nd November that same year and Eastleigh assumed responsibility for its family of 'Terriers'. The ultimate sanction materialised four years later, when the Hayling Island branch witnessed its last public passenger train on 2nd November 1963. By that time No.32640 had already been transferred to Brighton and had even shunted Littlehampton Wharf for a few days in mid-June 1963 when diesel power was not available. Later that year, on 21st September, came the dreaded call from Eastleigh.

By now No.32640, in course of its varied career, had amassed such an extraordinary melange of service that Eastleigh could hardly be reproached for its decision to withdraw the locomotive:

LB&SCR (1878–1901)	522,583 miles
IWCR (1902–1922)	198,746 miles
SR (IOW) (1923–1947)	294,601 miles
Mainland (1947–1963)	148,794 miles
Total	1,164,724 miles

Scrapping was accordingly fixed for February 1964.

In due course both offences, No.2640's prolonged absence from Fratton *and* its dingy livery, were expunged. The 'Terrier' reported back to Fratton under its own steam on 17th February 1951 and within a month, it entered Eastleigh Works for general repair and repaint. Given fresh BR lined livery, renumbered 32640 and still clinging to its IWCR chimney, it then lay for some months at Eastleigh pending decision as to its future. *(Author's Collection)*

Fortunately, however, the spirit of preservation was waking throughout southern England by now and execution was stayed long enough for Messrs Butlin's to stake a claim. The 'Terrier' was duly sold, taken back into Eastleigh Works for restoration to LB&SCR yellow livery and on 30th July 1964, it was observed passing through Snow Hill, Birmingham on a goods train, *en route* to public display alongside LMS 'Pacific' No.6203 at Butlin's Pwllheli Holiday Camp. Over the years small boys were amused. Then came 1972, when Butlin's, tiring of responsibility for their static exhibits, were persuaded to lend No.32640 to the Wight Locomotive Society for a period of ten years. Better still, outright purchase at £3,500 followed in 1976.

Quite incapable, of course, of being steamed, No.32640 left Pwllheli Camp by road on the evening of 26/27th January 1973. Down south, meanwhile, a warm welcome was being planned and a brass band preceded the 'Terrier' through Portsmouth on its way to Fishbourne Ferry. Once across the Solent, the locomotive was then quietly lodged in British Rail's Ryde Works. Time passed. The 'Terrier' was repainted, but only partially repaired, when events forced local enthusiasts' hands: the up sidings at St John's Road, Ryde were due to be lifted.

Thus, on 17th January 1975, a combined rescue operation by BR and Society members saw No.32640 transported from Ryde Works to the Isle of Wight Railway Company's HQ at Haven Street. There, willing hands got busy, and cosmetic restoration was effected in time for the Ryde and Newport Railway Centenary celebrations in August that year. A fibreglass IWC chimney replaced the old Drummond one, frontsteps and handrails were removed and, now painted in IWCR unlined black and carrying the number 11, the 'Terrier' was publicly unveiled at Haven Street station on 24th August 1975.

The ultimate acquisition of a new workshop building at Haven Street encouraged Society members to make a start, in 1978, on the immensely difficult and expensive task of restoring No.11 to operational condition. A year later, work was suspended to give preference to the rather easier job of restoring 'Terrier' No.46 *Newington*, and did not seriously recommence until January 1981. By the summer of 1983, estimates were that a further £7,000 would be required to get No.11 back in running order. Miraculously, funds were forthcoming and the time consuming task got under way. Latterly, a diesel generator was installed to supply machine tool electricity. Even the dismantling of the 'Terrier' presented incommensurate problems, thanks to the locomotive's long exposure to sea air at Pwllheli.

Today the 'Terrier' still remains under cover at Haven Street. But make no mistake: much is happening and members of the Isle of Wight Railway Company predict with every confidence that one fine day in the not too distant future No.W11 *Newport* will again grace Isle of Wight Central Railway metals.

Nos.78 *Knowle* and 71 *Wapping*, two of the 'Terriers' employed on Hayling Island and East Southsea branch work at the time, pose proudly at Portsmouth shed around the turn of the century. *Knowle*, in beautiful condition, has lost its condensing gear; this was restored later, when the 'Terrier' was adapted for motor-train work. *(National Railway Museum)*

(6)78 KNOWLE — Built July 1880. Later SR No.678, W4/W14 *Bembridge* and 2678. BR No.32678. Presently Kent & East Sussex Railway No.32678

One of the last eight 'Terriers' built, No.78 *Knowle* was already equipped with Westinghouse brake and iron brake shoes when it left the Erecting Shops at Brighton on 23rd July 1880. New Cross shed claimed it initially for work on the East London line. Over the next decade, however, as increasing numbers of 'D' and 'E' class Stroudley tanks descended on London, the need to retain a large complement of 'Terriers' around the capital diminished and, like others, No.78 found itself obliged to move out into the country. April 1887 saw it transferred to Tunbridge Wells shed. Then, during the early 1890s, the 'Terrier' moved on to Portsmouth, where, in conjunction with three other 'Terriers', *Gipsy Hill*, *Leadenhall*, and *Wapping*, it worked the Hayling Island and East Southsea branches. New 14in cylinders came *Knowle*'s way in 1894 and condensing pipes were removed.

The year 1907 ushered in a considerable change of circumstance for *Knowle*. Apart from being fitted with Marsh's push-pull gear, the locomotive's cylinders were reduced to 12in diameter, and condensing pipes were restored. Alas, repainted in new Marsh livery and renumbered 678, the 'Terrier' also lost its name. Next, in November 1911, by which time No.678 had run a total of 763,933 miles, it was reboiled to A1X class, the second conversion of that nature, at a cost of £926. From there it moved on to Horsham on Bognor motor-train duty. A move to Littlehampton followed in 1916; then, in November 1918, a call nearer London brought it to West Croydon. By Grouping, however, it had moved back to Horsham and mileage, as it entered

Southern Railway stock on 1st January 1923, stood at 949,056, a good average where 'Terriers' were concerned. Post-Grouping years were uneventful in that many 'Terriers' were placed in store and No.B678, having entered that category in September 1925, lay idle in Preston Park paint shop for the next 3½ years.

The wisdom of the SR's policy in laying up 'Terriers' came to the fore in 1927 when, soon after disposing of several ex-IWCR Beyer Peacock tanks, the Isle of Wight section found itself short of light engines. More 'Terriers' were needed — and No.B678 was one of three which were ultimately selected. New 14in cylinders were fitted at Brighton on 28th February 1929 and, duly furnished with injectors, an IOW extended coal bunker and a complete repaint in Island style, the 'Terrier', now renumbered W4, crossed the Solent in May that year. The name *Bembridge*, previously earmarked for a IOW Beyer Peacock 2-4-0T, since scrapped, was transferred to W4, together with bronze nameplates. The latter were sited below the legend 'SOUTHERN RAILWAY' at Ryde Works and 'push-pull' operating equipment was also fitted. Then, fully fit for Island action, No.W4 *Bembridge* was released briefly into the custody of Ryde shed before moving on to Newport. There, it joined other local 'Terriers' in working the more lightly laid lines ie Newport–Freshwater, Merstone–Ventnor West, and Brading–Bembridge.

The locomotive situation in the Isle of Wight remained highly volatile over the next year or two. Even before Grouping a party of LSWR officials had quietly visited the Island and assessed its railway system. Their report had been none too complimentary and subsequent Southern Region policy of relaying and upgrading lines had paved the way for a steady invasion of heavier O2 0-4-4Ts. By mid-1925 such major services as Ryde Pier Head–Ventnor were already firmly in their grasp. The Island

102

'Terriers', fighting a rearguard action over the years which followed, continued doggedly to handle light branch work and goods traffic. Conversely, really adverse winter conditions threw merciless light on the little locomotives' limitations when they were called upon to deal with other than a moderate load of freight. For a while Eastleigh continued to tolerate double-heading and divided goods trains. Then, in July 1932, action was taken and three more powerful E1 0-6-2Ts were despatched from the mainland. A fourth followed in June 1933.

The newly imported E1 tanks, free now to take up numbers W1 to W4, were intended primarily for goods duties on the Island. They soon, however, displayed a useful aptitude for passenger work into the bargain. Rather ironically, such threat as this posed to the 'Terriers' was largely defused when three more veteran IOW tanks were withdrawn in 1932–33. But a much greater threat, the upgrading of the Freshwater and Bembridge lines, lay imminent. Crisis duly arrived in 1936, when the installation of a new 25ft turntable at Bembridge finally opened both 'Terrier' strongholds to yet another invasion of O2 tanks. It was all too much and in May 1936, a sad procession of four IOW 'Terriers', Nos W9, W10, W12, and W14, stripped of their nameplates, wound its' weary way back to Eastleigh. The name *Bembridge* was transferred to newly arrived O2 tank No.W33. Obviously, No.W14's days on the Isle of Wight were over.

At Eastleigh, decisions duly emerged. One of the 'Terriers', No.W10, was condemned out of hand; strangely, it was not broken up until March 1949. First instincts were to deal with *Bembridge* similarly in December 1936. Then a change of heart saw the locomotive reprieved; taken into Works, reboilered, renumbered 2678, and painted full passenger green, it moved on to Fratton shed in July 1937. The latter, as it happened, was hardly short of 'Terriers' and consequently, less than a year later, No.2678 was tried out at Guildford as shed pilot in lieu of 0-4-0ST *Ironside*. Rather surprisingly, the 'Terrier' proved to be the least useful of the two; so the old Southampton Dock warrior was recalled, and No.2678 went back to Fratton. Regular Hayling Island branch line duties then ensued — until February 1940, when the 'Terrier' was sent on loan to the Kent & East Sussex Railway. The 'loan' proved to be a long-term one; when British Railways took the K&ESR over on 1st January 1948, No.2678 was still there!

Life on the Kent & East Sussex possibly achieved a certain measure of rationality under BR auspices. But it was never dull — as many a 'Terrier' could testify. On Sunday, 19th September 1948, for instance, a through hop-pickers Special ran from Northiam to London Bridge. The train, consisting of an ex-SE&CR six-coach set plus a utility van, was hauled unaided to Robertsbridge by No.32678. The only pity was that the 'Terrier's' feat, admirable in normal circumstances, was somewhat overshadowed by the fact that the seven mile run took 72 minutes! Fortunately, No.32678's good name was cleared when a subsequent post mortem revealed that half that time was spent at stations, including 27 minutes at Salehurst for ticket inspection! None the less, No.32678 came a real cropper the following year, when track subsidence derailed it at Wittersham on 29th March and the 'Terrier' finished up on its side on marshy ground, below track level. Eventually, the Ashford breakdown train tiptoed up the lightly laid metals and with considerable difficulty, No.32678 was extricated from its unenviable predicament. Not greatly damaged, it was returned to Rolvenden shed. A few weeks later it proceeded to Brighton for repair and, in the process, was painted BR lined black. It was then stored awhile at Ashford.

As a measure of rationalisation, No.W4 *Bembridge* was renumbered W14 in April 1932, and is seen here at Ryde. The locomotive's further stay on the Island was, however, to prove comparatively brief and by May 1936 it found itself back on the mainland. (*Author's Collection*)

Back once more in action, No.32678 paid an unexpected visit to its old haunts on 9th June 1950, when it worked a weed-killing train from Robertsbridge to Tonbridge via Headcorn. The load on this occasion was two tank wagons, one 25 ton brake and a spraying van. Six months later, the 'Terrier' was sighted at Eastbourne shed. This time, it transpired, it was travelling from Ashford to Newhaven, where it was due to stand in for No.2647. Peripatetic duties came to an end on 24th May 1951, when No.32678 was again allocated to Rolvenden.

No.32678's versatility surfaced again briefly in July 1953 when, after repair and repaint at Brighton Works, the 'Terrier' deputised as Works Pilot while No.377S was undergoing repair. Then back to Kent it went and on 2nd January 1954, it joined No.32655 in the Kent & East Sussex line's last day of public passenger service. Thereafter, only freight trains worked between Robertsbridge and Tenterden and three 'Terriers' were usually kept at St Leonards for that purpose. But each year, in late Autumn, the hop-picking season still had to be respected and special trains were still being run entirely for hop-pickers benefit. On Sunday, 23rd September 1956, No.32678 joined No.32636 in double-heading such a train, the 5.14pm 'empty', between Bexhill West and Robertsbridge. After reforming fore and aft in true K&ESR tradition the two 'Terriers' then worked forward to Bodiam as the 5.40pm 'up special'. A year later, another special, the 6.40pm Bodiam–London Bridge, ran for three Sundays in similar fashion. In preparation, two 'Terriers', Nos.32678 and 32670, worked the empty stock from Hastings to Roberts-bridge, then took up their time-honoured positions to reach Bodiam.

A rather different 'special' materialised on 12th April 1958, when a four-coach train sponsored by the Branch Lines Society entered Tenterden Station — the first to do so since regular passenger services ceased in January 1954. No.32636 had hauled the empty coaches from Hastings to Robertsbridge, whence No.32678, freshly off the morning Tenterden goods, hopped on in front to see the special down the branch. Later that day the two 'Terriers' double-headed the empty stock back to Hastings.

Two months later, Stage 2 of the Hastings diesel scheme was implemented and St Leonards ceased to function as a main shed. Its engines were officially reallocated as from 9th June 1958, whence diesels took over regular freight services. No.32678's immediate fate was a reposting to Fratton on 2nd June and re-

acquaintance with Hayling Island branch duties. Despite that, however, the locomotive contrived to maintain contact with the Kent & East Sussex line on at least two further occasions: 1958 was the last year for hop-pickers specials and although No.32678 was not initially involved it managed somehow to deputise for No.32662 on 14th September.

Return to Fratton brought little joy to No.32678; that shed closed on 2nd November 1959 and its allocation of 'Terriers' moved under the protection of Eastleigh shed, with one stabled overnight at Fratton to handle early morning Hayling Island branch duties. No.32678 next entered Eastleigh Works for overhaul and in June 1961, re-entered local activity. Certainly it was seen in steam, with two other 'Terriers', at Fratton on 11th February 1962. Traffic was heavy that summer, and No.32678, with two other companions, was kept busy handling three and four-coach Hayling Island trains. It missed the branch's closure on 2nd November 1963, though, for by May that year it had been transferred to Brighton and was currently employed shunting the West Quay at Newhaven.

On 22nd and 25th July 1963, No.32678 even had the satisfaction of standing in for a diesel when it worked the evening parcels special from Seaford to Newhaven. The noose finally tightened, however, on 10th August, when Newhaven's West Quay line, with its famous swing bridge, was closed. Wagons were cleared and, on 18th August 1963 No.32678 left for Brighton bearing many chalked inscriptions of farewell and regret. Less than two months later, on 5th October, it put in a morning's work as coal stage pilot before leaving for Eastleigh, coupled to M7 tank No.30379. The 'Terrier', by now, had run a total of 1,389,447 miles.

It says much for the spirit of the times that No.32678 was spared the M7's ultimate fate. Early in 1964 came word that at least two 'Terriers' were in the process of being restored at Eastleigh Works for preservation by Messrs Butlin's. Some months later, fact replaced hope when, *en route* to Butlin's Holiday Camp at Minehead, No.32678 was loaded on to a low wagon and left Eastleigh on the 12.22am Eastleigh–Salisbury–Fisherton freight. Already painted in a form of Stroudley yellow, it arrived at Minehead on 25th July 1964.

A decade later came Butlin's decision to disburden themselves of their static locomotive exhibits. Deep in Somerset, a preservation group had set up a Trust with a view to eventual

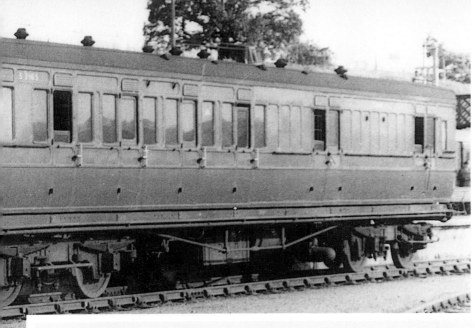

April 1952 — and a peaceful scene obtains at Robertsbridge as No.32678 arrives with its one-coach train from Tenterden; note the running number painted on the rear of the bunker. This was a reversion to a Brighton Works practice which had been discontinued before World War II. Standard 6in transfers were used, but the habit, presumably considered uneconomic, was soon dropped under BR auspices. (Lens of Sutton)

On 19th October 1958, No.32678 joined No.32636 in handling a four-coach special, the 'Rother Valley Limited', for the Locomotive Club of Great Britain. No.32678 is seen here at the rear of the train after its arrival at Rolvenden. Meantime No.32636, heading the train, prepares to take liquid refreshment in the distant rear. (Steamchest)

restoration of the Taunton-Minehead branch. Thus, after appropriate negotiation, No.32678 was sold to the West Somerset Railway Company. The 'Terrier' left Minehead Camp by road in April 1975, and proceeded to Williton, where it was stored in an old goods shed pending restoration. The engine was not in good shape, however. Serious deterioration had affected the front end of the boiler and by early 1983, the prospect of restoring the dismantled 'Terrier' had to be abandoned on financial grounds. The Somerset group then suggested that the Bluebell Railway might take over the task. A party representing the latter Railway visited Somerset but, after inspecting No.32678, decided that such a project was not for them. Fortunately, a director of RESCO (Railways) Ltd, a restoration firm based on Woolwich, stepped in to buy the locomotive and in April 1983, the dismantled remains of No.32678 were transferred to London.

Yellow liveried, but still bearing its BR numberplate, 'Terrier' No.32678 was quite dwarfed at Minehead Holiday Camp by the massive adjacent presence of LMS 'Pacific' No.6229 Duchess of Hamilton. Fortunately, both locomotives have since been rescued from this plight. (Steamchest)

72 FENCHURCH — Built September 1872. Later SR No.636, 2636 and BR No.32636. Now Bluebell Railway No.72 *Fenchurch*

When *Fenchurch* and *Wapping* left Brighton Erecting Shop on 28th August 1872, *Wapping* made the first trial run; but cylinder trouble obliged it to concede to *Fenchurch* the honour, on 7th September, of becoming the first 'Terrier' to enter traffic. Meanwhile, the fact that all six built that year were named after East London districts did not debar them in the slightest from being deployed on South London line service. Indeed, their energetic involvement in that area produced a collective mileage of 183,466 in 1873 alone. *Fenchurch,* contributing 34,647 miles to that figure, topped the list. Nine years later, with well over 300,000 miles under its belt, the pioneer 'Terrier' still held pride of place at Battersea.

Beneath this aura of hustle and bustle, however, all was not well; such was the erratic nature of the 'Terrier' steam brake that most train crews soon learned to rely on exclusive use of hand brakes when operating on the extremely tricky South London line. Stroudley, well aware that only introduction of a reliable continuous braking system could solve the LB&SCR's London suburban problem, watched and waited. In the event, enthusiastic co-operation in the Newark brake trials of 1875 was to convince him that the Westinghouse automatic air brake should be introduced at Brighton. Before that, however, he had *Fenchurch* fitted as a precaution, in October 1875, with a rival apparatus, Barker's Hydraulic Brake, and the locomotive was subjected to a lengthy series of trial runs between Victoria and London Bridge. The tests having clearly proved the superiority of the Westinghouse equipment, *Fenchurch,* later stripped of Barker gear, was then restored to normal duties at Battersea. In August 1879 it again received new cylinders, albeit still leading the original batch with a cumulative mileage of 279,794. As it happened, the little 'Terrier' was to complete nearly 26 years on South London service (and run some 600,000 miles in the process) ere the next major event in its life occurred.

The event could hardly have produced a greater change of circumstance. One moment in 1898, *Fenchurch* was bustling

When the Newhaven Harbour Company purchased its 'Terrier' in 1898, only number plates and Westinghouse brake were removed from the locomotive it Brighton Works. Hence, when it reported for Harbour duties on 27th June that year, *Fenchurch* still carried both name and Stroudley livery. *(Author's Collection)*

around South London; the next it was peacefully engaged in shunting duties at Newhaven Harbour.

The latter was, of course, at all times a close concern of the LB&SCR, though legal difficulties compelled it to be controlled by an independent Harbour Company. Initially, horses were used for quayside shunting. By 1888, however, these were largely supplanted by two saddletanks. In this context, Brighton offered every assistance in the way of locomotive maintenance and crew training. That, however, did not prevent Newhaven Harbour metals, innocent as they were of signalling, from witnessing many a minor accident. A particularly damaging one on 23rd March 1888 put both locomotives out of action and two 'Terriers', Nos.69 *Peckham* and 79 *Minories,* had to be borrowed from the LB&SCR until repairs were effected. Even then, despite Brighton's best endeavours, the Harbour Company's renewed lease of locomotive independence was to prove shortlived. One saddletank, hopelessly run down, went for scrap in December 1892. The other, though repaired at Brighton and Newhaven in May 1892 and March 1895 respectively, formally gave up the ghost in February 1898. While *Peckham* stood in once again as temporary replacement, Harbour management and Brighton went into conclave — as a result, *Fenchurch,* by now a veteran of 599,297 miles, changed hands for a consideration of £350.

Fenchurch got off to none too auspicious a start. Within a year or so, extensive repairs to Harbour defences so dislocated quayside work that, once again, other 'Terriers' had to be brought in to assist. Then, much to everyone's relief, work on the sea walls came to an end in February and *Fenchurch* was left to assume sole command. Thereafter, only periodic visits to Brighton Works interrupted years of peaceful daily Harbour routine. In the course of the first, in February 1904, the locomotive exchanged its 13in cylinders for new 14in ones. A second visit early in 1910 saw *Fenchurch* reliveried in black, relieved only by red lining.

The next move came in April 1913 when, at the request of the Harbour Company, the locomotive was reboilered to A1X class at a cost of £1,195. A subsequent visit to Brighton Works in April 1917, however, produced considerable cosmetic change. Apart from losing its name, the 'Terrier' was turned out in unlined black and a new (non-automatic) Westinghouse brake was fitted. One year later the legend 'Newhaven Harbour Company' was painted on its side tanks. By this time, cumulative mileage was in excess of 800,000. The inhibiting effect of Harbour duties, however, so degraded the locomotive's traditionally sprightly performance that by the end of October 1922, total mileage had only risen to 826,110.

The next major event in the railway calendar, the advent of Grouping in January 1923, purported to leave *Fenchurch* unaffected. But the air was full of changes — and a significant one duly occurred in 1926, when the Southern Railway, with the expenditure of £383,000, gained complete control of Newhaven Harbour. The railway fraternity promptly considered an intriguing question: what possible use could lie ahead for a 54-year old 'Terrier'? As it happened, the SR's answer to that poser came as a surprise and delight to many.

One more visit was made to Brighton in June 1929. In 1935, however, a modest supply of ex-LB&SCR gilt numerals were unearthed at Brighton Works. *Fenchurch* was one of a few chosen to benefit and in December that year, fresh '2636' numerals were added at Eastleigh. They were to be left undisturbed right up to 1950.

In 1926 *Fenchurch*, valued now at £575, was quietly absorbed into SR stock and the 'Terrier' entered Brighton Works in December that year. Contrary to normal Brighton practice, it was renumbered B636; for the more logical number, 672, was already owned by an ex-LSWR tank. Painted Southern Railway black to remind all and sundry of its non-passenger status, but none the less fully equipped with Westinghouse brake and vacuum ejectors, out ventured No.B636 to resume time-honoured duties at Newhaven Harbour. In this lovely study, the locomotive has paused awhile between shunting operations on the west side of the Harbour. (O. J. Morris)

The Southern Railway's faith in No.2636 did not go unrewarded, for the locomotive completed another 100,000 miles without serious mishap ere it again entered Eastleigh's doors, in 1949. By now, of course, Nationalisation had taken its course, and in June 1950, Brighton Works attended to *Fenchurch's* new BR lined black livery. Swanking a little now as the Southern Region's oldest locomotive, back went No.32636 to Newhaven Harbour. Life, as it happened, was never to be the same again.

The year 1952, for instance, ushered in a significant event, the celebration of Brighton Works' Centenary and in preparation for working special trips to Kemp Town in this context, No.32636 was despatched to Eastbourne on 27th July. There, attached to a Brighton motor-set, the 'Terrier' was tried out on evening trips between Eastbourne and Hailsham over a period of five days. In the absence of 'push-pull' gear, the locomotive had to run round after each journey. No difficulty was experienced, however, in maintaining schedules. *Fenchurch's* crew must, in fact, have been rather sorry when indisposition on the part of Newhaven's reserve 'Terrier' compelled their return to base on 5th August. A second crisis then arose towards the end of that month and No.32636 was hurriedly despatched to Ashford to assist in Kent and East Sussex hop-picking traffic. True to form, the 'Terrier' returned to Brighton in good time for the October 1952 celebrations and worked three specials each Sunday from Brighton to Kemp Town and back. The two coach 'push-pull' set used was brought specially from Gillingham.

Having thus reacquired a taste for passenger work, the erstwhile 'Goods tank' was by no means averse to officiating on the Hayling Island line periodically during the early months of 1953. It was temporarily fitted with coal rails during its ten week sojourn. Indeed, its performance there earned it a transfer to St Leonards shed that Autumn, again to help with hop-picker traffic on the Kent & East Sussex line. One particularly interesting turn was the 8.30am 'Empty', a six-coach corridor train handled between Hastings and Robertsbridge by No.32636 and a pilot. The train then became the 10.00am to Northiam, and left with No.32636 in front and a Rolvenden 'Terrier' at the rear. Unfortunately, lack of steam heating facilities precluded *Fenchurch* from working passenger trains during winter months and it was reluctantly returned to Newhaven at the end of the hop-picking season. It was still there when Newhaven shed was reduced to being a stabling depot on 19th September 1955.

In 1936, 'Terrier' No.2647, formerly *Cheapside*, joined *Fenchurch* at Newhaven in what was to be a fifteen year long partnership. In this photograph of the 'inseparables', taken at Newhaven shed on 11th June 1949, note how the two 'Terriers' differ in chimneys and coal bunkers. *(Steamchest)*

Right — As No.32636 lay damaged at Brighton shed early in 1962, few could have entertained future hopes for the 90 year old 'Terrier'. The greater, therefore, was the pleasure of all concerned when, in May 1962, No.32636 stepped forth from Eastleigh Works, repainted and fully repaired. As can be seen, a Hayling Island type spark arrester was also fitted. *(Steamchest)*

No.32636's next port of call was St Leonards. Various adventures followed. One day it was observed struggling manfully with the daily freight between Robertsbridge and Tenterden; the engine was steaming freely enough, but its train of seven wagons and a brake van had to be twice divided ere the 1:52 gradient into Tenterden could be surmounted. Eventually it returned to Brighton shed, but on 10th January 1957, when it was sent to Littlehampton to assist in quayside shunting, the 'Terrier' failed at Worthing with a broken damper. Class E2 tank No.32101, ex-Works and awaiting trial run, was given the unusual task of towing No.32636 back to Brighton. There, all must have been forgiven, for later in the year, No.32636 left Brighton Works within a month of its 85th birthday, the better for general overhaul and repaint. It was probably the last locomotive to receive such generous treatment; Brighton Works was due to give way to the production of Isetta 'bubble cars' in May 1958! Still, out again on loan and looking very smart indeed, No.32636 celebrated on 12th April 1958 by heading a passenger special into

Tenterden — the first since regular service ceased in January 1954. Having worked the empty four coach special from Hastings, No.32636 was joined by No.32678 at Robertsbridge whence, proceeding in customary K&ESR echelon, the two veterans took the train forward to Tenterden. At the end of the day the gallant pair reworked the special to Robertsbridge — then calmly double headed the empty stock back to Hastings.

Came 9th June 1958 and No.32636 was again sad witness to the demotion of a main line shed when, thanks to the implementation of Stage 2 of the Hastings diesel scheme, all steam engines at St Leonards were officially reallocated. A week earlier, diesel trials had been held on the Kent & East Sussex line. *Fenchurch*, in fact, had worked the last steam trips there on 31st May. From now on, it was decided, things would be different — and No.32636 was only to be retained at Ashford as a 'standby'.

So much for good intentions! The 7th June soon saw No.32636 back again on KE&SR metals. Then, one month later, resident diesel No.11223 got in such a state as to require

The only slight snag on the 'Sussex Special Rail Tour' occurred at Seaford, where No.32636's fireman had too little time to clean his fire. Thus, poor old *Fenchurch* finished up at Brighton Central with only 60 lb of steam in its boiler. On the outward journey the double-headed Special had rollicked down Falmer bank at 50mph! (*G. W. Sharpe*)

Ashford's attentions. So, No.32636, instructed to report back to St Leonards, stepped in, as to the manner born, to work the K&ESR branch for the next two days. Assiduously following the diesel's roster, it even took care of an early morning van trip from Crowhill to Bexhill West! On 22nd September 1958, up popped the 'Terrier' again, this time with No.32662, at the head of a Bodiam hop-pickers special. Less than a fortnight later, Rolvenden's diesel was again in trouble and No.32636 came to the rescue by working the Saturdays only Robertsbridge–Northiam shuttle. One final flourish followed on 19th October when a heavily laden passenger special, the 'Rother Valley Limited', laboured between Robertsbridge and Rolvenden with Nos.32678 and 32636 operating fore and aft.

The year 1959 was interesting. On 5th September, No.32636 travelled light from St Leonards to Eastbourne shed and, two days later, was used as a goods pilot in place of an E4. Placed in shed, out of steam for a month, it then proceeded to Fratton via Brighton. There, it worked on the Hayling Island branch, despite Fratton shed's closure in November 1959. Now under Eastleigh's aegis — and willing as ever to flaunt the merits of vintage steam — No.32636 soldiered on, until it was replaced by No.32655 on 27th March 1960. Ironically, Brighton, No.32636's next domicile, promptly reintroduced it to its old haunts at Newhaven Harbour where, one morning in February 1962, it learned a bitter lesson when it and a train of empty wagons being propelled by a 350hp diesel collided.

The revitalised 'Terrier' was soon in action. When Eastbourne shed's diesel shunter failed on 20th June No.32636 not only stood in for the defective diesel, but hauled it back to Brighton on the 23rd! On 7th October that year the 'Terrier' further flexed its muscles by joining another veteran, E6 class tank No.32418, in hauling an RCTS 'Sussex Special Rail Tour' over the Brighton–Seaford section.

Early in 1963, No.32636 stood in awhile at Lancing Works. Then it left for Fratton on 13th June. Where else could a hard-working 'Terrier' go! The locomotive's last public appearance on BR service coincided, appropriately enough, with closure of the Hayling Island branch. The Locomotive Club of Great Britain was quick to sponsor a 'Hayling Farewell' special, to be run on 3rd November 1963, 24 hours after public service ceased. Accordingly, that Sunday morning, with No.32636 leading and No.32670 trailing, five coaches laden with railway enthusiasts wound a leisurely way from Havant to Hayling Island. Photographic stops were made and hundreds of local inhabitants gathered to meet its arrival. Eventually and reluctantly, to the accompaniment of exploding detonators, the last up non-stop train to Havant was allowed to leave Hayling Island. Later that month, with a final tally of 1,109,513 miles to its credit, Britain's pioneer 'Terrier' was officially withdrawn by BR and on 4th January 1964, sister 'Terrier' No.32662 towed No.32636 from Fratton to Eastleigh. Both had been in store since the Hayling Island line closed.

The story should, but does not, end there. For yet one more chapter in *Fenchurch*'s long life opened up on 11th May 1964, when the 'Terrier' was instructed to proceed light from Eastleigh to Brighton. Two days later, it was spotted propelling an

ex-LB&SCR fruit van, No.270, up the weed-infested metals which still linked Ardingly and Horsted Keynes — and realisation dawned that both engine and van had been purchased by the Bluebell Railway Preservation Society. The investment, at £750, was to prove a sound one.

The first action of the Sheffield Park shed staff was to black out the BR emblem on the locomotive's tank sides and remove the first digit on smoke numberplate and cab sides. Thus, the 'Terrier' was restored as near as possible to its '2636' Southern Railway days. Then came further alterations.

On 12th July 1964, the number 72 was restored, the name *Fenchurch* reappeared on the left hand tank side, and the right hand side was given the inscription 'Newhaven Harbour Company' — to remind all who saw *Fenchurch*, or travelled behind her, of the two Companies the 'Terrier' had served so long and faithfully. Thereafter, No.72 joined sister 'Terrier' No.55 *Stepney* in handling Bluebell Railway traffic. *(Steamchest)*

---

(6)50 WHITECHAPEL — Built December 1876. Later SR Nos.B650, W9 *Fishbourne* & 515S. Also BR Nos.D515 & 32650. Presently Kent & East Sussex Railway No.10 *Sutton*

Curiously, this 'Terrier' was a sixty year old veteran in Southern Railway harness ere its career began to assume what one might call a chequered dimension. From the moment that *Whitechapel* entered East London and Croydon traffic at New Cross on 14th December 1876, life under LB&SCR colours was blameless and orthodox to a degree. Like *Martello*, No.50 served New Cross well and remained there practically until the end of the century. Then things began to happen.

Modification in the form of new 14in cylinders came in 1893, as did a revised number, 650, in June 1901. The latter half of 1905, however, saw the 'Terrier' feature in both the Surplus List and the LB&SCR's withdrawal programme — and into store it went. Two years later, a welcome change in Brighton policy brought about a reprieve; motor-fitted and liveried afresh, all in Marsh fashion, the 'Terrier', now nameless, resumed active

service. In March 1912 a transfer to Fratton found No.650 and two companion 'Terriers' working the Hayling Island line as to the manner born and, just over a year later, its 'push-pull' equipment gave way to the Westinghouse compressed air system. The World War I years inevitably brought change and, posted to Bognor shed in December 1916, No.650, in conjunction with No.680, worked in the mid-Sussex area for the next 3½ years.

The almost immediate resumption of holiday traffic in postwar years brought No.650 back to Fratton. There, it witnessed the end of 'push-pull' working on the Hayling Island branch and completed its 867,984th mile, before Brighton Works summoned it in May 1920 for reboilering. Thanks to postwar inflation, a new 'A1X' boiler now cost £1,195. The next development, Grouping, found the 'Terrier' at Portsmouth, with 951,269 miles to its credit, but apart from a minor number change in 1926, life for No.B650 continued largely as before. A real sea-change, however, loomed ahead in 1930 when, in response to a shortage of light engines on the Isle of Wight, authorities at Eastleigh decided to transfer three 'Terriers' from the mainland.

A long term resident of New Cross shed from the time it entered service on 14th December 1876, *Whitechapel* was renumbered 650 in 1901. *(Author's Collection)*

No.B650 was the last to go. In May 1930 it entered Eastleigh Works for repair and to receive the livery and extended bunker required for Island service. It duly re-emerged carrying a new number, W9, and space was left on its tank sides to accommodate the name *Fishbourne*. When steamed, however, the boiler gave cause for concern and was quickly replaced by that of No.B662. Ryde Works attended to the fitting of neat nameplates and, thus equipped, *Fishbourne*, allocated to Newport IOW shed, entered a new lease of life on the Island's more lightly laid branches. What no one envisaged was that the lease would prove to be such a short one. By 1936, in conditions already described under *Bembridge* (formerly *Knowle*), more powerful ex-LSWR tanks had succeeded in supplanting all but three of the Island's 'Terriers'. No.W9's services were no longer required. Thus, in May 1936, with a total mileage now standing at 1,069,877, it joined three others in a sorry trek back to the mainland. All were placed in store at Eastleigh.

After lying inert at Eastleigh for several months, No.W9 was taken into the Works for repair. To the astonishment of many, it re-emerged as Service Stock No.515S and, still bearing its green livery, was despatched to Lancing Carriage Works in April 1937 as Works Pilot.

Life at Lancing was fairly uneventful even at the best of times — and certainly so during the years of the Second World War. Victory, though, brought its own problems: witness the year 1946, when a nationwide shortage of locomotive coal prompted a Government ordinance that all four main line Companies should undertake a limited measure of oil firing. For its part, the Southern Railway was given a quota of 110 locomotives and, faced with unfamiliar problems, Eastleigh Works hurriedly modified N15 class 4-6-0 No.740 *Merlin* for crew training purposes. Meanwhile, in an effort to gain such additional experience as was possible in the short time available, No.515S was also con-

In this study, obtained during World War I, No.650 offers a stirring sight as it sweeps into Barnham Junction with a branch train from Bognor. The respective proportions of the 'Terrier' and a Marsh 'balloon' coach are clearly defined and four more coaches, plus three brakes, complete the little locomotive's not inconsiderable load. *(Derek Brough Collection)*

verted to oil-burning at Lancing Works in August 1946. Externally, the 'Terrier' looked no different, for the requisite oil tank was installed inside the bunker. By the end of 1947, 31 of the SR's programmed 110 locomotives were duly converted.

Reactions to oil burning were, however, mixed. Firemen appreciated a nice clean footplate, but passengers were less happy as oil fumes seeped back along a train. In any case, the

Three of the Isle of Wight's four redundant 'Terriers', Nos.W9, W14, and W10, shorn of nameplates, make a sorry group as they await their respective fates. No.W9 was, in fact, condemned by Eastleigh in December 1936, but a change of mind saw it given a general overhaul and the 'Terrier' was absorbed into Service Stock as No.515S. *(Author's Collection)*

whole programme petered out within a year when a new menace, oil shortage (!), took precedence. Having presumably yielded experience, No.515S could be found lying dead in Lancing sidings by the end of 1946, and February 1947 arrived before it was again observed working.

In August 1947, No.515S was repainted unlined black and a little later it reverted to coal burning. Five months after that, Service Locomotive No.680S arrived to take over as Lancing Works Pilot, and No.515S again lay awhile, dead, in the Works yard. Latterly it reported to Brighton Works for repair and boiler

change and in February 1952, the 'Terrier' was renumbered under British Railways auspices. Its new number, DS515, now appeared on the bunker sides and the side tanks, still unlined black, bore the inscription 'C&W LANCING WORKS'.

'Terrier' No.515S is caught going about its duties at Lancing. The LMS tender in the background is a former LNWR one which had been introduced to the Works Yard as a water tank during early World War II years. The tender remained at Lancing until the 1960s, when it was replaced by one of SE&CR origin. *(Author's Collection)*

August 1953 saw a healthy, and interesting reversion. Thanks to No.DS515's sound mechanical condition — and the fact that it still retained its Isle of Wight extended bunker — the 'Terrier' was taken back into general service. Departmental locomotive No.DS681, formerly *Cheam*, took its place at Lancing Works, whereupon No.DS515 made its way to Brighton Works. When it left there, on 6th November 1953, it carried both lined black livery and a new number, 32650. Then, posted, almost inevitably, to Fratton, No.32650 found useful employment over the next decade on the Hayling Island branch. By Whitsun it and four other Hayling Island 'Terriers' were required to adopt spark arresters and, in February 1957, No.32650 received a final repair and repaint at the much threatened Brighton Works. That same month, the LCGB elected to run a heavily laden 'Southern Counties Special' between Marylebone and Portsmouth and the revitalised 'Terrier' celebrated by joining No.32636 in handling a six-coach diversionary trip from Havant to Hayling Island and back. Fratton shed 'closed' on 2nd November 1959, but No.32650, stationed overnight as required, carried on working the Hayling Island branch. Holiday traffic on the Island was still flourishing, with normal weekday summer service of fifteen return trips stepped up to 24 at weekends.

So, quite gently, life moved on towards eventual closure of the Hayling Island branch. No.32650 was certainly observed to be fully employed through July 1963 and was still working the branch, with No.32646, halfway through September. Then the axe descended and on 2nd November 1963, the last day of public working, No.32650 joined Nos.32662 and 32670 in coping with a particularly large influx of farewell visitors. The last six-coach up train that evening left Hayling Island Station to the strains of 'Auld Lang Syne'. Two 'Terriers' worked fore and aft and the smokebox of the leading engine was draped with laurel wreath and headboard. All three 'Terriers' were officially withdrawn that month: No.32650 with a final tally of 1,271,019 miles. By mid-1964 rumour had it that No.32650 would be sold to Butlin's. In the event it was purchased by the Borough of Sutton and Cheam for ultimate exhibition at its new town centre.

Sold to the Borough via the Kent & East Sussex Preservation Society — and duly tidied up at Eastleigh — No.32650 then embarked on quite a remarkable journey to Robertsbridge. On the first day, 18th September 1964, it ran light under its own steam from Eastleigh to Eastbourne. Next morning it left about 10.00am and proved itself nimble enough to keep ahead of the 8.45am Victoria–Ore between Eastbourne and St Leonards. There, content to bow the knee, it was shunted into the diesel depot to let an electric train past. Later that day it arrived at Robertsbridge where the Mayor of Sutton and Cheam awaited official acceptance. A month or so later it was spotted lying dead in Robertsbridge yard. A little further up the branch, in the Flour Mill sidings at Northbridge Street, its future companions in K&ESR service, 'Terrier' No.32670 and P class No.31556, also lay awaiting developments.

No.32650 continued to lie at Robertsbridge until Whitsun 1966 when, restored to steam, it served a useful double purpose by hauling carriage stock to the KE&SR's establishment at Rolvenden. There, apart from being officially named *Sutton*, little happened until the 'Terrier' was taken into Rolvenden shops for overhaul in 1968. A new, locally cast, dome was fitted and, renumbered 50, *Sutton* re-entered service with the Borough of Sutton crest surmounting the painted name on its tank sides. Regular service then ensued between 1969 and 1972, when further workshop attention was required. This time, in addition to mechanical overhaul, *Sutton* was renumbered 10, albeit the green livery survived. Further repair work was effected in the spring of 1973, but the locomotive was back in good fettle in time for Christmas service. Good, too, was 1974 during which *Sutton* ran 278 miles. The K&ESR also re-opened for public traffic on 3rd February that year.

Appropriately, the K&ESR gave 'Terrier' No.32670 back the title it once bore in Colonel Stephens' service — K&ESR No.3 *Bodiam*. No.32650, still on loan from the Borough of Sutton and Cheam, was renamed *Sutton*, and allocated K&ESR's first blank number, 10. The Borough crest also appeared above the painted name, as can be seen from the above study of both K&ESR 'Terriers' at rest. *(Lens of Sutton)*

Further attention given at the end of the 1974 season included a fresh repaint and the provision of new nameplates, as a result of which, the 'Terrier' did not re-enter service until December 1975. None the less, *Sutton's* 100th birthday was appropriately celebrated in December the following year. The engine responded by excelling itself during 1977, when it ran 1,216 miles and spent nearly 500 hours in steam. In course of a subsequent boiler inspection, steam heating equipment was fitted and 'Santa Specials' were jubilantly tackled over the 1978 Christmas period. Boiler trouble emerged during the 1979 season but 1st February 1980 arrived before *Sutton* was withdrawn for extensive repairs. In May 1980, however, the Borough of Sutton lifted the gloom a little by granting the K&ESR a 30 year lease on the locomotive at a peppercorn rent. The overhaul, meanwhile, turned out to be more time consuming and expensive (£15,000) than was anticipated and No.10 did not return to service until 28th May 1984. On that occasion the Mayor of Sutton unveiled new brass name plates before the 'Terrier' left on the 12.10pm train.

Before proceeding further with *Sutton's* activities, it might be as well, at this stage, to consider the enormous obstacles which had been overcome by the Kent & East Sussex Preservation Society over the previous two decades. Formed immediately British Railways closed its Robertsbridge–Tenterden section in July 1961, the Society found BR reasonable enough to deal with. Unfortunately, impedence of a proposed new main road by a railway level-crossing at Junction Road, 2½ miles beyond Robertsbridge, was anathema to the Ministry of Transport. Thus, transfer of the K&ESR's old Light Railway Order to the Kent & East Sussex Railway Association was firmly refused — see above. Faced with such a brick wall, the Association responded by transforming itself in 1971 into a new Tenterden Railway Company Ltd. Appropriately armed with charitable status, it then declared its intention to re-open the line between Tenterden and Bodiam, just short of Junction Road. Things then began to happen. Such items of Company stock as remained at Robertsbridge were moved up the line, BR then lifted the track between Robertsbridge and Junction Road and, in July 1972, contracts were exchanged anent the purchase of the Junction Road–Tenterden section. The price — an enormous one for the

Association to raise — was £60,000 and, of course, ultimate success hinged on another very important proviso — the granting of a Light Railway Order. Happily, the story from thereon is one of hard work, consolidation, and success. The LRO covering the section between Tenterden and Bodiam was duly granted on 19th November 1973 and, so swift was progress, a full-scale public re-opening of the metals between Tenterden Town and half a mile beyond Rolvenden took place in 1974. Ten years later, when a two day 10th Anniversary Gala was held on 2nd and 3rd June, No.10 *Sutton* was a very active participant.

A year passed and in June 1985, *Sutton* joined the K&ESR's other 'Terrier' No.32670, the one time *Poplar*, in working an evening 'Wine & Dine' train. Then withdrawn from service early in 1987 with a cracked cylinder, *Sutton* reappeared in November that year repainted in Southern Railway lined green. Unfortunately, the cylinder repair was unsuccessful and No.10 had to re-enter K&ESR workshops a second time before it was able to resume service on 19th April 1988. During October that year Sunday trains employed both 'Terriers', working bunker to bunker on mixed trains consisting of two coaches, sundry wagons, and a guard's van.

The intention to penetrate right to Bodiam, however, never weakened and in May 1990, metals which by then had reached Wittersham Road (four miles), were extended publicly to reach Northiam. The K&ESR was now seven miles long. Current long-term ambitions are to carry on three more miles to Bodiam. Thanks to the difficulty of financing such a project, however, six more years are likely to elapse (written in 1994) before work can commence.

Looking ahead at the even longer-term ultimate K&ESR ambitions to reach Robertsbridge, (13½ miles), it is intriguing to note that BR did not apply for an Abandonment Order when it sold off its Bodiam–Robertsbridge section. Thus, the original LRO covering that 3½ miles still remains legally in force and probably could be, were the case valid, transferred afresh to the K&ESR. Estimated costs of some £600,000 to restore this section would have to be met, however, ere K&ESR locomotives find their way back to their old haunts at Robertsbridge. Meanwhile, a considerable accumulation of locomotives and rolling stock has been released into active service over the last ten years.

Sent new to Battersea in 1877, *Newington* was plunged straight away into South London line activity. It is seen here thus engaged after losing its condensing gear in 1894. Meanwhile, the Kensington branch had stepped in to claim the bulk of the 'Terrier's' attentions. *(Author's Collection)*

(6)46 NEWINGTON — Built January 1877. Later LSWR No.734, FY&NR No.2, SR Nos.W2/W8 *Freshwater* & BR No.32646. Presently Isle of Wight Railway Company No.W8 *Freshwater*

There is a peculiar appropriateness about the fact that the last 'Terrier' to be described in our chronological review endured *seven* changes of ownership ere it reached its present safe haven in the Isle of Wight. Yet, oddly enough, not a hint of the itinerant lifestyle which was to come *Newington's* way betrayed itself during the first 25 years of the locomotive's existence. As No.46, it entered the South London suburban circuit straight from Brighton Works on 11th January 1877 and, running anything up to 28,000 miles a year, it simply remained a Battersea stalwart right through, and beyond, the following decade.

Duplicate Listing followed, innocuously enough, in April 1902. Then, less than a year later, Dugald Drummond intervened — and life assumed a vastly different hue for LB&SCR No.646. The sequence of events which persuaded the LSWR to invest in a brace of 'Terriers' has already been described (see under *Clapham*). Suffice to say that *Newington*, with a track record of 574,266 miles, arrived in full Brighton livery at Nine Elms Works on the morning of 12th March 1903. It and companion engine *Clapham* were photographed for posterity's sake ere they disappeared inside and were again subjected to official record when they re-appeared on 2nd May, looking extremely smart in Drummond passenger livery.

For once in their lives, the two 'Terriers' failed to meet the bill. Their light axle weight was satisfactory enough, but the sharp curves of the LSWR's newly opened Lyme Regis branch offered too much resistance to six-coupled tanks. Four-coupled O2s were progressively introduced and by July 1906, No.734, excused Lyme Regis duty — temporarily at least, could be found working local trains around Yeovil. A month later it was reduced to station piloting at Bournemouth. Then in May 1907, 'Terrier' links with Lyme Regis finally snapped. Three O2 tanks assumed full responsibility for the branch and Nos.734 and 735 were laid aside at Exmouth shed; No.734 remained idle the

longer of the two. Next, in September 1907, it found a new home at Eastleigh, were it worked the Botley-Bishops Waltham branch. Some time during that period its bunker was fitted with three coal rails. But little more was heard of the 'Terrier' until it was summoned in December 1911 to join No.735 at Eastleigh Works. Inspection followed, an order was placed for two new boilers (complete with Drummond pattern dome top safety valves) and both 'Terriers' were reboilered in 1912. Each received new 13in cylinders and blast pipe, but the original short smokebox, copper-capped chimney and wooden brake shoes were all retained. In practice the new boilers were not a success. They steamed less freely than their Stroudley predecessors and were a constant source of priming. Within months, both 'Terriers' acquired an unhappy reputation amongst LSWR enginemen. There can be little doubt, therefore, that few Eastleigh hearts wilted when another chapter opened in No.734's life and the locomotive vanished on loan to the Freshwater, Yarmouth & Newport Railway on 25th June 1913.

On *loan*? Needless to say, there was a background. Since its inception in 1899, the FY&NR had traditionally relied upon its more affluent neighbour, the Isle of Wight Central Railway, to provide engines and rolling stock; the price was 45% of gross receipts. Yet, as so often happened in such circumstances, inter-Company relations left much to be desired and a final explosion in 1913 produced an ultimatum from IWCR that current working arrangements would cease on 30th June. Having previously brazened things out by implying it could work the line itself, the FY&NR Board was then left with no alternative but to search for suitably priced secondhand motive power. It was no easy task. Two locomotives subsequently offered by the IWCR (!) were declined as being too expensive an indulgence though, in fact, some carriages and wagons did eventually change hands.

One of the most intriguing of all 'Terriers', *Newington* passed into LSWR ownership in 1903 and, renumbered 734 at Nine Elms, is seen here in full South Western splendour. Westinghouse brake gear and Brighton work plates have gone and the locomotive is now nameless; but the Stroudley chimney remains. *(Author's Collection)*

Two more, put up by the LB&SCR (including 'Terrier' No.637 at £725), were also rejected as requiring heavy boiler repairs. Latterly, almost in despair, the FY&NR invested £725 in a six-coupled Manning Wardle saddle tank, *Northolt*, formerly employed by Pauling & Co. With Company funds thus exhausted, the FY&NR then turned to a more friendly LSWR and hired 'Terrier' No.734 with effect from 1st September 1913, as a very necessary second line of defence. The hire charge of £1-6s-8d (£1.33) per day embodied an option to buy in the following Spring for £900.

Duly landed at St Helen's and taken by road to Newport, No.734 did not let its new employers down. Clad still in LSWR livery, it worked on hire until March 1914, when outright purchase at £900 was arranged. In fairness to the LSWR, a quick calculation suggests that this apparently inflated figure very likely included nine months hire charge. Whatever, the agreed medium of payments spread over three years at 5% interest explains why No.734 had to wait until February 1917 before it could receive emerald green livery and its new number, FY&NR 2. In the interim, it and saddle tank, FY&NR No.2, worked the twelve mile single line jointly. They never functioned together, though, for double-heading was forbidden on the FY&NR's lightly laid track. Both locomotives shared the same maximum load restrictions: nine passenger coaches, ten mineral vehicles, twelve goods wagons, or 22 empty wagons. Relations with the 'auld enemy' improved none in the meantime — witness the fact

that the FY&NR's request, in April 1918, to have locomotive No.2 overhauled at Newport Works, was met by blank refusal on IWCR's part. All in all, it was probably something of a miracle that the smaller Company managed to hang on until Grouping. Even then, the FY&NR Board chose to challenge the £50,000 compensation it was offered and demanded £70,000! The dispute had to be referred to arbitration before the Southern Railway was able to assume official control, at *its* price, as from 1st September 1923.

By now the FY&NR's saddle tank, banished to Medina Wharf, had been superseded by ex-IWCR 'Terrier' No.W10 *Cowes* and, content to forgive and forget, the two Stroudley tanks were sharing Freshwater line services. Steam carriage heating and motor train equipments were fitted when No.W2 underwent heavy overhaul in January 1927 and in October 1928, when the 'Terrier' acquired the name *Freshwater*, auto-gear was also installed. In January 1932 there came a further real life-saving change, when Ryde Works removed No.W2's Drummond boiler and replaced it with a new Brighton one of 'A1X' pattern. In accordance with usual Island practice, however, no change was made to sanding arrangements. *Freshwater* was then returned to traffic on 18th April 1932 as No.W8. For the next five years it led a peripatetic existence on the Island and at some stage front steps were fitted. The next time it visited Ryde Works, however — December 1937 — it paid a modest price for its new lease of life by forfeiting its copper-capped chimney and receiving one of Marsh pattern *in lieu*. No.W8 was also painted Maunsell green. Its normal employment by now was on Merstone–Ventnor West auto-trains, though occasionally it stood in on Freshwater services and Medina cement trains.

For a decade from 1926 onwards, the Island's 'Terrier' population remained at seven. Then, as O2 and E1 tanks began to

Changes soon followed after Grouping and FY&NR No.2 became No.W2 in Southern Railway books. Then, in March 1924, the 'Terrier' was painted Maunsell green, its bunker was extended IOW fashion and vacuum brake was superseded by Westinghouse. The locomotive still carried its Drummond type safety valves when this photograph was taken at Newport on 21st September 1926.
(LCGB — Ken Nunn Collection)

press home their superiority on the upgraded Freshwater and Bembridge lines, four IOW 'Terriers' were sent back to the mainland in May 1936. Fortunately for *Freshwater*, it was one of the three survivors. Another narrow escape came in 1938, when *Freshwater*'s nameplates were removed in expectation of a similar fate, but for some reason, the transfer was cancelled and the nameplates were reinstated. The next real crisis, however, World War II, was not far off and its eventual eruption in September 1939 had a traumatic and immediate effect on Island traffic. In conjunction with many other locomotives, No.W8 was placed in store for some months and work during the war years was spasmodic to a degree. Came 1946 and No.W8, clad in austerity black, could be seen lying dead at Newport shed; this despite the fact that Island railway activities by now had picked up very smartly indeed.

Rebuilt as Class A1X at Ryde Works in 1932, No.W8 *Freshwater*, formerly No.646 *Newington*, was photographed at Eastleigh in the late 1930s. *(Author's Collection)*

At Nationalisation, by which time only two 'Terriers' remained on the Island, No.W8 entered Ryde Works for general overhaul. By sheer good fortune its original copper-capped chimney had been found in the works, and this was refitted before the engine returned to traffic on 13th August 1948, with 'BRITISH RAILWAYS' emblazoned high on its side tanks. In April 1949, however, the subsequent arrival of two more motor-fitted O2 tanks clearly presaged the end of Island service as far as 'Terriers' were concerned. Local speculation was that both Nos.W8 and W13 would end their days on the Kent & East Sus-

What now? A distinct air of uncertainty hangs over IOW 'Terriers' Nos.W8 and W13 as they lie inert on Eastleigh's 'dump'. Fortunately, both lived to fight another day. Seen here early in May 1949, both entered Eastleigh Works for overhaul a week or two later. *(Author's Collection)*

sex section. Events proved otherwise. True, the Isle of Wight's last two 'Terriers' were shipped to the mainland by floating crane on 13th April 1949, but after being unloaded at Southampton Docks, they found their way eventually to Eastleigh Works 'dump'.

Rendered nameless, fitted with vacuum ejector and stripped of 'push-pull' gear, the former IOW No.W8 left Eastleigh Works in August 1949 bearing BR No.32646 and proceeded straight to Fratton to assume Hayling Island duties. It was still liveried in unlined black, but at least a new number plate shone on its smokebox. Two years at Fratton sufficed. No.32646 was transferred to Newhaven shed in August 1951 and, four months later, it paid a rare visit to Brighton Works for repair and boiler change. In June 1953 the Railway Correspondence & Travel Society, on occasion of its 25th Anniversary, entertained high hopes of re-introducing the 'Terrier' to its old Lyme Regis haunts. Unfortunately, No.32646 was unable to complete its journey west from Newhaven and No.32662 deputised.

In the event, the return of No.32646 to Newhaven shed in May 1954 did not last long, for that shed was closed on 19th September 1955 and its engine duties became Brighton shed's responsibility. Still deemed capable of useful employment, however, No.32646 moved back to Fratton and resumed Hayling Island branch duties. These lasted until February 1958 when the 'Terrier' was given a last overhaul at Brighton Works before the latter finally closed.

Since the year 1957, No.32646 had, in fact, been wandering a little. It went to Brighton on 17th September 1957 and was seen at Eastbourne two days later. Thence, it pressed on for Newhaven and on its way home to Fratton, found employment

on 4th October, working a special horsebox train from Brighton to Worthing. On the 29th day of the following month, Fratton sent it to Brighton, to act as Works Pilot during No.377S's absence. Relieved of this duty by No.32662 one month later, No.32646 then called in at Brighton Works for a repaint before returning to Fratton. It was one of six 'Terriers' which were displaced when that shed lost its independent status on 2nd November 1959. During the week ending 3rd January 1960, No.32646 also assisted at Lancing Works when, for some reason, that establishment required four regular engines.

Despite Fratton shed's official 'closure', traffic on the Hayling Island branch was still quite brisk and on 1st July 1962, No.32646 was observed working hard, with two other 'Terriers', on holiday traffic. Trains were still heavy in the summer of 1963, despite increasing road competition and, oblivious to the fact that the branch was destined to close in November that year, No.32646 was seen working there on Saturday, 14th September 1963.

One year later, two 'Terriers', Nos.32646 and 32650, lay at Eastleigh Works 'awaiting restoration'. It soon transpired that, despite an abortive £750 bid by the Hayling Terrier Fund, No.32646 had, in fact, been sold to the Sadler Railcar Company of Droxford. Duly tidied up, the locomotive undertook the comparatively short journey to Droxford under its own steam late in November 1964. There, it was probably the first 'Terrier' to run on any part of the one-time Meon Valley line. Unfortunately, the Meon Valley project was not a success and, eighteen months later, the 'Terrier' was purchased by Brickwoods, the Portsmouth brewers. Thus, on 13th May 1966, No.32646, hauling a Southern Railway restaurant car, made one last journey from Droxford to Knowle Junction and back. Four days later, on Tuesday 17th May, it was shunted by diesel to Wickham, then transported by road to Hayling Island where, repainted in Stroudley livery and given back its old name *Newington*, it became a set piece in the forecourt of a new 'Hayling Billy' public house.

In this study, No.32646's previous sojourn in the Isle of Wight is advertised by the high position of the legend 'British Railways' on its side tanks. The 'Terrier's' livery remained unlined black until February 1958. *(W. Gilburt)*

After receiving BR lined livery at Brighton Works in February 1958, No.32646 returned to Fratton. As seen here, a coal rail has been added to its bunker and it now sports the obligatory Hayling Island spark arrester. Late in 1956, an axle failure on No.32646's part had caused tests to be made on all 'Terriers'. Despite that, No.32646 was still there when the Hayling Island branch closed on 3rd November 1963. *(Steamchest)*

Right

Once the opening ceremony of the 'Hayling Billy' public house was conducted by two drivers who handled the last train on the Hayling Island branch in November 1963, attention switched to No.46 *Newington*, which had been placed on a plinth in the forecourt. The 'Terrier' remained there for thirteen years. *(R. Stumpf)*

Full of steam and nimbly running round its train as in days of yore, SR No.W8 *Freshwater* will be ready shortly to convey another train load of visitors to Wootton, 1¾ miles away. The Society is deeply preoccupied, meanwhile, in restoring a second 'Terrier', *Newport*, not to mention an impressive collection of vintage carriage bodies. Thus, the old Isle of Wight spirit lives on — and it will be a memorable day for the Isle of Wight Railway when *Newport* emerges to complete a quite remarkable locomotive trinity. *(Steamchest)*

Newington proved to be a popular exhibit. But years of exposure in the open air soon ravished its pristine condition and, as in the case of Butlin's, the 'Terrier' became something of an unexpected liability. Fortunately, Brickwoods' successors, Whitbread Wessex Ltd, were urgently reminded of the historical value of the locomotive — not least by Isle of Wight enthusiasts(!) — and generously decided to donate it to the Wight Locomotive Society. Thus, painted SR green *in situ*, *Newington* left by low loader on 18th June 1979. The motion had been disconnected to prevent cylinder damage *en route*, and, delayed slightly by a Sealink labour dispute, the engine arrived back on IOW rails on the 25th. On 9th August, *Newington* was officially handed over to the Wight Locomotive Society by a representative of Whitbreads at a ceremony which was held at Haven Street.

Over the next two years an immense amount of hard work at Haven Street shops saw *Newington* restored to working order. On 21st June 1981, liveried once more in Southern green, it steamed again, as No.8 *Freshwater*, on ex-IWCR metals. After hauling a special 12.45pm train for Society members and invited guests, it then took on the 1.30pm normal scheduled train. A willing workhorse, it completed 887 miles before the running season ended and suffered only one minor Westinghouse fault.

Further repair work was carried out that winter and a return to traffic in June 1982 saw another 980 miles completed. Easter 1983 marked a resumption of service and, still running reliably, *Freshwater* ran 1,177 miles that year. Came Spring 1984 and No.8, the only Society locomotive in serviceable condition, though handicapped by the poor quality coal which resulted from the miners' strike that year, triumphed over the odds by running 1,097 miles. After some cylinder attention that winter, *Freshwater* then made 1984 a vintage year by registering a mileage of 1,097.

In this 1930s Isle of Wight scene 'Terrier' No.W11 *Newport* (formerly *Brighton*) is truly on home ground as it saunters through Newport (IOW) Station on a coal train for domestic consumption inland. The neat brass nameplate on the side tanks and bunker side numerals were features introduced by the Southern Railway late in 1928. They remained with the locomotive until it was shipped back to the mainland in February 1947.

POSTSCRIPT

Even as we go to Press important announcements have been made which should ensure that at least four working 'Terriers' will soldier on well into the 21st century. Firstly, collaboration between the Kent & East Sussex Railway and the Isle of Wight Steam Railway has resulted in an order being placed, at a very favourable price of £70,000, with Israel Newton Ltd., the well known Bradford specialist boiler-makers, for two new all-steel boiler and firebox assemblies. With delivery expected in mid-1996, one set will go to *Bodiam* (ex-*Poplar*), and the other to *Freshwater* (formerly *Newington*). Equally stirring news comes from the Bluebell Railway, who, by employing patterns made from National Railway Museum archive drawings, intend to have new cylinder blocks made for its two 'Terriers', *Stepney* and *Fenchurch*. The latter had already been revitalised, of course, in 1980 with a new firebox, supplied by Luggs of Billinghurst.

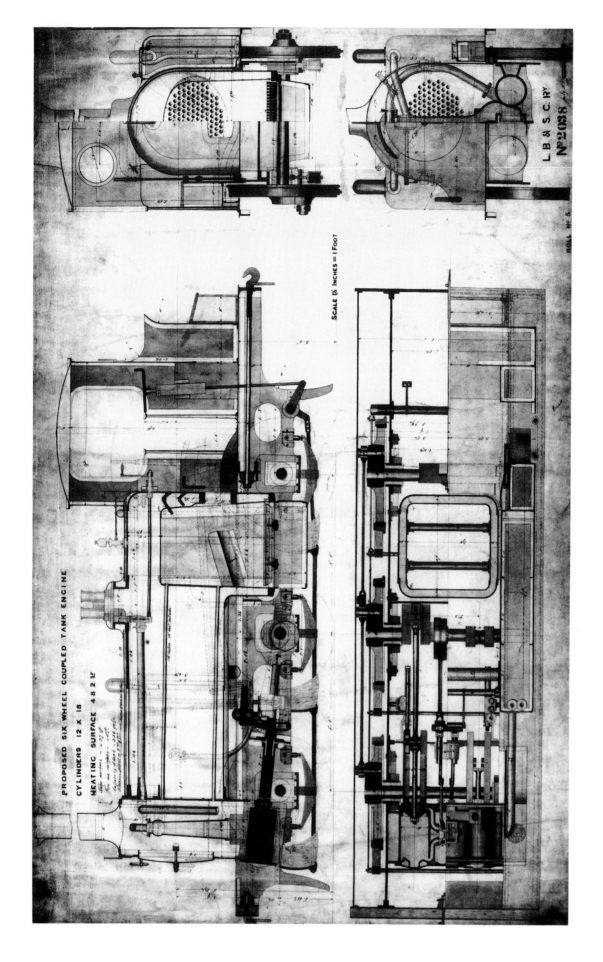

Stroudley's first drawing, dated June 1870, postulated a diminutive 0-6-0 side tank with a domeless boiler and Adams patent safety valves mounted on a raised manhole cover.

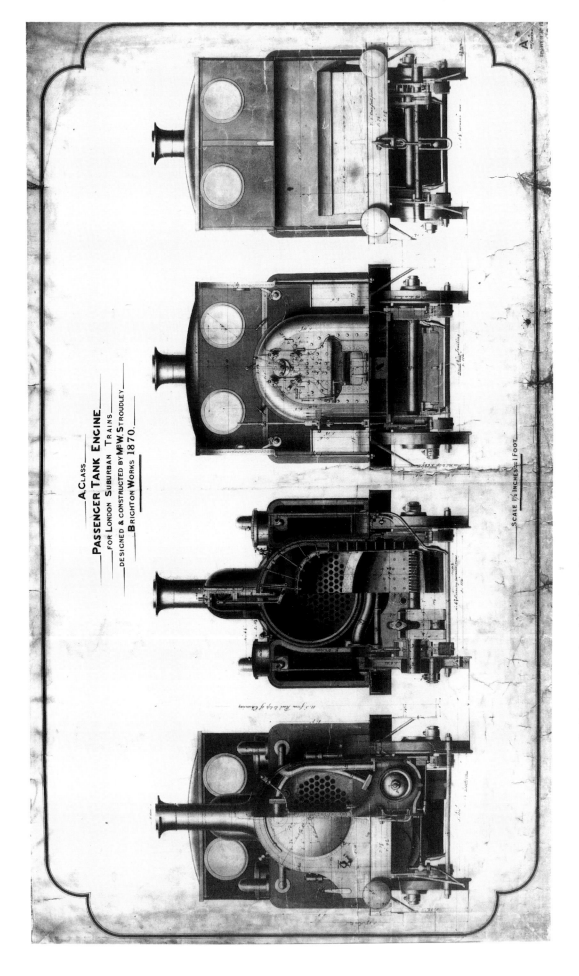

A.CLASS

PASSENGER TANK ENGINE

FOR LONDON SUBURBAN TRAINS

DESIGNED & CONSTRUCTED BY Mʳ W. STROUDLEY

BRIGHTON WORKS 1870.

SCALE 1½ INCHES = 1 FOOT

End view and sectional drawings showing the date 1870 must have been drawn later and dated retrospectively as the domed boiler illustrated was not adopted until 1872.

Other drawings have been placed within chapter 2. A Southern Railway weight diagram of the original engines will be found on page 23 while the modified A1X class is covered with a LB&SCR weight diagram on page 26. A general arrangement drawing to half an inch to the foot scale will be found across pages 24 and 25.

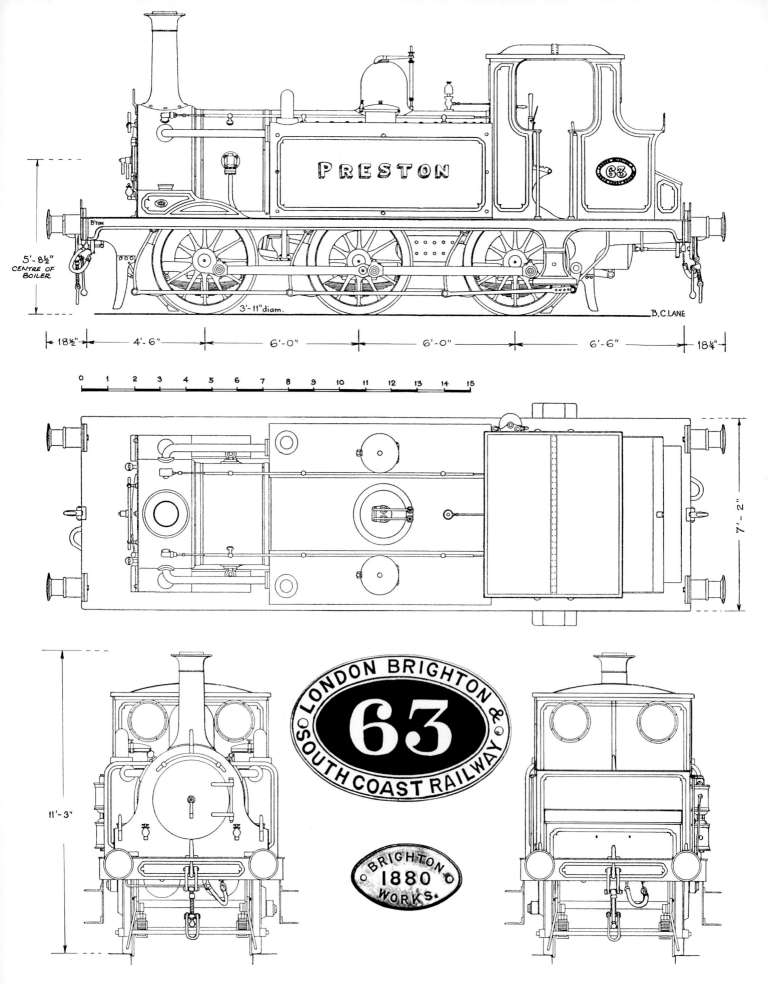

PRESTON

63

5'-8½"
CENTRE OF
BOILER

B'TON

3'-11"diam.

B.C.LANE

18½" | 4'-6" | 6'-0" | 6'-0" | 6'-6" | 18¼"

0 1 2 3 4 5 6 7 8 9 10 11 12 13 14 15

7'-2"

11'-3"

LONDON BRIGHTON &
63
SOUTH COAST RAILWAY

BRIGHTON
1880
WORKS.

INDEX

Numbers in Bold Italic type refer to illustrations